Parallel and
Distributed Computing

WILEY SERIES ON PARALLEL AND DISTRIBUTED COMPUTING
Series Editor: Albert Y. Zomaya

Parallel and Distributed Simulation Systems / Richard Fujimoto

Surviving the Design of Microprocessor and Multimicroprocessor Systems: Lessons Learned / Veljko Milutinović

Mobile Processing in Distributed and Open Environments / Peter Sapaty

Introduction to Parallel Algorithms / C. Xavier and S. S. Iyengar

Solutions to Parallel and Distributed Computing Problems: Lesson from Biological Sciences / Albert Y. Zomaya, Fikert Ercal, and Stephen Olariu (*Editors*)

New Parallel Algorithms for Direct Solution of Linear Equations / C. Siva Ram Murthy, K. N. Balasubramanya Murthy, and Srinivas Aluru

Practical PRAM Programming / Joerg Keller, Christoph Kessler, and Jesper Larsson Traeff

Computational Collective Intelligence / Tadeusz M. Szuba

Parallel and Distributed Computing: A Survey of Models, Paradigms, and Approaches / Claudia Leopold

Fundamentals of Distributed Object Systems: The CORBA Perspective / Zahir Tari and Omran Bukhres

Parallel and Distributed Computing

A Survey of Models, Paradigms, and Approaches

Claudia Leopold

A Wiley-Interscience Publication

JOHN WILEY & SONS, INC.

New York / Chichester / Weinheim / Brisbane / Singapore / Toronto

For ordering and customer service, call 1-800-CALL-WILEY

Library of Congress Cataloging in Publication Data is available.

ISBN 0-471-35831-2 (alk. paper)

10 9 8 7 6 5 4 3 2

Contents

Preface   *ix*

1 Introduction   **1**

   1.1 Parallel and Distributed Computing   *1*

   1.2 Motivation for Parallel and Distributed Computing   *6*

   1.3 Key Characteristics   *8*

   1.4 Models and Paradigms   *19*

   1.5 Remarks on the Organization of the Book   *27*

2 Architectures   **31**

   2.1 SIMD Computers   *31*

   2.2 Symmetric Multiprocessors   *33*

   2.3 Cache-Coherent NUMA Architectures   *35*

   2.4 Distributed-Memory Parallel Computers   *37*

   2.5 Computer Networks and Protocols   *38*

   2.6 Clusters   *45*

   2.7 Loosely Coupled Distributed Systems and Grids   *47*

3 Data Parallelism   *51*

    3.1   SIMD Parallelism   *53*

    3.2   Data Parallelism on Arrays   *56*

    3.3   Nested Data Parallelism   *64*

    3.4   Collective Operations and Libraries   *65*

    3.5   More on This Topic   *69*

4 Shared-Memory Programming   *73*

    4.1   Thread Models   *76*

    4.2   Structured Shared-Memory Programming   *84*

    4.3   Distributed Shared Memory   *89*

    4.4   One-Sided Communication Models   *92*

    4.5   More on This Topic   *93*

5 Message Passing   *95*

    5.1   Interprocess Communication   *100*

    5.2   Task Management   *103*

    5.3   Interoperability   *105*

    5.4   Very Low-Level Models   *106*

    5.5   More on This Topic   *108*

6 Client/Server Computing   *111*

    6.1   The Client/Server Paradigm   *113*

    6.2   Sockets   *118*

    6.3   Remote Procedure Calls   *122*

    6.4   More on This Topic   *125*

7 Code Mobility   *127*

    7.1   Enhanced Client/Server Computing   *132*

    7.2   Mobile Agents   *135*

    7.3   Parallel Mobile Code   *139*

7.4   Transparent Migration   142

7.5   More on This Topic   143

8   Coordination Models   **145**

8.1   Tuple-Based Coordination   146

8.2   Channel-Based Coordination   151

8.3   More on This Topic   155

9   Object-Oriented Models   **157**

9.1   Distributed Objects   159

9.2   Active Objects   167

9.3   More on This Topic   172

10   High-Level Programming Models   **177**

10.1   Automatic Parallelization   177

10.2   Skeleton Models   182

10.3   Compositional Models   186

10.4   Functional Programming Models   189

10.5   Logic Programming Models   193

10.6   More on This Topic   197

11   Abstract Models   **199**

11.1   Network Models   201

11.2   Parallel Random-Access Machine   205

11.3   Bulk-Synchronous Parallel Model   209

11.4   The LogP and QSM Models   214

11.5   Locality-Centric Models   216

11.6   Graph-Based Models   219

11.7   More on This Topic   221

12   Final Comparison   **223**

References   **229**

Index   **255**

Preface

Since computer networks and clusters are becoming more and more ubiquitous, the use of parallelism is no longer the privilege of a few scientific programmers with access to powerful supercomputers. Parallelism promises significant performance increases, and almost every application domain can profit. Despite this opportunity, parallel computing is only slowly entering the mainstream.

Part of the reason is the diversity of the field. The areas of parallel and distributed computing have traditionally evolved separately, with parallel computing focusing more on performance aspects, and distributed computing focusing more on the use of remote resources. Moreover, there are several streams within each of the two fields. In consequence, a variety of programming models and paradigms have been suggested: data parallelism, message passing, client/server computing, code mobility, to just name a few. These models have overlapping goals and characteristics.

An application programmer who intends to exploit parallelism faces the question as to which model to use. The question is difficult to answer, because differences are subtle at times. There is no universal best approach, and the choice must be based on properties of the particular application, the available architecture, the maturity of programming environments, etc.

This book surveys the models and paradigms in the converging area of parallel and distributed computing. It is meant to help in the organization of the field, by treating the diverse approaches within a common context. What sets this book apart is a big-picture view. The book covers a comprehensive set of models and paradigms, and skims lightly over more specific detail. Thus the novice reader is able to quickly grasp a balanced overview. Many good books about the individual topics are available and complement the present text. This book pays much attention to comparisons between the models, trying to convey a feeling for the coherency of the parallel and distributed computing field.

In the presentation, emphasis is placed on those models and paradigms that are used in practice. These are explained in such a way that the essential concepts can be understood by beginners. The book is both an introduction and a survey. As an introduction, it conveys the central concepts, problems, and ideas. As a survey, it gives a comprehensive picture that includes many less well-known proposals. The proposals are briefly put into context, and many references are given.

The book is intended for different audiences. First, it can be used in teaching, where it is meant to not be the sole textbook, but a framework within which individual topics can be elaborated upon, according to particular needs and interests. For instance, the book can be extended by a programming course in MPI and/or threads programming. Alternatively, the various topics can be illustrated and exercised with examples of Java programming environments, which meanwhile exist for almost all of the models. Second, the book is intended for application developers who want to first get an overview before choosing a particular programming style to study in depth. Third, the book is directed at researchers who are working in a particular subarea and want to get an overview of the others. In general, the book can be used by everybody who is interested in a survey instead of a particular subarea of parallel and distributed computing.

No specific prerequisites are needed for reading this book. One should, however, be familiar with elementary concepts of computer science, such as knowledge of an imperative language and a basic understanding of computer architecture.

Acknowledgments   I would like to thank everybody who has directly or indirectly contributed to the idea and realization of this book project. In particular, I thank Thomas Rauber, Stefan Kauer, and Peter Braun for carefully reading and commenting on all or parts of an earlier draft. Going a few years back, I thank Todd Heywood who originally introduced me to the topic of parallel models. I'm especially grateful to the anonymous reviewers who made many suggestions that have significantly improved the contents and presentation of the book. On the more technical side, I thank Elizabeth Kley for numerous hints on improving the English, Jutta Jäger for some assistance in completing the references, and Antje Kempf for drawing most of the figures. My thanks as well go to the staff at John Wiley & Sons, especially to Philip Meyler and Andrew Prince, for their help and cooperation. Part of the work has been done with support from a Habilitation Fellowship of the German Research Foundation DFG.

CLAUDIA LEOPOLD

Jena, Germany

Trademarks

ActiveX, Microsoft, and Windows NT are trademarks or registered trademarks of Microsoft Corporation.

Aglets, IBM, OS/2, and TSpaces are trademarks or registered trademarks of IBM Corporation.

AltaCluster is a trademark of Alta Technology Corporation.

Brazos is a trademark of The Brazos Project at Rice University.

Cilk is a trademark of the Massachusetts Institute of Technology.

CORBA, IDL, IIOP, OMG, and ORB are trademarks or registered trademarks of Object Management Group, Inc.

Cray T3E is a trademark of Cray Inc.

Intel, Pentium, and Pentium Pro are registered trademarks of Intel Corporation. Pentium III Xeon is a trademark of Intel Corporation.

Java, JavaSpaces, Jini, ONC, ONC+ , Sun, Sun Enterprise, and Sun Microsystems are trademarks or registered trademarks of Sun Microsystems, Inc. in the United States and other countries.

FORGE is a trademark or registered trademark of Applied Parallel Research, Inc.

Linda is a trademark of Scientific Computing Associates, Inc.

Linux is a registered trademark of Linus Torvalds.

MasPar is a registered trademark of MasPar Computer Corporation.

NUMA-Q and Sequent are registered trademarks of Sequent Computer Systems, Inc.

occam is a trademark of a company belonging to the SGS-THOMSON Microelectronics Group.

OpenMP, Origin, and SGI are trademarks of Silicon Graphics, Inc.

Paradise is a registered trademark of Scientific Computing Associates, Inc.

PGCC and PGF77 are trademarks or registered trademarks of The Portland Group, Inc.

UNIX is a registered trademark of The Open Group in the United States and other countries.

Voyager is a trademark of ObjectSpace, Inc.

All other trademarks are the property of their respective owners.

1

Introduction

This chapter provides general background on parallel and distributed computing, and specifies the subject of this book. We start with a characterization of the properties parallel and distributed, and relate them to each other. Then we go on with basics: motivation, objectives, and other elementary concepts. The second part of the chapter explains the terms model and paradigm from the book title, and outlines design goals and classification schemes.

1.1 PARALLEL AND DISTRIBUTED COMPUTING

This section describes the subject of parallel and distributed computing, and relates the two subareas to each other. After some historical remarks, we discuss both differences and common grounds that lead to convergence. Finally, parallel and distributed computing is contrasted with related fields.

The Traditional Area of Parallel Computing

Parallel computing refers to solving a task faster by employing multiple processors simultaneously. Driven by the continual desire for more computing power on the one hand, and the availability of appropriate technologies on the other, parallel computing became popular in the late 1980s and early

1990s. Several new companies were founded, and existing companies included the production of parallel machines in their program. Parallel computing was considered a promising field with enormous potential for increased performance.

Unfortunately, it soon became obvious that being able to build fast parallel hardware was not enough. The real challenge turned out to be software. Early parallel programming environments were difficult to use, and moreover they were often tied to a particular architecture. As a consequence, parallel programming was only practiced in areas with a very high demand for computing power—mainly science and engineering. Despite of government support, this market was too small, and most of the companies, among them leading vendors such as Thinking Machines and Kendall Square Research, had to file for bankruptcy or take parallel machines out of their program.

Fortunately, the outlook of parallel computing is much better than what one would expect from this brief history. Currently we are observing that networks of commodity PCs or workstations, so-called *clusters*, are gaining wide acceptance as affordable hardware platforms for parallelism. In many cases they are taking over the role of the earlier expensive supercomputers.

Computer networks have historically been the realm of distributed computing. We will now take a brief look at that area, and afterwards discuss the relationship with parallel computing.

The Traditional Area of Distributed Computing

A distributed system is a collection of autonomous computers that are interconnected with each other and cooperate, thereby sharing resources such as printers and databases. Distributed computing evolved during the 1980s and became ubiquitous during the 1990s.

Distributed systems are frequently used in commercial and data-processing applications. They range from small client/server configurations over organization-wide networks of various scales up to the Internet. Distributed systems can be coupled as loosely as a network of autonomous PCs that access the same printer, or so tightly that the user has the view of a large homogeneous computing resource.

In many cases, distributed systems are not sold as a whole, but grow naturally and incrementally. Individual computers are interconnected to local-area networks, and local-area networks are interconnected to wide-area networks, as the need arises.

The rise of distributed computing created a number of new problems that are addressed in research. Elementary problems include the absence of a common clock and the possibility of transmission failures. On a higher level, the access to shared resources must be managed so that different user programs do not interfere. Other problems relate to the heterogeneity of distributed systems, according to which distinct hardware, operating systems, and languages should be able to interoperate. Finally, security issues are of considerable and increasing concern.

Comparison Between Parallel and Distributed Computing

Although the two fields have traditionally evolved in separate ways, they have many common characteristics:

- Multiple processors are used.

- The processors are interconnected by some network.

- Multiple computational activities (processes) are in progress at the same time and cooperate with each other.

Indeed, the terms parallel and distributed are sometimes used interchangeably, and some authors consider parallel computing as a subfield of distributed computing [142]. Although many computations can be characterized as both parallel and distributed, we make a distinction in this book and associate the terms with slightly different properties. The difference can be summarized as follows:

> Parallel computing splits an application up into tasks that are executed *at the same time*, whereas distributed computing splits an application up into tasks that are executed *at different locations*, using *different resources*.

The distinction may look artificial, but it will later help us to classify the approaches. The distinction is derived from the respective subjects of the traditional fields. To summarize them, parallel computing places emphasis on the following features:

- An application is split into subtasks that are solved simultaneously, often in a tightly coupled manner.

- One application is considered at a time, and the goal is to speed up the processing of that single application.

- The programs are usually run on homogeneous architectures, which may have a shared memory.

Distributed computing, in contrast, places emphasis on the following features:

- The computation uses multiple resources that are situated in physically distant locations. Resources can, for instance, be processors, memories, disks, and databases.

- A distributed system runs multiple applications at a time. The applications may belong to different users.

- Distributed systems are often heterogeneous, open, and dynamic. Open means that the system comprises diverse hardware and software from different vendors; dynamic means that the system structure can change over time.

- A frequent concern is hiding system internals so that the distributed system looks to the user like a single large machine. This feature is called the *single system image*.

- Distributed systems do not have a shared memory, at least not at the hardware level.

To underline some differences, parallel computing refers to a single application, and thus the program execution is more predictable than it is for distributed computing, where nondeterminism and dynamic behavior are typical. Parallel computing aims at speeding up the execution of a single application, whereas distributed computing emphasizes the aspect of increasing the system throughput. As a general tendency, performance plays a larger role in parallel than in distributed computing.

Convergence of Parallel and Distributed Computing

Despite these differences, the areas of parallel and distributed computing have a significant overlap, as already noted. Since about the mid-1990s, the areas have been converging, and are described more and more as being one field. This convergence is increasingly visible in that:

- The areas increasingly use the same architectures. On one hand, the invention of fast network technologies enables the use of clusters in parallel computing. On the other hand, parallel machines are used as servers in distributed computing.

- The issues of parallelism and distribution are often intertwined and consequently researched together.

- There are joint research meetings as well as joint research institutions.

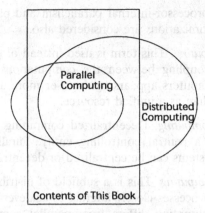

Fig. 1.1   The relationship between parallel and distributed computing.

Parallel and distributed computing is normally considered to be the union of the two fields. Nevertheless, this book focuses more on the intersection. Several topics that are relevant for only one of the fields are either skimmed or omitted altogether. For instance, we discuss neither processor-internal parallelism, nor networking applications with straightforward interaction such as email exchange. Figure 1.1 depicts the relationship between parallel and distributed computing assumed in this book.

Related Notions

The following fields could potentially be confused with parallel and distributed computing:

- *Concurrent Computing.* Concurrent computing focuses on the existence of multiple threads of control. It investigates the implications of multiple computations being in progress at the same time. A central issue is the conflict-free sharing of resources. The computations can be executed in parallel and on a distributed system, but they can also run in a time-shared manner on a sequential machine. The latter scenario is called *pseudoparallelism*. Concurrent computing emphasizes the competition aspect between the processes or threads, whereas parallel and distributed computing emphasizes the cooperation aspect.

- *Highly Parallel Computing.* The term means the same as parallel computing, except that a large number of processors must be present. The counterpart is lowly parallel computing, with the current borderline being arguably somewhere between 100 and 1000 processors [215, 338].

- *High-Performance Computing* or *Supercomputing.* Here, the focus is on the speed of execution. Whereas parallelism is an important means to achieve speed, processor-internal parallelism and parallelism-unrelated performance optimizations are considered also.

- *Networked Computing.* This term is used instead of distributed computing when the coupling between the computations is loose, and the collection of computers appears to the user more as a set of independent machines than as a unified resource.

- *Decentralized Computing.* Decentralized computing is characterized by the absence of a central controlling entity. Parallel and distributed programs and systems can be centralized or decentralized.

- *Collaborative Computing.* This is a subfield of distributed computing, in which users or processes closely interact to achieve some common goal. Collaborative computing differs from parallel computing in that the processes are more autonomous and specialized, and the interest is in combining their strengths. Typically, different processes represent different users.

1.2 MOTIVATION FOR PARALLEL AND DISTRIBUTED COMPUTING

This section lists reasons for deploying parallel and distributed computing, and mentions some application areas. In any particular application area, the advantages are relevant in varying degrees. This variety is a major cause for the diversity of the field.

Absolute performance A classic reason for the use of parallel computing is the demand for ever increasing computing power. The demand comes especially from scientific and engineering applications, such as climate and weather modeling; astrophysical simulation; and the design of materials, cars, and airplanes. Simulation tasks, in particular, show a correlation between accuracy and computational expense: More computing power allows scientists to study natural phenomena in more detail, and engineers to recognize more properties of their designs in advance, during simulation.

Performance is also important in commercial applications such as databases, as well as in combinatorial optimization, artificial intelligence, and many more areas. Performance can even be useful if the speed requirements are low, since it enables the use of more comfortable but slower program development tools.

Price/performance ratio Parallel computers are cheaper to build than sequential computers with the same level of performance. Designing a new processor is expensive, and thus it pays to use it in large quantity in a parallel machine. Moreover, parallel computers reach a high level of performance even if they deploy older processors instead of the fastest and most expensive ones available at the time.

Technological reasons   At least with current technologies, there are physical limitations to the integration density of chips, which may possibly limit the performance growth of sequential architectures. El-Rewini and Lewis [142, p. 46] predict that the performance growth curve will peak around the year 2005.

On the positive side, processors and hardware components have become so cheap that one can use them in large quantities. Significant progress has been made in network technologies so that fast, large, and long-distance networks can be built at a reasonable price.

Another restriction of sequential architectures is the fact that the access time to memory limits the overall performance, the so-called *von Neumann bottleneck*. Access time is a problem of both main memory and disks, and it is likely to get worse in the future. Parallel and distributed computing helps insofar as that it increases the cache and main memory capacities as a by-product of adding processors. Moreover, it allows data to be processed close to the location where they were generated, which reduces the amount of traffic to a system-wide memory.

Inherently parallel or distributed applications   The wide adoption of distributed computing can be chiefly attributed to the existence of a large number of inherently distributed applications. Information systems of companies and organizations are examples, as are seemingly all computer applications in which people cooperate over distance. Since the data are generated at different places, part of the processing is naturally done there. Since some computations need data from different places, cooperation between the computers is necessary.

Similarly, parallelism can be the most natural approach for modeling real-world systems in which parallel activities are going on.

Resource sharing   In a distributed system, multiple users or computational tasks can share resources—both hardware resources such as servers and printers, and software resources such as databases and programs. Resource sharing has two faces. On one hand, users get access to a *large number* of resources such as processors, memories, and disks. On the other hand, users get access to *specialized* resources, for instance to supercomputers.

Availability   Parallel and distributed systems contain multiple components of the same kind. If one of the components breaks, another component can, at least in principle, take over its function. Similarly, during maintenance, the system can continue operation while some components are being replaced.

Of course, a system must be specifically designed to provide such functionality. High availability is especially important in commercial applications, where, for instance, databases should always be accessible.

Incremental growth Parallel and distributed systems are scalable, that is, in most cases one can add processors or other components after the system was purchased.

Other reasons Another advantage is *scavenging*. It is based on the observation that a lot of computing power is wasted, particularly outside business hours. By integrating the computers into a distributed system, the excess computing power can be made available to other users or applications.

Finally, parallel and distributed hardware is often purchased for carrying out sequential computations. In this case, multiple serial programs are run concurrently on a single parallel machine—a computing style that is referred to as *serial program*, *parallel system* (SPPS [338]), or as throughput-oriented computing.

1.3 KEY CHARACTERISTICS

This section covers central objectives, major problems, and basic notions of parallel and distributed computing. The listed issues guide the design of system components at various levels, ranging from hardware and operating systems over algorithms up to programming models, languages, and tools. The purpose of this section is not so much to introduce concepts for later use, as to convey the flavor of the field in general, that is, to put the more specialized topic of models and paradigms into context. The relative importance of the various issues listed below depends on the application area.

Basic Notions

A *task* is a program or a part of a program in execution. It is one of the afore-mentioned computational activities that take place at the same time and/or at different locations. The typical task has a single thread of control, but sometimes the term is also applied to computational activities that contain subtasks. The term *process* is used synonymously with task, except in Ch. 4, where tasks are distinguished as processes and threads. In contrast to a task, a *job* is a whole, usually sequential, program in execution.

A *node* or *processing element* is an entity that is able to compute. Depending on the architecture, it may be a single processor; an ensemble that consists of an application and a communication processor; or an autonomous computer that comprises memory, disks, software, etc. In most parts of this book, we take a high-level view in which the internal structure of the nodes is either not important or clear from context. Thus the more common word *processor* is sometimes used as a synonym for node.

Further basic notions are introduced in the following subsections, along with a discussion of related issues.

Single-Application Performance

An obvious measure is the *running time*, also called the *execution cost*. Another frequently used measure is the *speedup*, which is defined as the ratio between the sequential and the parallel running time:

$$speedup(P) = T_1/T(P) \ .$$

In this formula, $T(P)$ denotes the running time of the parallel program on P processors, and T_1 denotes the running time of a sequential reference program. Ideally, the reference program is the fastest sequential program that solves the problem. In practice, other reference programs are used as well, and one must take the respective definitions into account when comparing speedups.

An alternative measure is *efficiency*, which is defined as the ratio between speedup and number of processors:

$$efficiency(P) = speedup(P)/P \ .$$

Unrelated to that definition, the term *efficient* is also used in an informal setting as a synonym for having good performance.

Ideally, one would expect the speedup to grow linearly, and the efficiency to be 1 for all P. Such cases do indeed exist. There even exist cases in which the speedup is *superlinear*, that is, k processors solve a task in less than $1/k$-th of the sequential running time. Such behavior can be explained by the increased cache capacity that was already mentioned. Unfortunately, linear and superlinear speedups are rare. Even worse, for the large majority of programs, the speedup curve lags far behind the ideal case, as shown in Fig. 1.2.

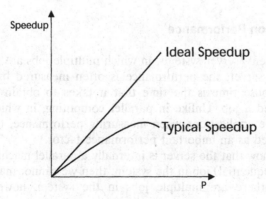

Fig. 1.2 A typical speedup curve.

There are several reasons for the gap between ideal and real speedup:

- *Amdahl's Law*. This observation, attributed to Gene Amdahl [20], states that each computation contains a "serial portion", that is, some part s of the code is not amenable to parallelization. No matter how many processors are used, the execution time cannot be reduced below s. Consequently, the speedup is bounded from above by the constant T_1/s. Fortunately, the implications of Amdahl's law are less limiting than what one might expect. A second observation, called the *Gustafson-Barsis law* in [142], states that a parallel program is often used to solve a larger instance of a problem than its sequential counterpart. Hence, as the number of processors grows, T_1 grows while s remains almost constant. Therefore T_1/s is often not a constant in practice.

- *Task Management and Load Balancing*. Managing the set of tasks induces a certain overhead. Furthermore, it is often difficult if not impossible to split the work evenly between processors.

- *Communication and Synchronization*. Parallelization introduces the need for communication and synchronization. In all current architectures, these activities are slow compared to computation, often by orders of magnitude. The communication costs are measured in terms of latency and bandwidth. *Latency* is the time that it takes to transmit a message from one location to another. *Bandwidth* is the amount of data that can be transferred per unit of time in a stable state. The communication costs comprise the physical transmission costs and the protocol overhead. The latter is particularly high in heterogeneous networks, where data may have to be converted to another format. The communication costs can be reduced, but they cannot be avoided. In theoretical work, Papadimitriou and Ullman [328] have shown an example problem for which each algorithm with optimal computation costs necessarily has nonoptimal communication costs, which dominate the total running time.

Multi-Application Performance

Especially in client/server systems, in which multiple jobs are independently submitted to a server, the performance is often measured by the *response time*. The response time is the time that it takes to obtain a result after having submitted a job. Unlike in parallel computing, in which one avoids running multiple applications when measuring performance, the number of jobs is recognized as an important performance factor.

Assume for now that the server is internally a parallel machine. If there is only a single (sequential) job in the system, then we cannot make use of that parallelism. If there are multiple jobs in the system, however, then we can—by running the jobs on different processors. In other words, the advantage of parallelism is the server's ability to accommodate a higher load. This observation is analogous to the Gustafson-Barsis law: the performance potential is exploited especially in those cases in which the computational demand grows.

The ability of a system to handle high loads is referred to as *throughput*. It is measured as the number of tasks that are accomplished per unit of time. Performance can also be measured as *resource utilization*, for instance as *processor utilization*.

Applications such as video–on–demand critically depend on the availability of resources that they share with other applications, for instance bandwidth and buffer space. *Quality of service* (QoS) is concerned with providing a guaranteed amount of the required resources.

Performance Optimization

In addition to reducing the computational expense as in sequential computing, new performance issues must be tackled. They are outlined in the following text, which is also summarized in Fig. 1.3.

First, *load balancing* is directed at assigning the same amount of work to each processor. It is not sufficient to assign the same number of tasks, because task sizes may vary. If the task sizes are known in advance, load balancing can be accomplished statically at compile time; alternatively the tasks are assigned dynamically at run time. A task can be assigned to a processor once and for all, or it may be allowed to migrate to another processor when the system load changes.

The majority of performance optimization techniques concerns *communication optimization*. We distinguish three major approaches: latency reduction, latency avoidance, and latency tolerance.

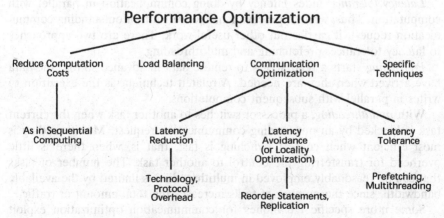

Fig. 1.3 Performance optimization techniques.

Latency reduction comprises those techniques that improve the latency or bandwidth of the system. In addition to technological advances, reduction of protocol overhead falls under this heading.

Latency avoidance makes use of a concept that is known as locality. Locality, generally speaking, is the property of data accesses to cluster in space and/or time. Almost every program exhibits a certain degree of locality. Latency avoidance, also called locality optimization, rearranges a program, for instance by reordering the program statements, so that the degree of locality is increased.

To make the concept of locality more concrete, we observe that memory appears to each processor as a hierarchy. The hierarchy can, for instance, consist of a small but fast cache; a larger but slower local memory; and a remote memory, which comprises all the memory modules that are accessible over the network. The access time to the remote memory modules can moreover depend on the network distance. Details of the memory hierarchy are architecture-specific; as a common characteristic, the capacities and access times are increasing from level to level. Latency avoidance comprises all techniques that increase the percentage of references that go to fast memory modules.

A notable latency avoidance technique is *replication*. Normally, when several processes need access to the same data, the data are transferred back and forth, which is inefficient. With replication, multiple copies of the data are held in different locations, and different processes work with different copies. The idea of replication can be extended to computations; in this case the same computation is run on multiple nodes, which saves the communication of results. A well-known example of replication is *caching*, the insertion of an additional fast memory level that holds frequently used data. Caching is not only used in the design of basic computer architectures, it is also a technique for speeding up the web. The drawback of any form of replication is the necessity to maintain consistency of the replicated data.

Latency tolerance hides latency by doing communication in parallel with computation. Thus, while a processor has to wait for an outstanding communication request, it carries out other useful work. There are two approaches to latency tolerance: prefetching and multithreading.

Prefetching starts a read access to remote data in advance so that the data have arrived when they are needed. A related technique is the execution of writes in parallel with subsequent computations.

With *multithreading*, a processor switches to another task when the current task is blocked by an outstanding communication request. Multithreading is most efficient when context switching is fast, that is, when there is little overhead for transferring the control to another task. The number of tasks that can be reasonably employed in multithreading is limited by the available bandwidth, since the number of tasks increases the total amount of traffic.

Some more specific techniques for communication optimization exploit particular features of the network or transmission protocol. For instance, it is often faster to transmit one large message instead of multiple small messages, and it can pay to aggregate messages prior to sending.

Performance optimization is characterized by tradeoffs. A famous tradeoff exists between load balancing and locality optimization. In the extreme, a parallel program runs on a single processor—locality is perfect, but load balancing is poor.

Due to the complexity of performance optimization, it is useful to concentrate changes on performance-critical program sections, especially on program sections that are executed repeatedly. These sections can be located with the help of profiling and performance visualization tools. Another set of tools allows for performance prediction, that is, developers can assess the performance of their programs in advance, ideally in early design stages.

Complexity of Program Design

Not only performance optimization but program design in general is more complex than in the sequential case. This subsection gives a survey of the new issues which, briefly stated, are similar to those in managing a group of people: splitting the work up into tasks, assigning the tasks to the group members, organizing the communication, etc.

In many practical programming environments, only some of the issues are handled by the programmer. The other issues are committed to automatic tools such as compilers and run-time systems, which find more or less satisfactory solutions. The division of responsibility between programmer and tools is resolved differently in the various programming models.

First, the application must be split into individual tasks. This step includes the choice of an appropriate *granularity* or *task size*. Depending on the granularity, programs are referred to as *fine-*, *medium-*, or *coarse-grained*. Tasks of different sizes can be combined in the same program.

In general, the advantage of coarse-grained programs is a high computation-to-communication ratio. This advantage is due to the locality principle, according to which any one task tends to repeatedly access the same set of data. The advantage of fine-grained programs, on the other hand, is a higher amenability to load balancing, because smaller units can be combined more flexibly into approximately equal loads. The choice of granularity is highly intertwined with the choice of a programming model, since each programming model is tied to a particular range of task sizes. The choice of granularity also interacts with the other issues of program design outlined below.

The next issues are *task scheduling*, the assignment of tasks in a spatial sense to processors and in a temporal sense to start times; and *data distribution*, the assignment of data to processors. Both task scheduling and data distribution have a large influence on performance.

Perhaps even more important is the *management of communication and synchronization*; these activities are also called *coordination*. Only through coordination can processes cooperate and share resources.

Besides performance optimization, *correctness* is an important issue when coordinating processes. Parallel and distributed programs can give rise to so-called *race conditions*, that is, the same computation can produce different outcomes when it is run repeatedly on the same input. Race conditions are due to insufficient synchronization and should be avoided in most cases. A race condition occurs for instance if two processes are each sending a message to a third process, and the output of the third process depends on the order in which the messages arrive. In some rare cases, race conditions are desired, namely when different program runs produce different outputs, and any of the outputs represents a correct result.

An especially detrimental effect is *deadlocks*. A deadlock occurs when processes wait for each other so that the program is unable to proceed.

All the issues listed above, as well as the choice of programming model, software environment, and hardware architecture, interact and should ideally be addressed together. This combination is what creates the severe difficulties encountered in parallel program design.

Intractable Problems

Obviously, one would like to commit as many issues as possible to automatic tools. Unfortunately, there are essential limitations here.

To give an example, Pelagatti [334] surveys a group of intractability results that refer to task scheduling, more specifically to the mapping of program graphs onto architectures. In a program graph, nodes represent processes, and arcs represent precedence constraints and/or communications. The architecture is described by a graph, too—nodes represent processors, and arcs represent communication links. The objective is to find a mapping of the program graph nodes onto the architecture graph nodes, which minimizes some performance cost function. For several practical relevant performance cost functions, the problem is NP-hard and nonapproximable. Simply stated, it takes prohibitively long to find an optimal solution or a solution that is guaranteed to be close to optimum.

Support for Software Development

Parallel programs have typically been small, and thus their software engineering aspects have not yet been sufficiently addressed. As programs become larger, this must change. The same software engineering goals as in sequential computing must be addressed. For instance, large teams must be able to collaborate on a software project, and software components should be reusable. The variety of tools for software development that exists in the sequential domain should be transferred to the parallel domain. The situation is much better in distributed computing, where standards such as CORBA have been developed with software engineering support as an explicit concern.

For parallel and distributed computing, software engineering support is even more important than for sequential computing, because:

- Program design is more complex.

- Larger problems are tackled (especially in distributed computing).

- The field is new to many programmers.

- The idea of decentralized systems seems to be counterintuitive to human thinking, as argued in Resnick [358].

The transition from sequential computing to parallel and distributed computing is supported by extending sequential programming languages instead of inventing completely new ones. This approach also facilitates the reuse of existing programs.

Transparency

Transparency is the hiding of aspects of a system's functionality from the user or programmer. The hidden functionality is managed automatically, so that the user does not need to deal with the corresponding details. On the other hand, the user loses control over the functionality. A different degree of transparency is exhibited to users and programmers who work on different levels of a system. For instance, a programmer can manage the distribution of data among processors, and thereby implement a user interface in which the distribution is transparent.

The concept of transparency closely resembles that of a single system image: We speak of a single system image if the system exposes a certain (not exactly specified) degree of transparency. Well-known forms of transparency include:

- *Location Transparency.* A user does not see which particular resource he or she is using. In particular, the user does not see whether the resource is local or remote (access transparency).

- *Concurrency Transparency.* The fact that several users or processes are sharing a resource is hidden from the user. So the user does not need to deal with the corresponding synchronization issues. If the system contains multiple resources of the same kind, the assignment of processes to individual resources is hidden as well.

- *Failure Transparency.* Elementary failures such as transmission faults are typically handled transparently. Transparency can also be provided for other failures such as the temporal unavailability of a certain processor.

- *Parallelism Transparency.* At present, it is rarely a good idea to hide the existence of multiple processors from the programmer. It may, however, be a useful abstraction for users of application programs.

Obviously, transparency is desirable. If it comes, however, at the price of too high an overhead, then the user may prefer to manage the corresponding functionality him- or herself. Since transparency is based on automatic mechanisms that must work for all cases, self-made solutions for a concrete case are potentially superior. Transparency is sometimes undesirable, for instance when a user wants to access a particular printer. The pros and cons of transparency will be further discussed in later chapters, especially in Ch. 4.

Code and Performance Portability

Loosely speaking, a program is *portable* if it runs on a variety of architectures, including future ones. Portability has clear advantages:

- The effort of writing the program amortizes over time if the program is widely used and has a long life span.

- One can easily switch to a more powerful architecture if more computing power is needed.

- One can easily switch to an alternative architecture if the original system breaks down.

- Programs can be developed on relatively cheap platforms.

Most of the programming languages and tools that are in frequent use today enable the writing of portable programs in the above sense. We call this interpretation of the term *code portability*; it says that programs must produce the same results on a variety of architectures. Code portability is achieved through standards that are widely adopted and remain stable over a long period of time.

A second aspect of portability, *performance portability*, is not yet sufficiently resolved. Performance portability requires a program to run on a variety of architectures in such a way that the observed performance reflects the performance potential of the respective architecture. Performance portability is difficult to achieve, since portability and performance are conflicting goals: If a program runs on several architectures, then the programmer cannot exploit the specifics of a particular machine. The compiler and run-time system can exploit the specifics, but such automatic support is more difficult to implement.

Scalability

Scalability is an obvious goal with a rather fuzzy meaning. Confusion arises in that a variety of definitions are used in different contexts. In general, a system is called *scalable* if its resources can be expanded to accommodate greater computational power.

Resources can be expanded at different levels. At the hardware level, a typical expansion is the addition of processors. Architectures that support this expansion are called scalable. When adding processors, it is often necessary to improve the communication system as well.

The term scaling is used not only for resource adding, but also for the replacement of resources by more powerful ones. At the software level, for instance, an operating system can be replaced by a new version thereof.

When applied to programs, the term scalability is especially confusing. Scaling a program can mean that the program is given more processors, that it is run on a more powerful machine, and/or that the input size is increased. In either case, it can be profitable to adapt the program to the new situation, for instance by choosing a different algorithm.

When scaling a system or a program, one expects a certain performance increase. The term scalability may or may not imply a guaranteed level of increase.

Due to the variety of meanings, only a few general statements can be made about scalability. One is that centralization should be avoided. Centralization creates bottlenecks and limits the degree of parallelism, as we have seen with Amdahl's law.

Heterogeneity

A system is *heterogeneous* if it is composed of dissimilar hardware and software. Heterogeneity can be contrasted with portability: A program that works in a heterogeneous environment must deal with various hardware and software components at the same time, whereas a portable program must run on different systems at different times. Many distributed systems are heterogeneous, whereas parallel programs are often written for homogeneous machines. The widespread use of clusters increases the importance of heterogeneity in parallel computing.

A related notion is *interoperability*. It denotes the ability of different components, possibly from different vendors, to interact. The components can be hardware components such as individual computers; they can also be software components such as application programs or parts of application programs. Of particular interest is the interoperability between program parts that were written in different languages.

In order for components from different vendors to interoperate, the vendors must have agreed on some standard interfaces. A system is called *open* if the manufacturer of the system has made provisions for users or third parties to later add or replace components. Interoperability and openness are concerns in sequential computing, too, but their importance grows in parallel and distributed computing due to the higher system complexity.

An advantage of heterogeneity is the opportunity to combine specialized components. A disadvantage is a possible performance degradation, which is due to the need to transform data between different representations and to recompile programs.

Dependability

Dependability is a broad topic; it covers all issues that are related to the occurrence of faults and other unintended events. Since parallel and distributed systems are complex, there is a lot that can go wrong: On the lowest level, hardware components can break in both the nodes and the communication network, the system can be physically damaged, or the electricity supply can be interrupted. Next, messages sent through the network can be lost or be corrupted during transfer. On a higher level, software can fail due to programming errors or unhandled inputs. Another possible reason for failures is the insufficient provision of resources such as bandwidth. Finally, the failures can be caused by adversary actions.

Dependability comprises reliability, safety, and security. *Reliability* is concerned with the continuation of service in the presence of faults. The goal is to maximize the *availability*, which is the fraction of time that the system is usable. Next, *safety* is concerned with the prevention of catastrophic failures. Finally, *security* deals with the avoidance or tolerance of deliberate attacks. Distributed systems are more susceptible to such attacks than are sequential systems, since distributed systems are accessed by many people and from many locations. Also, the network can be subject to unauthorized eavesdropping.

Dealing with failures involves *fault avoidance*, *fault detection*, and *fault recovery*. Fault detection is especially difficult for transient (nonpermanent) failures, and for Byzantine failures. We speak of Byzantine failures when the faulty component continues working but produces wrong outputs.

If it is not possible to cope fully with a failure, then the system should allow for graceful degradation, that is, it should continue to operate with reduced functionality. Techniques for recovering from faults include *redundancy* and *checkpointing*. Redundancy means having substitutes for the system components in reserve so that the computation can switch to the substitute if an original component breaks. Checkpointing means saving the state of a program from time to time so that, in the event of a failure, the system can resume from a previous state.

Dependability is an important and large area. It is not further discussed in this book. Instead, the interested reader is referred to specialized books such as [30, 346, 380]

General-Purpose versus Special-Purpose Systems

A special-purpose system is one that was specifically designed for a particular application area. For other applications it either is not useful at all or offers suboptimal performance. Application areas that frequently use special-purpose systems include real-time systems and image processing. This book deals almost exclusively with general-purpose systems, that is, with systems that can be used for a variety of application areas.

1.4   MODELS AND PARADIGMS

What are Models and Paradigms?

This book treats models and paradigms. In a sense, it thus covers almost the whole area of general-purpose parallel and distributed computing, and in another sense it covers only a small fraction thereof. This section explains what that means.

Let us first look at Fig. 1.4, which gives a simplified view of the area. The figure shows how parallel and distributed computing mediates between technology (at the bottom), and applications (at the top). Although the figure mentions only a few illustrative concepts, one can see that the conceptual distance to be bridged is very large. Moreover, both the technologies and the

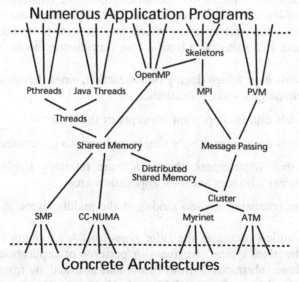

Fig. 1.4 A simplified (and incomplete) view of the parallel and distributed computing field. The purpose of the figure is to illustrate the concept of model hierarchy.

applications are diverse and constantly evolving. Altogether, the field of parallel and distributed computing is very complex.

To manage the complexity, a number of conceptual levels have been introduced in between technology and applications, as shown in the figure. We call such an abstract view a *model*. Models are used widely in science. According to *The Oxford English Dictionary* [385], a model is "a simplified or idealized description or conception of a particular system, situation or process". This is the meaning of the word that we assume here.

In Fig. 1.4, each model describes a selected set of features or capabilities of the system or model below it, and hides other features. The selection of features is driven by a purpose, which derives from the intended usage of the model by the level above it. In this sense, the model provides an abstract view of both the levels below and those above it. Taking it further, a model provides an abstract view of both the technologies and the applications; in other words, it defines a compromise between their respective requirements and opportunities.

Figure 1.4 illustrates yet another fact: The relationship between the models is rarely one-to-one. Many programming models can be realized on several architectures, and many architectures support several programming models. This keeps the field coherent.

In addition to the conceptual hierarchy of models, there is a real hierarchy of systems and interfaces through which programming languages and environments are implemented. The systems and interfaces serve a similar purpose to that of the conceptual models: managing complexity and facilitating a division of labor. Yet, the two hierarchies are different.

The models more towards the bottom or top of the conceptual hierarchy are called low-level or high-level, respectively. This book concentrates on models at about the *middle* levels, which have several favorable properties that make them well suited as a basis for an introductory book:

- The models have a high degree of abstraction, since they omit details of both technologies and applications.

- The models express important concepts of the field.

- The models are comparatively simple and easy to understand.

- Due to their abstractness, the models are relatively stable in face of technological advances and new application areas.

- There are comparatively few models at the middle levels.

A second notion occurs in the title: *paradigm*. A paradigm is a kind of model that describes typical structures or patterns of application programs. As argued above, abstractions from below and abstractions from above are combined in the design of a model. Thus the distinction between models and paradigms is rather vague.

Of course, the term "middle level" is vague as well, and some of the inclusions and omissions in this book are probably arguable. Essentially, the term stands for two classes of models:

- Programming models, which describe a programmer's view of the parallel or distributed system, and

- Abstract models, which have associated cost measures and are used in algorithm design.

Programming models   Only a few programming models were explicitly suggested and formulated as models by their inventors. The large majority, in contrast, were implicitly defined through the definition of a programming language or library. In fact, each programming language, together with libraries, run-time system, etc., defines a programming model.

In many contexts, the term *application programming interface* (API) is used instead of programming model. The difference between the terms consists in the focus on underlying principles in the case of a model, as opposed to the explicitness about usage details such as function names, parameter types, etc. in the case of an API.

Due to the abstractness of models, there is in general not a one-to-one correspondence between programming models and programming languages/environments. On one hand, a model can be realized by several languages/environments. We will later see the example of message passing, which can be coupled with both C and Fortran. On the other hand, a single language can realize several programming models. The most prominent example is Java, which, partially through extensions, supports almost all of the major programming models that we discuss in this book.

The term programming model has a different meaning in other areas of computer science. In particular, it often stands for the complete semantics of a language and includes issues such as typing, inheritance, and security. In this book, the term is restricted to those aspects of a language or environment that are related to the management of parallelism/distribution. It is often difficult to untangle the parallelism/distribution issues from the multitude of software engineering and other issues. In favor of a short and focused book, I have nevertheless tried to do so, and only briefly mention other considerations, even though they are often important aspects of the respective approaches.

In summary, this book covers a horizontal slice of the parallel and distributed computing field. The advantage of this approach is the opportunity to overview the whole field within a relatively short text. My hope is that this view will help to emphasize the central and unifying ideas. Of course the approach also has a distinct disadvantage: The book does not cover any of the subjects in sufficient depth to allow one to start working with them immediately. Hence, after reading this book, one should continue reading more specialized books on whatever the particular field of interest is. There are currently many excellent publications that treat particular programming paradigms, architectures, methodologies for software design, algorithms, etc. The purpose of this book is to give the overview that is necessary to decide on a particular subarea to study, and to provide general background.

Bridging models Models give the programmer or algorithm designer a simplified but hopefully sufficiently correct view of a system whose complexity he or she would otherwise not be able to manage. Since models define a compromise between hardware capabilities and software requirements, they must be *designed*.

With the rise of parallel computing, model design has become a research topic. The situation was different in sequential computing, where a single model, the von Neumann computer, was established early, and was thereafter relied upon throughout the field. The need of a comparable central unifying model for parallel computing was recognized in the late 1980s and early 1990s. Hardware [381], as well as software [395] and algorithm [422] designers felt that they needed a standard model (or at least a small number of fundamental models [381]) as a basis for their work. Such a standard model is sometimes called *bridging model* [422] and serves several purposes:

- It tells hardware designers which functionality they should support.

- It tells software designers which functionality they can assume to be provided by each architecture.

- It gives algorithm designers a realistic model of the machines.

Hence, a bridging model facilitates the division of labor between hardware, software, and algorithm designers.

Now, about ten years later, a single bridging model or standard still does not exist. However, a relatively small number of major models have been established, which are quite stable and mature. Most models are at a slightly higher level of abstraction than the envisioned bridging model. Nevertheless, they serve a similar purpose: defining an abstract machine that software designers can assume and hardware designers strive to support.

Design Goals and Tradeoffs

People think in terms of concepts or paradigms. ... If one has the correct paradigms, ... solutions may be easy.

Shuey, Spooner, and Frieder [379]

In the following, we list design goals for programming models. Abstract models for algorithm design have slightly differing goals. Since abstract models are handled in a separate chapter of this book, we do not go into detail here.

Programmability A model should help make the programming task as easy as possible. Therefore, it should conceal architectural details. It should make the complexity of program design manageable for the programmer, by committing as many responsibilities as possible to the tools. This issue has already been discussed.

For programmability, a model should furthermore provide constructs in which programmers can directly express their algorithmic intentions. The constructs should facilitate the design of well-structured programs.

Other considerations include support for maintenance, reusability, and correctness. For instance, a model should try to make race conditions and deadlocks impossible or at least easy to detect.

Related with programmability is the goal that the definition of the model itself should be concise, since people prefer to work with simple concepts.

Reflectivity A model should give a realistic picture of the architectures that it describes. At a minimum, essential features such as the number of processors or the existence of special resources in a heterogeneous system should be made visible to the programmer. There is no universal answer to the question whether a particular feature should be represented or not. It depends on the capabilities of the compilers, run-time systems, and other tools, and also on specifics of the application. As a general rule, a model should represent those features that a programmer can use to significantly improve the performance or functionality of a program, but it should not represent those features that can almost equally well be exploited by automatic tools.

A model should guide the programmer in using the most appropriate features. In no case should it permit the exploitation of loopholes, that is, of mechanisms that appear to be simple in the model but are difficult to realize in practice.

Cost model Whenever programming requires some consideration of performance, which is almost always the case, it is useful for the programming model to include a cost model. Sometimes, the cost model can be rough. For instance, it may be sufficient that the programmer is aware of expensive constructs and avoids their excessive use.

In performance-oriented parallel computing, a cost model should represent, at least to some extent, the relative costs of computation, communication, and synchronization. It is still a matter of debate in how much detail these costs should be represented.

A cost model is needed by the programmer as a basis for making an intelligent decision in favor of one implementation variant out of several opportunities. The cost model can be supplemented by performance prediction tools, which estimate the costs of an implementation variant that has already been formulated as a program.

Architecture independence A programming model should describe a range of architectures. It should reflect these architectures as explained above. Architecture-independent programming models are a prerequisite for performance portability. Only architecture-independent programs can be translated by compilers/tools so that they run efficiently on a variety of architectures.

Flexibility Programming models should provide constructs that support a variety of application areas and higher-level programming styles. Flexibility is useful, since it keeps the number of programming models low. Also, different parts of an application can be handled in the same programming model.

Tradeoffs Obviously, the above goals are in tension with each other. Programmability and architecture independence require abstraction from architectural features, whereas reflectivity is facilitated by explicit representation. There does not seem to be a universally best tradeoff between abstraction and reflectivity. The tradeoff depends largely from specifics of a particular application. For instance, one may give less attention to communication costs if applications are coarse-grained.

The importance of performance depends not only on the contents of a program, but also on the context in which it is developed. Alpern and Carter [16] observe that the total costs of an application are composed of the development costs and the run-time costs. Depending on the number of program runs, one or the other should be focused on. Correspondingly, Alpern and Carter distinguish between performance programming and expedient programming.

The existence of different reasonable tradeoffs is one reason for the existence of different programming models. Another reason is the fact that different application areas utilize different architectural features. Heterogeneity, mobility, and even parallelism are currently exploited in only some of the applications.

Classification Schemes

There are relatively few widely used models for parallel and distributed computing, but many more research proposals or less well-known approaches. Naturally, this diversity calls for classification. In the following, I review some classification schemes from the literature. Although they were suggested in different contexts, they provide criteria that we can later use to assess the various models.

Flynn's classification scheme and extensions This scheme is simple but famous. It was introduced in 1972 by Michael Flynn [152] and distinguishes between four classes of computers: SISD, SIMD, MISD, and MIMD. In these abbreviations, the first two letters say whether multiple instructions can be carried out at the same time, and the last two letters say whether multiple data can be processed at the same time. For instance, SIMD stands for "single instruction, multiple data". SISD computers are von Neumann computers; MISD computers have probably never been built. Parallel architectures can be classified into SIMD and MIMD, but nowadays the large majority of machines are MIMD.

SIMD and MIMD are established terms and still widely used. Yet more often, you will see the abbreviations SPMD and MPMD. They stand for "single program, multiple data" and "multiple program, multiple data" respectively, which are subclasses of MIMD. In the SPMD paradigm, all processes carry out the same program on different data. In the MPMD paradigm, different processes carry out different programs. The borderline between SPMD and MPMD is fuzzy, as we will see later.

The extended Flynn classification is, in a sense, orthogonal to the level-of-abstraction classification that is represented by the model hierarchy. For instance, SIMD is a concept that characterizes both architectures and programming languages.

Classification scheme of El-Rewini and Lewis This scheme was proposed only recently in [142]. It refers to parallel and distributed computing, not merely to parallel computing like the previous scheme. The scheme uses two dimensions for classification: granularity, and degree of coupling in the system architecture. The first dimension distinguishes between fine-, medium-, and large-grained problems, and the second dimension distinguishes between tightly coupled, coupled, loosely coupled, and shared-database system architectures.

Classification scheme of Skillicorn and Talia This scheme is especially important for us, because it refers explicitly to programming models. The scheme was proposed in 1998 in [392] and focuses on parallel computing. The scheme uses two dimensions for classification as well. In the first dimension, models are classified according to their degree of abstraction, which is related to the level in the model hierarchy. Strictly speaking, the degree of abstraction reflects how many program design activities are the responsibility of the programmer and how many are the responsibility of tools. Six classes are distinguished in this dimension:

- Models with implicit parallelism: The programmer does not give any hints on the parallel execution of the program.

- Models with explicit parallelism but implicit decomposition: The programmer indicates potential for parallelism, but lets the tools decide whether it is exploited, that is, the tools define the parallel tasks.

- Models with explicit decomposition but implicit mapping: The programmer defines the tasks, but all other activities are committed to tools.

- Models with explicit mapping but implicit communication: Like the previous class, except that the programmer is also responsible for task scheduling.

- Models with explicit communication but implicit synchronization: The programmer is responsible for most of the activities. Only synchronization is supported to a certain degree.

- Models in which the full program design complexity is managed by the programmer.

In the second dimension, the classification scheme distinguishes between three classes:

- Models with a dynamic number of processes and with no limit to the communication volume. (Dynamic means unknown before run time.)

- Models with a statically fixed number of processes and with no limit to the communication volume. (Statically fixed means known at compile time.)

- Models with a statically fixed number of processes and with a limited communication volume.

The classification scheme has a total of 18 classes, of which 15 are exemplified by existing models in [392].

Language-based classification Frequently, programming languages (and with them their associated models) are classified from a language point of view into:

- Extended conventional languages with constructs for expressing parallelism, task scheduling, communication, etc. The extensions can take the form of

  - Libraries,

  - Compiler directives, or

  - Language constructs.

- New languages.

- Conventional languages whose implicit parallelism is exploited by tools.

Pros and cons of the various approaches will be discussed later.

1.5 REMARKS ON THE ORGANIZATION OF THE BOOK

The book is principally organized by placing each major programming model (or a group of related programming models) in a separate chapter. Less well-known models and approaches have been assigned to the major model they are most similar to. The placement decision was not always obvious, and in fact some topics could as well have been treated elsewhere. In particular, there is some overlap between the chapters, and several otherwise unrelated programming models have features in common.

By this style of organization, I do not intend to define a strict classification scheme. It is rather a loose framework for presentational purposes, in which related ideas are discussed together.

The book starts with some background knowledge on architectures. Then the various programming models are handled one after another. The order of the chapters is loosely based on the principle of going from low-level to high-level models. Abstract models are covered in a separate chapter. The book finishes with a final comparison of all models.

Throughout the book, I have included discussions and comparisons between the models. The assessments express my personal opinion and impression from studying the literature, and are arguable to a certain extent. Assessments are elusive because the properties of programming models depend on the concrete implementation, architecture, and application, and these may change over time. Moreover, several topics are under debate.

A major goal of this book is to convey the essential ideas of the parallel and distributed computing field without going into much detail. To achieve this, the presentation of concepts is occasionally simplified.

BIBLIOGRAPHICAL REMARKS

Basics of parallel and/or distributed computing have been treated in several textbooks: Almasi and Gottlieb [15], Baker and Smith [33], Coulouris et al. [119], Crichlow [120], El-Rewini and Lewis [142], Singh [386], Tanenbaum [408], and others. More exhaustive books in the area are Zomaya [455] and Hwang and Xu [220]. Other interesting readings include Pelagatti [334], and Skillicorn and Talia [392].

As yet, there is no generally agreed on definition for the notions of parallel and distributed. The definitions that are given in the literature differ, for instance, in whether they consider shared-memory parallel computers as distributed systems, and in whether they require distributed systems to provide a single system image. Definitions or characterizations are given, for example, in Agha and Kim [11], Almasi and Gottlieb [15, p. 5], Baker and Smith [33, p. 1], Coulouris et al. [119, p. 2], Crichlow [120, p. 2], Zomaya [455, p. 6], El-Rewini and Lewis [142, pp. 2–3], and Tanenbaum [408, p. 2].

The history of parallel computing is quite extensively treated in Culler et al. [124]. Early references that acknowledge the convergence of parallel and distributed computing include Blair [56] and Zomaya [456]. An interesting discussion of the relationship between the fields is also given by Pfister [338]. Concurrent computing is covered in textbooks and survey papers such as [32, 131], whereas a definition for supercomputers is given in Hord [215]. The notions of decentralized, networked, and collaborative computing are used, for example, in Wu [445] and Farley [146].

Section 1.2 draws on related presentations in Almasi and Gottlieb [15], El-Rewini and Lewis, [142]. Singh [386], Skillicorn and Talia [392], and Tanenbaum [408]. A relatively detailed account of various application areas is given in Baker and Smith [33].

Section 1.3 has adopted material from the following main sources, which are also suggested for further reference:

- Multi–Application performance: El-Rewini and Lewis [142].

- Complexity of program design: Pelagatti [334].

- Support for software development: Dubois [138].

- Transparency: Tanenbaum [408] and Singh [386]; for the original definition see the Reference Model of Open Distributed Processing (RM-ODP) [317].

- Portability: Baker and Smith [33] and Pelagatti [334].

- Scalability: Hwang and Xu [220].

- Heterogeneity: Shuey et al. [379].

- Dependability: Tanenbaum [408] and Wu [445].

A glossary of basic terminology is provided by Wilson [441].

The treatment of model hierarchy loosely follows a prior presentation in Heywood and Leopold [204]. The notion of models is also inspired by Akl [13], Pelagatti [334], Pfister [338], and Skillicorn and Talia [392]. The presentation of design goals for models draws on material from Pelagatti [334], Skillicorn and Talia [392], Heywood and Ranka [205], and Maggs et al. [277].

The extended Flynn classification is, for example, explained in Hwang and Xu [220] and Pfister [338]. Pelagatti [334] describes another classification scheme, which is similar in spirit to the scheme of Skillicorn and Talia. Further classification schemes are reviewed in Almasi and Gottlieb [15] and Crichlow [120].

2

Architectures

This chapter gives a brief overview of the major classes of parallel and distributed architectures. Whereas different classes had widely differing characteristics in the past, we are at present observing a convergence [124]. This chapter is nevertheless organized around the different classes, as their existence inspired the development of different programming models. The following classes are distinguished: SIMD computers, symmetric multiprocessors, cache-coherent NUMA architectures, distributed-memory parallel computers, clusters, loosely coupled distributed systems, and grids. An additional section provides preliminaries on network technologies. The chapter finishes with bibliographical remarks and references to less common architectures.

2.1 SIMD COMPUTERS

Early parallel architectures often followed the SIMD style of computing. These machines are composed of a powerful control processor and an array of relatively simple processing elements (PEs), as shown in Fig. 2.1. Memory is distributed, that is, each PE is in charge of a separate memory module.

SIMD computers maintain only a single copy of the program and a single program counter; both are stored in the control processor. As in a sequential machine, the control processor repeatedly issues a next instruction and decodes it. If the instruction refers to data in the control processor's own memory, then it executes the instruction as usual. Otherwise, it broadcasts

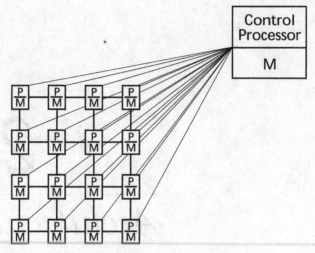

Fig. 2.1 A typical SIMD architecture. P stands for processor, and M stands for memory module.

the instruction to all the PEs, which thereupon carry it out on (different) data in their respective memories.

Due to the broadcast mechanism, it is not possible for two PEs to carry out different instructions in the same step. Nevertheless, a PE can sit idle for an instruction if, as a result of a prior condition evaluation, a certain flag was set.

Besides doing computations on local data, the PEs can also be instructed to communicate with one another. Therefore they are interconnected, often in a two-dimensional mesh scheme as in Fig. 2.1. If a communication follows the interconnection pattern (for instance, if each PE sends data to its right neighbor in the two-dimensional mesh), then the communication is comparatively fast. If the communication is irregular, however (that is, if the directions and distances of different messages differ), then the communication is slower, but it can nevertheless be accomplished.

Examples of SIMD architectures are the Connection Machine CM-2 of Thinking Machines [215] and the MasPar MP-2 of MasPar Computer Corporation [215, 282]. These machines belong to different generations. Whereas the CM-2 contains up to about 65 000 very simple PEs, the PEs of the MP-2 are more powerful but smaller in number.

The current trend is in the direction of using commodity processors and of supporting SPMD instead of SIMD. Pure SIMD designs seem to be disappearing as general-purpose platforms. They are being replaced by MIMD machines with explicit support for SPMD mechanisms such as fast broadcast and synchronization [124]. In special-purpose computing such as multimedia and real-time applications, however, the SIMD idea lives on. For instance, it is used in the Internet streaming SIMD extensions of the Intel Pentium III processor [410].

2.2 SYMMETRIC MULTIPROCESSORS

Symmetric multiprocessors (SMPs) have been in use since about the mid 1960s [124]. They are very popular now, especially as servers for commercial computing. SMPs are typically run in SPPS (serial program, parallel system) mode, but parallel computing is possible as well.

SMPs currently have between 2 and at least 64 processors, which are commodity processors. The architectures are either bus- or switch-based, as illustrated with three typical organizations in Fig. 2.2. In Fig. 2.2, the memory

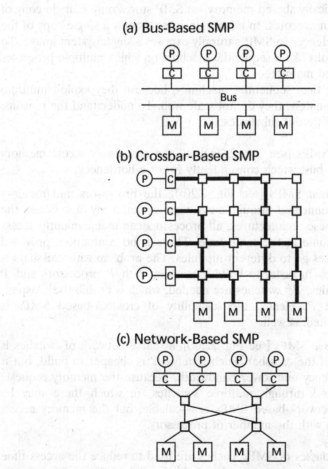

Fig. 2.2 SMP architectures. P stands for processor, C stands for cache, and M stands for memory module.

is split into several physical modules, as is often done in real machines. SMPs have the following characteristics:

- They have a *single address space*, that is, each processor can access each memory location via normal load/store instructions of the hardware.

- Processors communicate with each other by writing to and reading from the *shared memory*.

- The relation between processors and memory modules is *symmetric*, that is, the access time to a particular memory cell is the same for all processors. This symmetry is also called *uniform memory access* (UMA). Access to IO controllers is symmetric, too, but IO issues are not elaborated upon in this book.

Due to the physically shared memory, an SMP stores only a single copy of each program that it executes. In particular, it stores only a single copy of the operating system. Hence, an SMP naturally exposes a single system image. To a user, the SMP looks like a sequential machine on which multiple processes run in a time-shared manner.

SMPs are faster than sequential machines, because they exploit multiple processors. Unfortunately, they do not scale well. To understand the reasons, let us look at the different subclasses:

- In *bus-based* SMPs [see Fig. 2.2(a)], all the processors access memory over the same bus, which consequently forms a bottleneck.

- In *crossbar-based* SMPs [see Fig. 2.2(b)], the processors and memory modules are connected through a two-dimensional array of switches, the crossbar. In these architectures, all processors can independently access a memory module at the same time. There is no contention, provided that the accesses go to different modules. The problem with crossbars is hardware costs. In order to build a machine with P processors and P memory modules, P^2 switches are needed, which is prohibitively expensive for large P. Hence, the scalability of crossbar-based SMPs is practically limited as well.

- In *network-based* SMPs [see Fig. 2.2(c)], a sparse network of switches is used instead of the crossbar. Such a network is cheaper to build, but it has higher latency and lower bandwidth, because the memory requests must be routed through multiple switches, in which there may be contention. Network-based SMPs are scalable, but the memory access time increases with the number of processors.

In all three subclasses of SMPs, caches are used to reduce the access time to memory. As in uniprocessors, caches hold those data that are frequently accessed during some period of program execution. Data are replicated from the shared memory to the cache when they are accessed; they are overwritten when they have not been accessed for a while. To be more precise, data are transferred in units of *cache lines*, which are collections of a few consecutive data. As in uniprocessors, we often have two levels of cache: L1 and L2. The L1 cache is faster and smaller than the L2 cache, but the L2 cache is still faster and smaller than the main memory. Caches reduce the frequency of accesses to the shared memory, and hence they reduce the contention in bus-, as well as crossbar- and network-based SMPs.

The use of caches raises the problem of coherency. When a memory cell is written, cached copies of that cell become invalid, and the copy holders must be informed about that. Cache coherence is a large research area, and various, often sophisticated, protocols have been suggested over the years. With any protocol, the maintenance of cache coherence has a price in time and hardware costs. The price increases with the number of processors.

SMPs have the advantage of being comparatively easy to program, since data distribution is not an issue. The gain is smaller than what one might expect, however, since the programmer must still strive for locality in order to get performance. That is because, despite the symmetry, the access time to main memory differs from that to cache.

Examples of SMP architectures are the Intel Pentium Pro processor, which internally consists of up to four bus-connected processors [124], and the Sun Enterprise 10 000 Server, which consists of up to 64 processors and a proprietary crossbar interconnect [403].

2.3 CACHE-COHERENT NUMA ARCHITECTURES

As we have learned in the previous section, network-based SMPs have the same latency and bandwidth for all processor–memory pairs, but these measures deteriorate as the number of processors grows. Pfister [338] coins the term uniformly *bad* memory access (U*B*MA) in a similar context. Technically, it is easy to speed up *part* of the memory accesses, by directly connecting each processor to one of the memory modules. In terms of performance, this modification comes at no price, since the latency remains constant for the other accesses. Even better, as some accesses are fulfilled locally, the bandwidth requirements decrease. This design is thus very reasonable, and it is normally preferred to SMPs for large processor numbers.

The new design is called *cache-coherent nonuniform memory access* (CC-NUMA). It is visualized in Fig. 2.3. CC-NUMA architectures have the following characteristics:

- They have a *single address space*, that is, each processor can access each memory location via normal load/store instructions of the hardware.

- Processors communicate with each other by writing to and reading from the *shared memory*.

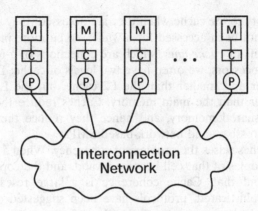

Fig. 2.3   CC-NUMA architecture.

- The relation between processors and memory modules is *not symmetric*. Each processor has an associated *local memory*, which can be accessed faster than the rest of memory, the *remote memory*.

The difference between the access times to the local and remote memories increases with the number of processors. There are two reasons: First, the size of the interconnection network grows. Second, the cache coherence protocol induces more and more overhead—cache coherence protocols are more complicated for CC-NUMA architectures than they are for SMPs.

When a processor reads data from a remote memory, the data are placed in the processor's cache so that consecutive accesses are fast. If the data later have to be replaced due to limited cache capacity, it depends on the operating system where they are written to. Normally, the data are just written back to the remote memory where they came from. The operating system may, however, decide to migrate the data to the local memory, since, due to locality, it is likely that the same processor will access the data again and again. Similarly, it may pay to replicate the data in order to facilitate concurrent access by multiple processors.

An example of a CC-NUMA architecture is the Sequent NUMA-Q 2000 [376]. It contains up to 64 Pentium III Xeon processors, which are internally SMPs. Another example architecture is the SGI Origin [262]. For this architecture, Laudon and Lenoski [262] give ratios for the access times to L1 cache : L2 cache : local memory : remote memory. The ratios are about 1 : 10 : 60 : 120 for a four-processor machine, and 1 : 10 : 60 : 180 for a 128-processor machine.

As in SMPs, it is not necessary to distribute the data, but a well-chosen data layout can speed up programs. The effect of the data distribution is stronger, because of the additional difference in the access times to local and remote memories.

2.4 DISTRIBUTED-MEMORY PARALLEL COMPUTERS

In this section, we treat parallel architectures with no or limited hardware support for the shared-memory abstraction. The generic structure of these so-called distributed-memory parallel computers is shown in Fig. 2.4. It is the same as that of CC-NUMA architectures, except that the hardware support for cache coherence is lacking. In the extreme, a distributed-memory parallel machine can be a collection of independent computers that are each composed of processors, memory modules, IO facilities, etc. This case corresponds to clusters and is treated in Sect. 2.6. The present section concentrates on more tightly integrated designs that are built and sold as a unit, although the borderline with clusters is fuzzy.

Distributed-memory parallel computers can be classified as *non-cache-coherent NUMA* (NCC-NUMA) and *no remote memory access* (NORMA) architectures. Both classes tend to deploy more processors than SMPs and CC-NUMA machines. They are easier to build on a large scale, since they do not need cache coherence hardware.

NCC-NUMA is similar to CC-NUMA in that both architectures have a single address space, interprocess communication goes through a shared memory, and the memory is physically distributed among the processors. NCC-NUMA architectures differ from CC-NUMA architectures in that only data from the local memory are written to cache.

Thus, operating-system support for page migration and replication is more important than in the CC-NUMA case. The corresponding functionality can alternatively be provided by run-time libraries, applications, or other software environments.

NCC-NUMA architectures are often classified as shared-memory, since the processors can access the remote memory via normal load/store instructions. In contrast, NORMA architectures have multiple address spaces, and

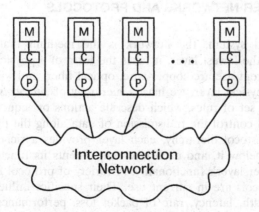

Fig. 2.4 Architecture of a distributed-memory parallel computer.

the processors access the remote memories via IO-like instructions. These instructions tend to be slower, but due to powerful optimizations the borderline is disappearing [124].

Many people feel that it is more difficult to program a distributed than a shared-memory machine, since the data distribution must be specified. Hence, much research has been conducted on implementing a shared-memory abstraction on top of a distributed-memory architecture by means of software. The concept is called *software distributed shared memory* or just *distributed shared memory* (DSM). It is dealt with in Ch. 4 of this book.

An example of a NCC-NUMA architecture is the CRAY T3E [383], which contains up to 2048 processors. An example of a NORMA architecture is the Intel ASCI Option Red Supercomputer [286]. The largest currently working machine of this type consists of almost 10 000 Pentium Pro processors, each being a two-processor SMP internally. The processors communicate through IO-like mechanisms, with specific options for the SMP pairs. At the time of this writing, the Intel ASCI Option Red Supercomputer is the most powerful computer in the world, according to the Top 500 list of supercomputer sites [416].

Summarizing the last three sections, we have a spectrum of MIMD parallel architectures that reaches from SMPs over CC-NUMA, NCC-NUMA, and NORMA architectures until clusters. The various architectures differ in their degree of hardware support for the shared-memory abstraction and for communication in general. The borderlines between the various classes are fuzzy. In recognition of increasingly similar techniques in hardware design, Culler et al. [124] speak of a convergence of parallel computer architectures.

Now we turn to distributed architectures, which are distinguished as clusters, loosely coupled distributed systems, and grids. Before the classes are introduced in more detail, the following section is devoted to preliminaries on network technologies and protocols.

2.5 COMPUTER NETWORKS AND PROTOCOLS

In a distributed system, the network is the medium that connects the computers. On the lowest layer, it takes the form of a physical transmission medium. In current use are copper wire, optical fiber, and wireless media.

Above the physical layer, we have a hierarchy of *protocols*. A protocol is an agreed-upon set of rules, which describe actions or sequences of actions that initiate and control the transmission of data along the physical connections. In the protocol hierarchy, each layer provides a richer functionality than the layer below it, and each layer implements its functionality on the basis of the lower layer's functionality. A variety of protocol hierarchies and individual protocols are in current use. Their specifics influence properties such as bandwidth, latency, rate of packet loss, performance advantage of long over short messages, existence of performance guarantees, etc.

Which physical media and protocols are used depends on the purpose of the network. The most important distinction is between *local area networks* (LANs) and *wide area networks* (WANs). A LAN connects relatively few computers within a small area, for instance within a building or campus. If the area is particularly small and if the connected computers are primarily used as a single system, we speak of a *system area network* (SAN). A WAN, in contrast, connects many computers within a large geographical area such as a country or continent. On an intermediate scale between LANs and WANs, we have *metropolitan area networks* (MANs). They are not treated here, and neither are other more specific classes.

A major difference between LANs and WANs can be seen in their interconnection topology. In LANs, the computers often communicate over a shared medium such as a bus, whereas in WANs, messages are sent through intermediate network nodes. These nodes take the form of bridges, switches, routers, or gateways, and are special devices or computers that control the path of the message through the network. Intermediate nodes can also function as firewalls, which block suspicious messages for reasons of security. WANs are hierarchically structured. They are irregularly composed of sub- and sub-subnetworks, and connections at higher levels typically provide larger bandwidths.

A message can normally take several paths from source to destination. Possible criteria for the selection of a path include dynamic factors such as the current congestion along different routes. In many networks, long messages are not transferred as a whole, but they are split up into several *packets* of a maximum size, and transferred separately. The activities concerned with moving packets from source to destination are referred to as *routing*.

Routing mechanisms can be classified into *connection-oriented* and *connectionless* schemes. In connectionless schemes, the packets of a message are moved independently, possibly along different paths. In connection-oriented schemes, they are routed along the same path, which is called a connection. The connection must be established prior to sending a message, and is released afterwards.

In connection-oriented routing, only the first packet holds the full destination address, whereas the others just need an identification of the connection to which they belong. Hence, less overhead information is moved around, and the processing of messages in the intermediate nodes is simplified. Connectionless routing, on the other hand, eliminates the need for connection establishment.

TCP/IP and UDP/IP

The major current protocol family for WANs is TCP/IP. It is very popular, since it is used in the Internet. TCP/IP is actually two main protocols, TCP and IP.

The Internet Protocol (IP) runs on a relatively low layer of the protocol hierarchy. It is a connectionless protocol and provides a so-called *best-effort* service. Best-effort means that IP tries to transfer all packets, but it does not give any guarantees. In particular, it is possible that packets get lost or become corrupted during transfer. Packet loss is frequently caused by congestion, since IP allows an intermediate node to throw away packets when it is overloaded.

The Transmission Control Protocol (TCP) runs on the layer above IP and expands the IP functionality into a reliable and connection-oriented service. TCP is concerned with the transfer of whole messages, which can be of variable size. The messages are first split up into packets at the source, then handed over to IP for transfer, and finally reassembled at the destination. TCP checks if all packets have arrived, and if their contents are correct according to some checksum. In case of errors, retransmission is requested. TCP also accomplishes flow control, that is, it adapts the speed of injecting packets into the network to the receiver speed.

Although the reliable service of TCP is desirable, it comes at the price of a high overhead that makes TCP slow. In several applications (e.g. multimedia), speed is more important than reliability. In these cases, the Unreliable Datagram Protocol (UDP) is a useful alternative to TCP. It runs atop of IP, too, but is connectionless and transmits data in packets that are called *datagrams*. UDP is a rather minor extension of IP that adds checksums and port numbers (explained in Sect. 6.2). As with IP, datagrams may get lost.

As shown in Fig. 2.5, applications can be built directly on top of TCP and UDP. Often, however, there is an intermediate software layer in between, which uses the TCP or UDP functionality to implement a different and more

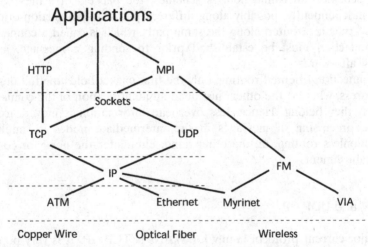

Fig. 2.5 Structure of the protocol hierarchy and typical relations between major protocols.

comfortable programming model. Intermediate layers also facilitate portability, since the same programming model can be implemented on top of various protocols.

As shown in Fig. 2.5, IP, TCP, and UDP are supplemented by other protocols. Some of them are treated below; many more protocols and protocol combinations exist. The protocol hierarchy resembles the hierarchy of models from Sect. 1.4 in that a variety of technologies and applications is unified by a few protocols (or models) at an intermediate level.

ATM

A major disadvantage of TCP and UDP is their reliance on the best-effort service of IP, so they cannot give performance guarantees. A well-known, although not yet widely used, alternative is the Asynchronous Transfer Mode (ATM) protocol.

ATM is connection-oriented and transfers data in very small units called *cells*. ATM still allows nodes to throw away packets, but it selects the packets on the basis of differing QoS (quality of service) requirements. Also, those packets that arrive are guaranteed to be in the right order. ATM was developed with several applications in mind, of which data exchange in the context of distributed computing is an example only. In addition to facilitating QoS, ATM has a speed advantage over TCP/IP.

LAN Technologies

ATM is a technology for both WANs and LANs. In the LAN case, it has a strong competitor, *Ethernet*, which has historically evolved into an ubiquitous technology. Ethernet comes in three variants: the original Ethernet, Fast Ethernet, and Gigabit Ethernet. The variants, which were introduced between the early 1980s and the end 1990s, differ mainly in their speed.

The basic mechanism of Ethernet assumes a shared medium such as a bus. All the interconnected computers can read from that medium at the same time, but only one computer can write to it. If a computer has a message to send, it waits until the medium is free and then starts writing. It can happen that two computers start writing at the same time. Such collisions are recognized by the writing computers, which then stop the transmission, wait for a random time period, and afterwards try to write again.

The Ethernet protocol is connectionless. QoS-oriented modifications are being worked on, but so far ATM is superior in that respect. Ethernet supports a range of message sizes. Instead of the bus, a central switch can be used (especially in the newer variants). By composing switches, hierarchical network topologies can be built up.

Another mechanism for LANs is the *token ring*. Here the network has the topology of a ring in which one or several tokens, possibly marked with some priority, circle round. A computer that is willing to send must first take possession of a matching token; it releases the token after the transfer.

General Issues

Now that we have become acquainted with some well-known technologies and protocols, it is time to consider their interrelationships and to discuss general performance issues.

Ethernet, ATM, and several other protocols focus on the lower layers of the protocol hierarchy. Although the notion of ATM is actually associated with a complete hierarchy, protocol hierarchies have the advantage that independently developed protocols can be combined. Typical combinations are TCP/IP on top of the lower ATM layers, and TCP/IP on top of Ethernet.

The opportunity to compose different protocols is useful for compatibility in heterogeneous networks. The drawback is a significant overhead, which is on one hand due to the fact that each layer must activate the next lower layer's functionality. On the other hand, it is likely that some functionality is provided twice. The existence of the protocol hierarchy makes statements of the form "Protocol X has bandwidth Y" difficult, since each additional layer adds overhead and consequently provides less bandwidth than the underlying protocol or technology would permit.

As was already noted, the latency and bandwidth of a network are determined by the speed of the physical transmission medium and by the protocol overhead. Often, the protocol overhead is the more decisive of the two factors. It is particularly high if the packets are small.

The communication speed is limited by both the latency and the bandwidth. The latency problem seems to be more fundamental, since the bandwidth can be increased to almost any value by adding more wires and switches. Latency improvement, in contrast, is eventually limited by the speed of light.

A very important performance factor is congestion. Particularly in WANs, the observed latencies and bandwidths are highly dependent on congestion that stems from unrelated users and applications—as we all know from the Web.

The situation is better in LANs, where the routing paths are shorter, heterogeneity is much less of an issue, and security is easier to maintain. Also, LANs are comparatively small, so that upgrades to new technologies are less costly and lie in the purview of a single organization.

Figure 2.6 presents a survey of major network protocols. Although the numbers are based on 1997 technology, the figure nicely reflects some general trends:

- The communication speed tends to fall with increasing size of the network.

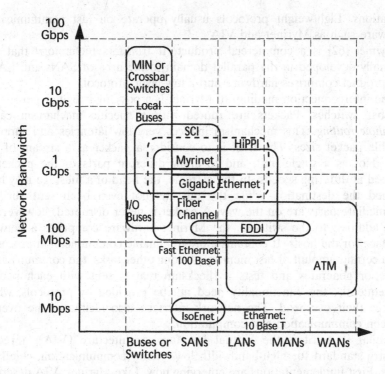

Fig. 2.6 A survey of network technologies. Reprinted, by permission, from K. Hwang and Z. Xu, *Scalable Parallel Computing*, [220, p. 274]. © 1998 The McGraw-Hill Companies.

- A technology can normally be used for a certain range of network sizes.

- The borderlines between the various classes of distributed systems are blurry.

SAN Technologies and Lightweight Protocols

In general, the performance of current networks lags behind the technological opportunities. This is partially due to the costs of modern technologies. It is also due to the design of the common TCP/IP protocols, which pay more attention to portability than to performance.

Particularly in LANs and SANs, the overhead of TCP/IP is disappointing in that the underlying technologies permit much better performance. *Lightweight protocols* are a relatively recent development that addresses this problem. Lightweight protocols improve the performance by orders of magnitude (a factor of 20 to 30 is cited in [107]), chiefly by bypassing the operating system in the communication, and by reducing the number of message copy operations. Lightweight protocols usually operate on fast communication hardware such as Myrinet and VIA.

Myrinet [62] is a commercial product. It transfers technology that was originally developed in the parallel domain to the area of SANs and LANs. The product comprises hardware and a low-layer protocol.

The interconnection medium of Myrinet is a possibly irregular network of crossbar switches. Packets are routed with a specific mechanism called *wormhole routing*. This mechanism induces very low latencies and supports variable packet sizes. The trick is to consider a packet as a stream of bits instead of as a single unit, and to allow different parts of the packet to proceed at differing speeds. In the extreme, the head of a message may have reached the destination while the tail has not even been sent yet and intermediate parts are on the way. A packet is never disrupted, however.

In addition to the switches, the Myrinet hardware comprises a network interface for the hosts. It contains a programmable communication processor and a certain amount of fast memory. Among other tasks, the communication processor generates and tests a checksum that is sent with each packet. Consequently, this functionality need not be provided by protocols, which reduces their overhead. The network interface also facilitates the overlap between communication and computation.

Similar in spirit is the Virtual Interface Architecture (VIA), a recent industry standard for high-bandwidth low-latency communication, chiefly in SANs. First implementations are emerging now. Like Myrinet, VIA describes a mechanism through which user processes can communicate without involvement of the operating system.

On fast communication hardware, the standard TCP/IP and UDP/IP protocols run faster than on other hardware. To fully exploit the power of the hardware, however, lightweight communication protocols are used. Although it is in principle possible for an application to directly access the very low layers, such as the Myrinet protocol, this is in most cases not a good idea. Low-layer interfaces are complex, which makes programming difficult and nonportable. Therefore, intermediate (lightweight) protocols are used, for instance Active Messages (AM) and Fast Messages (FM). These protocols are treated in Sect. 5.4.

A quite different approach to networking is represented by the Scalable Coherent Interface (SCI) technology [374]. SCI is a formal standard. It was proposed in 1992 and is supported by several hardware vendors. SCI compares to Myrinet roughly the same way as NUMA compares to NORMA. In other words, the characteristic feature of SCI is the opportunity to access the remote memory via read/write operations. SCI is used in both parallel computers (e.g. NUMA-Q, T3E) and clusters. Some SCI implementations support cache coherence, whereas others do not [76]. SCI is a fast technology and scales to large processor numbers.

Summarizing this section, we have seen the most common protocols that are used in current networks, and we have seen typical tradeoffs between portability and performance. Many other important protocols exist, for instance in the context of wireless computing and multicasting (one sender passes a message to multiple receivers). See Sect. 2.7 for further references.

2.6 CLUSTERS

Pfister [338, p. 72] gives the following definition of a cluster:

A cluster is a type of parallel or distributed system that

- Consists of a collection of interconnected whole computers, and
- Is used as a single, unified computing resource.

Although this definition is not universally agreed upon, it gives a fairly good idea of the concept.

In the definition, the term "whole computer" stands for a node that comprises one or several processors, a cache, a main memory, a disk, an IO interface, and an own operating system. Thus a "whole computer" can be a PC, a workstation, or even an SMP. The interconnection network uses either standard technologies such as Ethernet, or high-performance technologies such as Myrinet. The number of nodes varies widely, from two to a few thousand at present.

The term "single, unified computing resource" stands for what we have called a single system image (SSI) before. In particular the following SSI features are often supported:

- Single entry point—one can log in to the cluster instead of to a particular node.
- Single file system.
- Coordinated job queues and location transparency for SPPS processing.
- Single system image for system administration.

Typically the SSI features are provided by a middleware layer above the operating system, as depicted in Fig. 2.7. Alternatively, part of the functionality can be provided by the operating system, or also by hardware.

In many clusters, the SSI functionality is supplemented or partially replaced by high availability functionality, which is implemented in a similar way. Accordingly, clusters are frequently classified into high-availability and high-performance clusters. We restrict ourselves here to high-performance clusters, which can be run in SPPS mode or execute parallel programs.

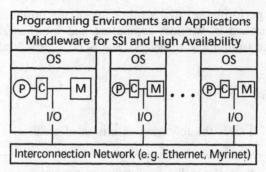

Fig. 2.7 A typical cluster architecture.

Clusters have several advantages over more conventional parallel architectures, the most important being their price. The price is comparatively low because clusters use commodity components. Other advantages of clusters are scalability and the fact that users can often stay with their usual environment. The distinction between clusters and distributed-memory parallel computers is a gradual one. It depends mainly on the degree to which the communication network is optimized and integrated into the system. Yet, some clusters rival the performance of distributed-memory parallel machines [133].

Cluster architectures vary widely. First, *dedicated clusters* are solely designed for use as parallel machines. They are often packaged compactly, that is, the nodes are located in a small physical area such as a single room and do not contain peripherals such as keyboard and monitor. Some dedicated clusters are built, sold, and technically supported as vendor products, whereas others are composed by the user. Examples are given below. Dedicated clusters are normally based on fast interconnection technology such as Fast Ethernet, Gigabit Ethernet, or Myrinet.

Second, *campus-wide clusters* are chiefly motivated by the potential for scavenging. They connect PCs or workstations that are normally run by a single user, standing on his or her desktop. To make use of idle cycles, the computers, together with the interconnection network that exists anyway, are additionally used as a cluster.

Obviously, campus-wide clusters are slower than dedicated ones. Thus, they are typically used for running large-grained applications, as well as for program development and teaching. Besides speed, another typical difference from dedicated clusters is the fact that the network is exposed, that is, both cluster-related and cluster-unrelated traffic goes along the same connections. Consequently, security is an important concern. Finally, campus-wide clusters are often heterogeneous, whereas dedicated clusters are homogeneous. In addition to dedicated and campus-wide clusters there are several intermediate forms.

We will now briefly look at some typical high-performance clusters: Beowulf clusters, HPVM clusters, and the ASCI Blue Mountain.

Beowulf clusters are a kind of dedicated clusters, in which the user buys and assembles the components him- or herself [44, 400]. The number of nodes ranges from below ten to a few hundred at present. Typically the nodes run the Linux operating system. Beowulf clusters are well known for their good price/performance ratio. Although SPPS mode is possible, they are often deployed for parallel computing.

HPVM stands for High-Performance Virtual Machine, a university research project. Within this project, cluster software such as the already mentioned FM protocol has been developed. Other project components address heterogeneity and support for QoS-oriented resource sharing [106]. An example of a HPVM system is the HPVM III cluster [105]. It comprises about 100 nodes, with each node being a two-processor SMP that runs the Windows NT operating system. HPVM III uses Fast Ethernet and Myrinet technologies for the internal traffic, and can be accessed from the outside via TCP/IP.

The ASCI Blue Mountain [29] is a vendor system from Silicon Graphics. At the time of this writing, it ranges third on the already mentioned Top 500 list of supercomputer sites [416]. The ASCI Blue Mountain comprises about 50 nodes, each of which is internally a 128-processor SGI Origin SMP. There are many more vendor systems, for instance AltaCluster [19] and HPCLINE [217].

2.7 LOOSELY COUPLED DISTRIBUTED SYSTEMS AND GRIDS

Like clusters, loosely coupled distributed systems are collections of whole computers that are interconnected by some network. The distinction from clusters is a gradual one, determined by the degree to which either the single system image or multiple system images predominate. As we have discussed in the previous section, the term cluster refers not only to some hardware configuration, but it includes the software, too. Since different applications can be based on different software, the same physical system can be used as a cluster by one application, and as a collection of independent computers by another.

Loosely coupled distributed systems have a comparatively slow interconnection network that is typically based on TCP/IP. Hence they are rarely used for parallel computing, except for a few cases with a large grain size. Instead, their main application area is distributed computing.

The systems can be composed of workstations, PCs, and other architectures. Most often they are heterogeneous. Dependability and security are important concerns. Security, in particular, is difficult to handle, due to the large and to some degree unknown user base. Many loosely coupled distributed systems lack a central control unit and have multiple system administrators.

The various systems can be classified according to their size into *intranets* and *internets*: intranets exist within an organization, and internets cross organizational boundaries.

Our last architectural class is *computational grids*. Grids do not exist yet, except for a few experimental ones such as the NASA Information Power Grid [117, 225]. Foster and Kesselman [156] give the following definition:

> A grid is a hardware and software infrastructure that provides dependable, consistent, pervasive, and inexpensive access to high-end computational capabilities.

The grid idea is to create an ubiquitous computing infrastructure that resembles the electrical power grid. Grids do not fit well into the framework that we have introduced so far. Probably they come closest to a large-scale cluster that incorporates many computing resources, memories, databases, etc. Like clusters, grids can be used for high-performance computing, but they can also be used for collaborative computing, high-throughput computing, and other applications.

Back to the definition, grids provide a *seamless* integration of resources, that is, they let the system appear as a unified resource. The concept of seamless integration resembles the SSI concept of clusters. It is, however, more difficult to realize, since grids are heterogeneous and decentralized.

Further, *pervasive* means that a user can at any time and from any location access the functionality of the grid, as is the case with electric power. *Dependable* has the usual meaning and moreover implies that the grid provides guarantees for functionality and QoS. *Consistent* means that a user gets the same services no matter when, from which location, and via which hardware he or she connects to the system.

The building blocks of a grid can be single PCs and workstations; more typically they are clusters and supercomputers. In particular, the connection of multiple supercomputers into a unified computing resource is referred to as *metacomputing*. Grids can contain special-purpose resources such as SIMD machines, which are more economically used in a grid than within a single organization.

Like clusters, grids facilitate scavenging, but on a much larger scale. Since grids connect many resources and run many applications at once, they are able to even up hot spots from different applications. The design of grid software, that is, of middleware that provides the seamless integration, is an important research area at present. One challenge is the dynamic nature of grids, that is, users can connect and disconnect at any time. Other research topics concern the exploitation of special resources, security, and pricing.

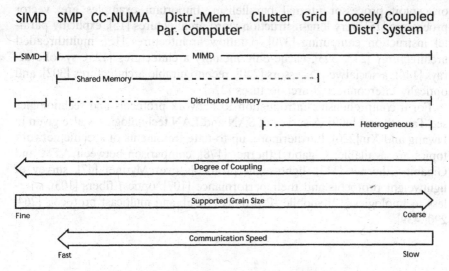

Fig. 2.8 Survey of parallel and distributed architectures.

First middleware systems have been suggested, notably Legion [266] and Globus [180]. The middleware systems can also be considered as *wide-area operating systems* [191]. We come back to some middleware systems in later chapters of this book.

Summarizing this chapter, a whole spectrum of parallel and distributed architectures is currently used. Figure 2.8 gives a survey of the various classes.

BIBLIOGRAPHICAL REMARKS

A comprehensive and up-to-date resource on parallel computer architecture is Culler et al. [124]. The current standard texts on clusters are Buyya [77, 78] and Pfister [338], and the primary reference on grids is Foster and Kesselman [158] (especially Ch. 2 of that book [156]). As a more general resource, Hwang and Xu [220] is recommended. From [220], I adopted the classification scheme of this chapter; that book also includes a concise introduction to clusters. SMPs and CC-NUMA architectures are covered well in Pfister [338]. SIMD architectures are treated, for example, in Jurczyk and Schwederski [240].

This chapter has surveyed those architectures that currently make up the mainstream of parallel and distributed computing. Many other interesting designs could be mentioned, which played a major role in the past, may play a larger role in the future, are mainly directed at special-purpose computing, or exploit processor-internal parallelism. Important examples are: vector processors [15], very long-instruction-word architectures [15], explicitly parallel instruction computing [370], dataflow architectures [15], multithreaded architectures [215, 393], cache-only memory architectures [125], systolic arrays [144], associative processors [240], reconfigurable architectures [302], and optically interconnected architectures [226].

For a comprehensive introduction to network protocols and technologies see Tanenbaum [409]. A survey of SAN and LAN technologies is also given in Hwang and Xu [220]. Furthermore, up-to-date treatments of specific network topics are available: Gigabit Ethernet [178], comparison between ATM and Gigabit Ethernet [113], lightweight protocols over Myrinet [47], survey of lightweight protocols and their performance [107], optical fibers [103], wireless technologies [12], mobile IP protocol [336], and multicast protocols [264, 290, 439].

3
Data Parallelism

Now that we have become acquainted with the objectives, problems, and hardware preliminaries of parallel and distributed computing, it is time to jump into the main part of the book. This chapter, like most of the following, starts with a general introduction of the current topic. The introduction explains the concept of data parallelism, contrasts it with other approaches, and outlines its strengths and weaknesses in a brief form. Then we move from the abstract to the concrete, and consider submodels and practical realizations in more detail. The chapter finishes with a survey of related work and with bibliographical remarks.

Data parallelism is actually more a paradigm than a model. The paradigm has, however, strongly influenced the design of a class of programming languages. Therefore it can as well be considered as a programming model now. The distinction between the paradigm and the model view is relevant insofar as the data-parallel paradigm is often expressed in non-data-parallel languages. Let us start with a definition:

> Data parallelism is characterized by the parallel execution of the same operation on different parts of a large data set.

The parallel operation can be elementary or complex. Accordingly, we distinguish between two basic styles of data parallelism: SIMD and SPMD.

51

Another classification criterion is the structure of the dataset. Whereas the established data-parallel languages are restricted to arrays, other approaches extend the concept to sets, lists, and other data structures.

The data-parallel programming model focuses on architectures with a single address space and a physically distributed memory. Thus, data distribution plays a major role, but program variables are visible to all processes. The model is most reflective of SIMD and NUMA architectures, but high-performance implementations also exist for SMPs and clusters [372].

The major advantage of data parallelism is program simplicity. Considering the overall structure of a program, we have only a single thread of control. Parallelism comes in via data-parallel steps, which are executed one after another, mixed with sequential steps. The principle is illustrated in Fig. 3.1.

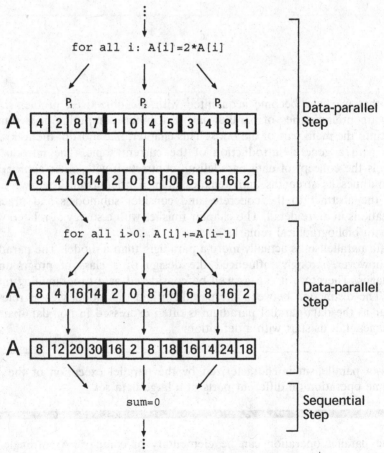

Fig. 3.1 The principle of data parallelism.

As shown in the figure, the data set is split into subsets (or domains), and each subset is assigned to a different processor. The splitting (or data distribution) must in most languages be specified by the programmer, who can choose from a certain set of options. The options are language-specific; examples are given later. As a general remark, the data distribution is not necessarily fixed once and for all: most programming languages allow for redistribution during program execution.

In each data-parallel step, the respective operation is applied in parallel to the various data domains. Ideally, the domains are operated upon independently. In reality, of course, many operations involve data from different domains, and thus communication is necessary. In a communication, the data are replicated, that is, the owner keeps the data and sends a copy to the requesting processor.

Obviously, not only the data but also the operations must be assigned to processors. Many compilers adopt the *owner-computes rule*, in which an assignment is carried out by the processor that owns the data on the left-hand side. In some systems, the programmer can explicitly specify the operation assignment, as we will see later.

The data-parallel paradigm can be contrasted with the *task-parallel* one. While data parallelism executes the same operation on different data, task parallelism executes different operations on the same or on different data. Task parallelism is normally expressed in non-data-parallel languages. Nevertheless, many data-parallel languages allow for a limited form of task parallelism: By placing complex operations within a conditional, a programmer can enforce the parallel execution of different tasks in a data-parallel step. Of course, this opportunity is not in the spirit of the data-parallel paradigm. Typically, data parallelism is more fine-grained than task parallelism. Thus it is a better fit for tightly coupled architectures than for distributed systems with a slow interconnection network.

3.1 SIMD PARALLELISM

Data parallelism originates from programming models for SIMD architectures. These early models closely imitated the SIMD style and are exemplified by C*, the MasPar Language MPL, and the architecture-independent language Parallaxis [142]. Due to the architectural trend away from SIMD, the development of SIMD languages was eclipsed by the emerging SPMD style. Hence, this section is mainly interesting for historical reasons; SIMD models do not play a significant role anymore in general-purpose computing. The section should nevertheless be read, since it introduces some concepts that will be used later.

We explain SIMD parallelism on the example of C*. Like most SIMD languages, C* was designed for a specific architecture, in this case the Connection Machine CM-2 that was mentioned before. C* extends the programming language C with constructs for declaring and manipulating parallel arrays. These arrays are distributed over the processor array of the CM-2.

As described in the introduction, a C* program is a sequence of data-parallel and sequential steps. In the case of C*, the data-parallel steps correspond to elementary operations. We will now look at the various language features.

Declaration and distribution of parallel arrays Parallel arrays are introduced through a *shape* declaration, which specifies the number of dimensions as well as their extent. The concrete values need not be known before run time. Based on the shape declaration, the data distribution is chosen automatically. A parallel array can be initialized by reading in the values from a sequential array, which is time-consuming; or by generating a regular pattern.

Data-parallel computations The parallel arrays are normally manipulated in loops. We call them *parallel loops*, although the term is a bit unfortunate in that the constructs are not iterative as loops normally are. Instead, the loop iterations are carried out in parallel, and the iterations are assigned according to the owner-computes rule.

An important construct is **where**. It selects the set of processors that take part in a data-parallel step. Consider, for instance, the following program fragment:

> **where** $(a < b)$
>
> > $c = a;$
>
> **else**
>
> > $c = b$

Here, a, b, and c are parallel arrays. Assume for now that we have as many processors as array elements and that processor i owns $a[i]$, $b[i]$, and $c[i]$. Then the first line says that each processor i independently evaluates $a[i] < b[i]$, and sets some flag according to the result. In the next line, those processors with *flag* = true execute $c[i] = a[i]$, while the remaining processors sit idle. Finally, those processors with *flag* = false execute $c[i] = b[i]$, while the formerly busy processors are idle now. After each elementary operation, a synchronization takes place. If more than one array element is stored per processor, the sequence of steps is repeated for each element. In the body of a **where** statement, any valid statement sequences of C* are permitted.

Communication Whereas in the example above, each processor was able to do its work independently, many other programs involve communication. The communication mechanisms of C* were inspired by the interconnection

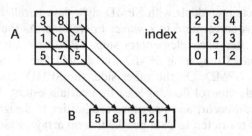

Fig. 3.2 A general communication with sum reduction.

network of the CM-2. Thus C* distinguishes between regular and general communications. In *regular communications*, all individual accesses have the same direction and stride with respect to the declared shape, such as in $a[i, j] = b[i + 2, j - 1]$ for $1 \le i, j \le n$ (not in C* syntax). For *general communications*, there is no such limitation. A communication is specified with the help of an index array, which lists for each individual datum the source or alternatively the destination, as in $a[i] = b[index[i]]$ or in $a[index[i]] = b[i]$. General communications can also involve arrays that have different shapes, as shown in Fig. 3.2. Compared with regular communications, general communications are more flexible, but their execution is slower and they are harder to specify.

Collective operations Collective operations describe common patterns of cooperation between processors and may involve both communication and computation. Collective operations are covered in depth in Sect. 3.4. To just give an example, *reduction* is a collective operation that transforms a vector into a scalar, for instance by adding its elements. Figure 3.2 illustrates this operation, in connection with a general communication.

Assessment A drawback of SIMD languages is their restriction to problems with a very regular structure. Due to the implicit synchronization after each elementary step, any use of task parallelism induces inefficiencies if it can be expressed at all. Although C* is architecture-specific, the language was also implemented on the CM-5, which is a MIMD machine. Remember the difference between code and performance portability. Although the SIMD language runs, it does not fully exploit the performance potential. Yet, the performance problem is smaller than one might expect, because some of the superfluous synchronizations can be eliminated through compiler analysis [200].

3.2 DATA PARALLELISM ON ARRAYS

The rest of this chapter deals with SPMD-style data parallelism, that is, the data-parallel steps correspond to *complex* operations. As there is no implicit synchronization after each elementary step, SPMD models are also called *loosely synchronous*. Comparing SPMD with SIMD, the performance is normally better with SPMD. On the other side, the SPMD model gives up the concept of a single control flow, at least to a certain extent. In consequence, race conditions can occur, and programs are harder to design and verify.

This section is restricted to data parallelism on arrays, which is much more common than data parallelism on other data structures. In particular, we outline the programming models of the HPF and HPF-2 languages. Nonarray approaches are treated in the next section, and also at the end of the chapter.

HPF

At present, many people associate the concept of array-based data parallelism with the language High Performance Fortran (HPF). Although not as popular as MPI or CORBA (which will be treated in later chapters), HPF has a certain practical significance. Several commercial and public-domain compilers, as well as debugging and performance profiling tools, are available.

HPF is an extension of Fortran 90, a language that can already be classified as data-parallel, although in a more limited sense than HPF. Fortran 90 is outlined in Sect. 3.4. HPF extends Fortran 90 with constructs for the explicit expression of data parallelism.

Most of the constructs take the form of *compiler directives*. When properly used, compiler directives do not change the semantics of a program, but they give the compiler hints for the generation of more efficient code. The compiler is free to use or ignore the hints. It can also identify and exploit additional performance potential. Despite advances in compiler technology, smart hints can speed up a program significantly. Let us now look at the individual HPF constructs.

Parallelism constructs Parallelism is specified through parallel loop constructs, called FORALL and INDEPENDENT, respectively. FORALL is a new language construct, not just a compiler directive. It works like a SIMD parallel loop; in particular, it executes an implicit synchronization after each elementary step. The FORALL construct is illustrated in Fig. 3.3, where it is also contrasted with the conventional (iterative) DO loop. In the diagrams, arrows indicate guaranteed execution orders, which are enforced through implicit synchronizations. Note that the synchronizations are carried out after each elementary step, not only at statement boundaries.

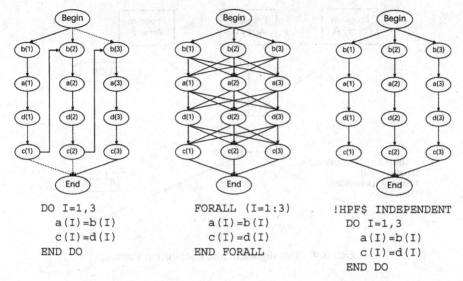

```
DO I=1,3            FORALL (I=1:3)        !HPF$ INDEPENDENT
  a(I)=b(I)            a(I)=b(I)            DO I=1,3
  c(I)=d(I)            c(I)=d(I)              a(I)=b(I)
END DO              END FORALL               c(I)=d(I)
                                           END DO
```

Fig. 3.3 Comparison between DO, FORALL, and INDEPENDENT in HPF. Adapted, by permission, from C. H. Koelbel et al., *The High Performance Fortran Handbook*. [254] © 1994 Massachusetts Institute of Technology.

The second parallel construct is a compiler directive called INDEPEN-DENT. If a loop is marked by that keyword, the intermediate synchronizations are omitted. Only at the end of the whole loop does an implicit synchroniza-tion take place. The INDEPENDENT directive is illustrated in Fig. 3.3 as well.

The INDEPENDENT directive is an assurance that the programmer gives to the compiler. It tells the compiler that the implicit synchronizations can be safely omitted, without risking correctness. In other words, the programmer guarantees that no branch modifies a variable that is read or written by another branch. If the INDEPENDENT directive is mistakenly specified other-wise, race conditions and erroneous programs may result. It is the user's responsibility to avoid that.

The FORALL and INDEPENDENT constructs can be nested. Within the body of the constructs, function calls are permitted, provided that the functions are free of side effects. The side-effect freedom must be declared explicitly by the programmer, by using the keyword PURE.

Communication The communication is implicit. Any Fortran statements induce communication if the operands are stored at different processors. Examples are A(I)=A(I-1) and A(I)=B(F(I)). In the latter case, the communication pattern is irregular.

Data distribution Reflecting the focus on NUMA machines, data distribu-tion is a major part of the language. The data distribution is specified in two

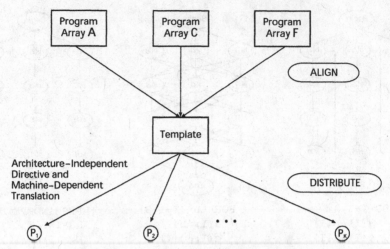

Fig. 3.4 The alignment and distribution steps.

steps, which are referred to as *alignment* and *distribution*, respectively. The steps are illustrated in Fig. 3.4.

In the alignment step, the programmer specifies the relative positioning of *different* arrays. Therefore, he or she maps the program arrays to a single array called a *template*. The template is either one of the program arrays, or a virtual array that is only introduced for this purpose. In the distribution step, the programmer partitions the template into domains such that each domain is assigned to a different processor.

An example is given in Fig. 3.5. The figure uses HPF syntax, which should be self-explanatory. Part (a) specifies an alignment that maps arrays A and B to a virtual template T. Compiler directives are introduced by !HPF$. The first line declares T; of course T must be large enough to hold A and B. In the next lines, A and B are aligned to T, as illustrated by the diagram below.

Figures 3.5 (b) and (c) depict different examples for the distribution step. Note that only T is partitioned explicitly, whereas the distribution of A and B follows from the alignment. Because of being virtual, T itself is not physically distributed and therefore omitted from the figure. Nevertheless, one must think in terms of T in order to understand the distribution of A and B.

The directives in Fig. 3.5 (b) and (c), respectively, illustrate the two basic distribution schemes that are available in HPF: *block* and *cyclic*. The schemes are architecture-independent in that they are stated without reference to the absolute number of processors. Thus they do not give explicit data domains, but describe a pattern according to which the compiler accomplishes the distribution when the number of processors is known. Both distribution schemes assign an approximately equal number of data to each processor. Block distribution assigns neighboring template elements to the same processor, whereas cyclic distribution assigns the data alternately—as shown in the diagrams.

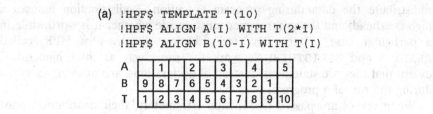

Fig. 3.5 An example for the alignment-distribution mechanism of HPF.

In addition to the block and cyclic schemes, there are variants. One variant represents a compromise between block and cyclic: It alternately assigns equal-sized data blocks of a user-defined size to the processors.

The same distribution patterns as for one-dimensional arrays are also defined for two- and multidimensional arrays. Here it is possible to choose different distributions for different axes, and to specify any rectilinear subblocks. Furthermore, one can exclude a dimension from the distribution so that, for instance, all elements of the same row of an array are assigned to the same processor. Similarly, one can require the replication of data. Through an additional set of directives, the programmer can give hints on the assignment of data domains to physical processors.

It should be emphasized that HPF gives the programmer explicit control over data distribution. Although the programmer is not forced to always make a choice, doing so will normally improve the performance. Formulating a useful directive is often difficult, since one needs detailed knowledge about both the communication structure of the program and the architecture of the machine. As a general rule, block distribution should be used when the application has a significant locality potential, and cyclic distribution should be used when the load balancing is otherwise poor. Cyclic distribution should in particular be used when neighboring elements have similar computational requirements.

The choice of data distribution is especially difficult when different program parts have different preferences. In such cases, it may be useful to redistribute the data during program execution. Redistribution induces a high overhead, and the programmer must decide whether it is worthwhile in a particular case or not. The redistribution directives of HPF, called REALIGN and REDISTRIBUTE, work the same way as their namesakes, except that they are statements instead of declarations, and are thus executed during the run of a program.

When arrays are passed as function parameters, their distribution must possibly be converted. The HPF language definition formulates a relatively involved set of rules for these cases.

Collective operations and extrinsic procedures HPF has a rich set of intrinsic functions, such as logarithm and square root, which are supplied together with the language. Some of these functions are well suited for parallel execution. An example is reduction, for which HPF allows not only basic combinators such as summation, but also complex user-defined combinators.

An extrinsic procedure is a program part that was written in another language. By incorporating extrinsic procedures into an HPF program, the pure data-parallel style of HPF can be supplemented by other programming styles. Of particular interest is the combination with message passing (see Ch. 5).

Assessment HPF is a performance-oriented language, with focus on scientific and engineering applications. Nevertheless, it has a comparatively high level of abstraction. The design of HPF was driven by the goal of making the programmer free from those tasks that a compiler can accomplish as well, but giving the programmer control over those tasks that cannot (yet) be handled automatically. The price to be paid for combining performance with ease of use was a restriction of applicability. HPF is only appropriate for applications with a regular structure, since in particular the data distribution constructs are restricted to regular patterns. This restriction was felt to be an important drawback; it motivated the design of an improved language, HPF-2.

HPF-2

The HPF-2 standard was published in early 1997 and is based on Fortran 95, the successor of Fortran 90. HPF-2 extends HPF with both regular language features and a large set of approved extensions. The approved extensions describe features that are desirable from an application programmer's point of view, but are difficult to implement in compilers. HPF-2 compilers are still rare, and none of them supports the complete set of extensions as yet. Nevertheless, in the following we refer to the whole standard, including extensions.

As was already mentioned, HPF-2 is motivated by the practical importance of irregular applications. Applications are called irregular if the progress
of work and the distribution of data do not follow simple patterns, but may
be input-dependent and evolve in an unpredictable way. In other languages,
irregular programs often deploy indirect addressing via pointers or index
arrays, and use sparse matrices and nonarray data structures. HPF-2 addresses some of the needs of these applications, some open problems are
mentioned later. In the following, we describe the new features of HPF-2.

Data distribution   First, the block distribution is generalized to blocks that
may have different sizes. Second, extending on that, HPF-2 introduces
indirect mappings. They are specified with the help of an index array, which
lists for each individual datum a processor to which the data is mapped. Here
we do not refer to physical processors, but to virtual ones, which are
described later. The generalized distributions are useful for coding irregular
applications. Moreover, they support load balancing on heterogeneous architectures.

There are yet more extensions, concerning in particular the distribution of
parameters in function calls. For instance, the user can assert that the actual
parameters have a certain distribution, or that the distribution fulfills certain
constraints.

Operation placement   In addition to the placement of data, the programmer can also specify the placement of operations. Therefore, he or she refers
to a *virtual-processor arrangement*. This concept was already present in HPF,
and is an important feature of HPF-2. A virtual-processor arrangement
defines a shape for the set of physical processors. Eight processors, for
instance, can be arranged as a 1×8 or a 4×2 grid. The extent of the shapes
depends on the number of physical processors, but it suffices that the number
be known at run time. The number of virtual processors must be the same as
or less than that of physical processors. In the latter case, the virtual-processor
arrangement describes a subset of the physical processors.

To place an operation, a programmer directly names a processor or a set
of processors on which the operation shall run. Alternatively, he or she can
request that the operation be run by the owner of a certain datum as in

```
!HPF$ ON HOME (Z(I))

   X(I-1) = X(I-1) + Z(I)
```

In the example, the statement is executed by the owner of Z(I), instead
of by the owner of X(I-1) as would be implied by the owner-computes rule.

Assertions for communication optimization   HPF-2 defines several new
assertions through which the programmer can give hints that the compiler

can exploit in communication optimization. Here are some examples:

- The programmer can assert that all inputs to an operation are stored locally.

- In connection with the INDEPENDENT directive, the programmer can assert that the updates to a certain variable may be executed in any order. The update can consequently be implemented as a reduction.

- The programmer can describe a rectilinear frame around a processor's data domain. Such a frame is called a *shadow*, and marks frequently needed data that are owned by other processors. The compiler can use this information to optimize memory allocation and communications.

Task parallelism HPF-2 supports the expression of task parallelism in a limited form: Disjoint processor subsets may be instructed to carry out different operations. Such task-parallel constructs may be nested. Furthermore, HPF-2 introduces the concept of private variables, which are only visible within a single branch of an INDEPENDENT loop.

Although the task-parallel facilities of HPF-2 are limited, some common task-parallel paradigms can be expressed. An important paradigm is *pipelining*. With pipelining, a computation is divided into stages such that each stage is responsible for a certain task, the data are flowing through the stages, and the different stages are working in parallel. The scheme is illustrated in Fig. 3.6. There, the computation of H(G(F(x))) is accomplished in three

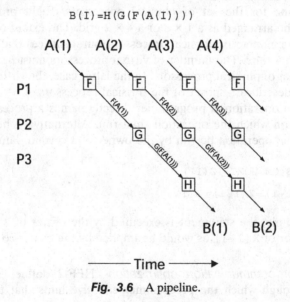

Fig. 3.6 A pipeline.

stages, which correspond to the functions F, G, and H, respectively. It is possible to express pipelining in HPF-2, as the following program fragment for the example of Fig. 3.6 demonstrates:

```
DO I=1, N

  IN1=A(I)

  !HPF$ INDEPENDENT

  DO STAGE=1, 3

    IF (STAGE == 1 .AND. 1<= I .AND. I<= N-2) THEN

      !HPF$ ON (P(1))

      OUT1=FUNCTION_F(IN1)

    ELSE IF (STAGE == 2 .AND. 2<= I .AND. I<= N-1) THEN

      !HPF$ ON (P(2))

      OUT2=FUNCTION_G(IN2)

    ELSE IF (STAGE == 3 .AND. 3<= I .AND. I<= N) THEN

      !HPF$ ON (P(3))

      OUT3=FUNCTION_H(IN3)

    END IF

  END DO

  IN2=OUT1

  IN3=OUT2

  B(I)=OUT3

END DO
```

Assessment   In HPF-2, the programmer can express many performance-relevant details of program execution, even sophisticated details of irregular programs. On the other side, this opportunity places a large burden on the programmer. Compiler design is a challenging task, too, if one expects the compiler to exploit the additional information.

Another problem with HPF-2 is the still-insufficient support for irregular applications. Whereas several important problem classes can be handled now, others do not seem to fit into the data-parallel framework at all. In particular, there is no efficient way to deal with a general form of task parallelism in which the number and communication behavior of the tasks are input-dependent and cannot be estimated by the programmer. The data-parallel model is directed at problems with a relatively predictable program structure.

Since the support for task parallelism is severely limited, Delves and Zima [130] suggest combining data parallelism with other programming models. More specifically, they propose to use data parallelism within small program units, and to couple the units with the help of a different coordination model. Such compositional approaches are treated in Sect. 10.3.

Yet another problem with HPF-2 is the focus on a two-level memory hierarchy. The distinction between the local and the remote memories does not seem to be sufficient for SMP clusters. Apart from this limitation, HPF-2 scores well on portability. Since the programmer expresses his or her suggestions in a largely architecture-independent way, code portability and, to some extent, also performance portability are supported.

Assessing the performance of HPF is elusive, since it depends heavily on the available compiler technology and the concrete application. Some numbers in [130, 372] indicate that the performance is comparable to or slightly worse than that of MPI on many regular and some irregular problems. MPI will be covered in Ch. 5; it is the major message-passing system in use today.

On the positive side, software development is comparatively easy in data-parallel languages. Since there are no explicit communication constructs, deadlocks cannot occur, and performance prediction is feasible. Also, the programmer need not handle the details of communication. An MPI programmer, in contrast, is responsible for activities such as the allocation of communication buffers

In summary, data parallelism, as exemplified by HPF-2, combines performance, ease of use, and portability for an important class of programs. Future developments will likely make use of advancing compiler technology and consider non-array-based data structures. Another promising direction is the combination with skeleton models for task parallelism, which are described in Sect. 10.2.

Although array-based data parallelism is at present chiefly based on Fortran, many of the described constructs are not Fortran-specific. Instead, the binding to Fortran can be attributed to the importance of data parallelism in scientific computing and to the prevailing role of Fortran in that domain.

3.3 NESTED DATA PARALLELISM

As we know, SPMD-style data parallelism carries out complex operations over the various data domains. If the data domains are themselves internally structured, and if the operations are internally data-parallel again, we have obtained a new programming model, nested data parallelism.

Nested data parallelism can be expressed in HPF, and also in Fortran 90/95. Prins et al. [348] give examples and discuss efficient implementation techniques.

Here we will look at an earlier language that adopts nested data parallelism as its central language concept: NESL [58]. NESL is a functional language, which was mainly developed for teaching purposes and algorithmic experimentation.

The main data structure of NESL is the sequence, a variable-length collection of data which all have the same type. Sequences can be nested, and this is where nested data parallelism comes into play.

In NESL, data parallelism is expressed through a *map* construct. It applies a given function to all elements of a sequence or subsequence. The function can be elementary or user-defined. It may contain other applications of *map*, recursively, so that one can easily express nested data parallelism. The *map* construct can be combined with a *where* construct which, like the *where* construct of C*, qualifies the set of data elements that take part in a data-parallel step. Furthermore, NESL defines collective operations, for instance reductions.

An important aspect of the NESL project was the definition of an associated cost model. With this model, the performance of NESL programs can be evaluated analytically. A reason why such an evaluation is feasible is the restriction to programs with a predictable computation and communication structure.

Nested data parallelism is a natural fit with *divide and conquer*. This paradigm is well-known from sequential computing, and it is also used for expressing parallelism. With divide and conquer, an algorithmic problem is split into multiple subproblems, the subproblems are solved independently, and the solutions are finally composed into an overall solution. The subproblems are similar in nature to the original problem, but smaller in scale. Divide and conquer proceeds recursively, that is, the subproblems are further split into sub-subproblems, and so on. Often, the subproblems operate on different subsets of the data, and thus there is a close correspondence to the NESL concept of recursively partitioning sequences into subsequences.

Nested data parallelism can also help in coding irregular applications. An example is given by Prins et al. [348], who consider sparse-matrix computations. They find it useful to store the matrices in a hierarchical data structure, and to formulate the operations in a nested data-parallel way.

3.4 COLLECTIVE OPERATIONS AND LIBRARIES

An operation is called *collective* if it is executed jointly by all or a subset of the processes. Collective operations do not fit well into the classification scheme of this book, because they are supported in various programming models: data-parallelism, shared-memory programming, message passing, and others. I treat the topic here because 1) collective operations are an important topic that should be handled at the beginning, and 2) collective operations are close in concept to data parallelism in that they adopt a global view of the computation.

A collective operation must be invoked by all the participating processes. Usually, each of the processes issues an explicit function call. In some languages, collective operations are invoked implicitly, for instance in C* (see Fig. 3.2). Conceptually, a collective operation starts execution only after all the function calls have been issued. Therefore, the operation normally forces the faster processes to wait for the slower ones. In practical systems such as MPI, it may occasionally happen that a function returns before all calls have been issued. Such behavior is due to optimizations and does not express the spirit of the model.

Collective operations describe simple patterns of cooperation that are frequently found in parallel programs. The concrete set of operations is language-specific. In the following, we survey some common examples.

Examples of collective operations   Perhaps the most elementary operations are *broadcast* and *multicast*. With broadcast, one process communicates data to all other processes; with multicast, the process communicates the data to a subset of the processes. Sometimes, the term broadcast is used for groups as well, and the difference can be more subtle.

A kind of counterpart is the *reduction* operation, which was mentioned before. A reduction combines multiple values from multiple processes into a single value at a single process. Typical combinators include addition, multiplication, AND, OR, maximum, and minimum. Some systems, such as HPF, allow user-defined operators. In any case, the operator must be associative and commutative so that the subcomputations may be executed in any order.

Barrier synchronization does nothing except to stop the fast processes until the slower processes have caught up. When a process reaches a barrier, it waits until all other processes have reached their corresponding barriers, too. Behind a barrier, one can be sure that all processes have reached a certain point of program execution.

The next pair of collective operations is targeted at architectures with a distributed memory: *Scatter* distributes a set of input data to several processes, and *gather* collects the results afterwards. Thus, scatter partitions a data set, which is originally stored at a single process, into approximately equal-sized subsets, and sends each subset to a different process. Gather does just the contrary: It collects multiple data subsets from multiple processes, and puts them together into a single data structure, which is stored in a single process. Figure 3.7 depicts several collective operations.

Assessment of collective operations and libraries   The functionality of collective operations can normally be simulated with other functionalities of the respective systems. Collective operations should nevertheless be pre-

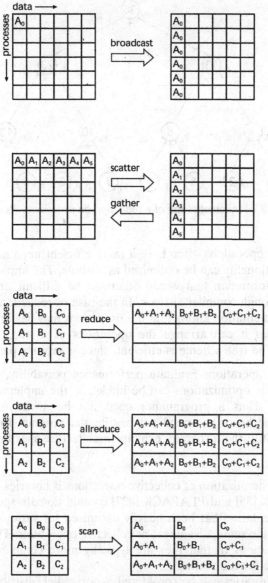

Fig. 3.7 Some collective operations. Adapted, by permission, from M. Snir et al., *MPI: The Complete Reference.* [394] © 1996 Massachusetts Institute of Technology.

ferred, for the following reasons:

- Collective operations ease program design and make programs clearer, since a single function call can stand for a complex operation. Clearness is an important advantage not only for program design, but also for verification, maintenance, and performance prediction.

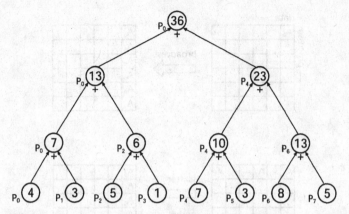

Fig. 3.8 Implementation of a reduction on processors $P_0, \ldots, P_7$.

- Collective operations often have a more efficient implementation, since their functionality can be optimized as a whole. The implementation can exploit information that would otherwise be difficult or impossible to obtain through compiler analysis. In the case of reductions, for instance, the implementation knows that the operations may be carried out in any order. Thus it can arrange the operations as a tree, as depicted in Fig. 3.8. The tree scheme is efficient, since it exploits parallelism.

- Collective operations facilitate performance portability, since architecture-specific optimizations can be hidden in the implementation of the functions. Thus a programmer need not be aware of architectural details, and he or she need not rewrite the program for a new architecture. Still the program exploits architecture-specific performance potential.

A natural generalization of collective operations is libraries. Libraries such as ScaLAPACK [55] and PLAPACK [423] contain domain-specific functions whose implementation has been heavily optimized for various architectures. Libraries have the same advantages as collective operations. They differ from collective operations in that they are typically more complex and describe domain-specific functionalities.

The use of libraries can be considered as a parallel/distributed programming model in its own right. In the extreme, all aspects of parallelism and distribution are encapsulated in library functions, and the programmer just invokes the functions in a sequential program. Where applicable, this is an elegant approach with many advantages. Unfortunately, it presupposes the existence of libraries that already contain the required functions.

In the library approach, the programmer codes the outer structure of a program, whereas the details are automatically filled in by the implementation. A related and in a sense opposite approach is *skeletons*. Here, the outer program structure is predefined and the details are filled in by the programmer. The skeleton model is dealt with in Sect. 10.2.

3.5 MORE ON THIS TOPIC

In languages such as C* and HPF, the programmer is explicitly concerned with the expression of data parallelism. Other languages are less explicit, but encourage a programming style that makes the automatic detection of data parallelism easy for the compiler. Well-known examples are Fortran 90 and Fortran 95, which are targeted at both sequential and parallel architectures. Fortran 90 and Fortran 95 are similar to each other, and hence we handle them together. In the Fortran 90/95 programming model, array operations can be specified in a closed form. Programmers write, for instance, A = B, instead of a loop like

```
DO I = 1, N
  A[I] = B[I]
END DO
```

From a closed form, the compiler can immediately conclude that the individual operations are independent and can hence be executed in parallel. Closed-form expressions are not restricted to whole arrays; they can denote array sections as well. For instance, a programmer can describe the set of elements in the left half of the even-numbered rows of an array. The programmer can even describe irregular array sections, with the help of an index array. Furthermore, Fortran 90/95 defines a *where* construct, which is similar to that of C*. Intrinsic functions are supported as well; some of them have a parallel implementation.

At the same time as HPF-2, the related HPF+ language was developed [43]. HPF+ deploys a one-step data distribution mechanism, which eliminates templates and permits the expression of some additional data distributions. Furthermore, HPF+ generalizes the shadow concept to irregular frames called halos.

HPF+ supports the *inspector/executor* scheme, which is a well-known run-time technique for implementing irregular communications that cannot be planned at compile time. In the scheme, a loop execution starts with a call to the inspector, which investigates the communication requirements of the loop and formulates a communication schedule. Thereafter, the executor accomplishes the actual work, according to the schedule. The inspector algorithm is time-consuming. Therefore, HPF+ introduces programmer assertions that can simplify the inspector code. A programmer can, for instance, declare that all iterations of a loop have the same communication requirements.

For irregular data structures, Brandes et al. [69] advocate the use of trees instead of the pointer-based structures that are known from other languages. They show that an HPF-2 compiler can generate an efficient implementation if it is aware of the tree structure.

Not Fortran-based, ZPL [96, 457] is another array-based data-parallel language. ZPL emphasizes performance predictability, and introduces a convenient description of shadow-like neighborhoods.

Quite a lot of research on data parallelism has been conducted within the context of object-oriented languages, mainly C++ and Java. C++ examples include C**, pC++, POOMA, and the Amelia Vector Template Library. These languages/libraries have several interesting features, for instance:

- Data parallelism for nonarray data structures such as trees, directed acyclic graphs (pC++), and special-purpose sets (particles in POOMA).

- An HPF-like alignment mechanism for general data structures (pC++).

The HPJava project [86, 88, 454] incorporates data parallelism into Java. It combines an HPF-like data distribution mechanism on one hand with explicit communication and an extended task-parallel model on the other. The task-parallel model includes local variables, which belong to a single process. Explicit communication means that, unlike in HPF, the programmer must use special library functions for communication. Thus, unlike in HPF, the programmer must distinguish between local and remote variables. This modification makes programming harder, but increases the programmer's awareness of expensive operations, and simplifies compilation.

Another approach for incorporating data parallelism into Java is described in Blount et al. [59]. Their language realizes nested data parallelism, via a *forall* construct and collective operations.

Skillicorn and Talia [392] give some references to earlier data-parallel languages that operate on sets and other nonarray data structures.

Closely related with data parallelism is the concept of *domain decomposition*. This term is frequently used in scientific computing, where it denotes the partitioning of a data set according to some physical relationship. The term is explained, for instance, in Baker and Smith [33].

BIBLIOGRAPHICAL REMARKS

Data parallelism is covered in many of the textbooks mentioned in Ch. 1. A concise description and classification is also given in Larus et al. [261]. The section on SIMD parallelism in this chapter draws on a C* course from Edinburgh Parallel Computing Centre [359]. Another useful resource is Hatcher and Quinn [200].

The standard references for High Performance Fortran are Koelbel et al. [254] and the HPF-2 standard document [207]. Reference [254] also includes an introduction to Fortran 90. Another good survey of Fortran 90, HPF, and other data-parallel languages is given in Hwang and Xu [220]. Several textbooks on Fortran 90 and Fortran 95 are available, for example Metcalf and Reid [294]. Information on Fortran-based languages can furthermore be obtained from compiler vendors, such as Portland Group, Inc. [339]. The pros and cons of HPF-2 are discussed in Delves and Zima [130].

A survey of libraries for linear algebra is given in Dongarra and Walker [135]. Java libraries for high-performance computing are described in Getov, et al. [173]. A comprehensive resource on data parallelism in C++-based languages is Wilson and Lu [442]. Further details on the pC++ language can be found in Bodin et al. [63].

4

Shared-Memory Programming

This chapter handles the first task-parallel model. Like the previous chapter, it starts with a general description and assessment of the model. Then we consider submodels. As usual, the chapter finishes with a survey and with bibliographical remarks. Let us start with a definition:

> In the shared-memory model, multiple tasks, often with a different functionality, run in parallel. The tasks communicate with one another by writing to and reading from a shared memory.

In other words, shared-memory programming is a task-parallel model that is characterized by the availability of a shared memory. The shared memory can exist physically, or be implemented as an abstraction for the programmer. All communication is indirect and goes through the shared memory, as illustrated in Fig. 4.1. Instead of talking to each other, the tasks are coupled through common data structures. Thus, a task need not know the identity of another task it is cooperating with. It need not even be aware of the fact that communication takes place at a given time.

Typically, only some of the variables and data structures are shared among the tasks. The others are private, that is, they are owned by a single task and are not visible to the outside. In some systems, variables may be shared among a subset of tasks.

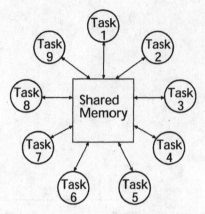

Fig. 4.1   The shared-memory model.

Comparison with data parallelism   Shared-memory programming resembles data parallelism insofar as both models use a single address space. Nevertheless there are fundamental differences. They can be delineated by the notion of tasks. Data parallelism does not normally use this notion, although the branches of an *independent* construct can be interpreted as tasks. As indicated by the keyword *independent*, data-parallel tasks do not explicitly coordinate their activities. Shared-memory programming, in contrast, places emphasis on the provision of intertask synchronization mechanisms. In dataparallel programming, tasks exist implicitly. The programmer has a global view of the program and does not think in terms of the individual tasks. In shared-memory programming, however, the notion of tasks is ubiquitous. The programmer is given explicit control over task management; he or she can, for instance, create and destroy tasks.

General properties   The majority of the shared-memory programming constructs deal with either synchronization or task management. No language support is needed for communication; it is expressed implicitly as in HPF. Shared-memory programming is on one hand simple, since

- The memory organization is the same as in the familiar sequential programming models,

- The programmer need not deal with data distribution, and

- The programmer need not handle communication details such as the allocation of buffers.

On the other hand, shared-memory programming raises specific difficulties:

- *Synchronization.* No assumption can be made about the relative progress of the various tasks. Not even communications induce an ordering, since they are indirect. To guarantee correctness, the tasks must coordinate their actions through explicit synchronizations. For instance, a task that needs a value computed by another task must possibly wait for that task. Two tasks that both modify the same variable by first reading and then writing it must make sure that their actions do not overlap. Shared-memory languages provide synchronization constructs, but the programmer is responsible for deploying them appropriately. Ensuring correctness is difficult, since the number of tasks can be large, and since the tasks may interact in ways that are hard to comprehend. Hence, the programmer must be careful to avoid race conditions and deadlocks. The same problems that make programming difficult also complicate debugging and maintenance. Another consideration is performance. Synchronizations slow down a program, not so much for their own costs, but because they require some task to wait. For efficiency, synchronizations should be avoided wherever possible.

- *Locality.* Although the programmer is not required to specify data distribution and task scheduling, he or she should take these issues into account for efficiency. This holds true for SMPs due to caching; it is even more important for NUMA architectures and distributed-memory parallel computers. The programmer must rely on indirect means to enforce locality, because explicit data placement directives like those in HPF are not available. The predominant means for locality optimization is code restructuring, that is, rearranging the operations of a program. In SMPs, for instance, one will rearrange the operations so that operations that use the same cache line are preferably carried out by the same task. Another means for locality optimization is the reorganization of data structures. A different data distribution can be enforced by, for instance, exchanging the rows and columns of a matrix.

Practical relevance and application areas   Shared-memory programming originated from concurrent programming of uniprocessors, and was later adapted to the emerging SMPs. The shared-memory model is a natural fit for SMPs, because of their hardware shared memory. Moreover, SMPs are frequently deployed as servers, and for that shared-memory programming is a good fit again, since it supports a large number of unrelated tasks. In this environment, intertask communication tends to be infrequent, and thus the issue of avoiding race conditions and deadlocks is less pressing than elsewhere. As SMPs have become widespread, the shared-memory programming model has become popular, too. A lot of experience has been gained, and much of the existing SMP software is written in this model.

The popularity and success of the shared-memory model on SMPs were a major motivation for the development of CC-NUMA architectures and software distributed shared memories. These architectures have the advantage of being scalable to large processor numbers, and still they are able to run the existing SMP software. Unfortunately, only code portability, not performance portability is meant here.

Shared-memory models have been implemented on SMPs, CC-NUMA architectures, NCC-NUMA architectures, distributed-memory parallel computers, and clusters. Grids may be added in the future. There is a certain bias towards homogeneous architectures, which is probably due to the SMP tradition and not necessarily inherent in the model.

Transparency Especially on distributed-memory architectures, shared-memory programming competes with the message-passing model that will be introduced in Ch. 5. A major difference between shared-memory programming and message passing is the degree of transparency. In shared-memory programming, data and task placement, as well as replication and migration, are transparent, whereas in message passing they are not. All what was said about transparency in the introduction applies here:

- Shared-memory programming is comfortable for the programmer, but the programmer loses control.

- The system mechanisms work well in the general case, but they are suboptimal in special cases.

- Transparency makes performance prediction difficult.

Submodels Within the shared-memory programming model, several submodels or streams can be distinguished. They differ in the architectures and applications for which they are primarily designed. The models can be classified as thread models, structured shared-memory models, distributed shared-memory models, and one-sided communication models. Each of the models is treated in a separate section below. Other streams and submodels exist. As usual, some of them are mentioned in the final survey section.

4.1 THREAD MODELS

Thread models are the oldest and most typical subclass. They focus on inherently parallel computations, and are quite closely tied to sequential and SMP environments.

Processes and threads So far, we have sloppily equated tasks, processes, and threads. It is now time to acknowledge their differences, because they are essential for the concept of thread models. Briefly stated:

> Threads have a shared memory, and processes do not.

Task is a generic term that covers both concepts. As a connotation, the term task stands more for logical units of the program, whereas process/thread stands more for the physical realization of these units. In this sense, a single process or thread can carry out multiple tasks during its lifetime.

For a deeper understanding of the difference between processes and threads, let us look at the area of operating systems, in which the notions were originally defined. In both parallel and sequential architectures, the operating system is responsible for the management of jobs that stem from different applications and users. These jobs are called processes. Processes are independent, operate on different address spaces, and normally do not want to know anything about each other. Processes are competitors that share the CPU and other resources.

The sharing of the CPU, say on a sequential machine, is managed by the operating system, which from time to time interrupts a process and transfers control to another. In such events, called *context switches*, state information is saved to let the process proceed later. The state information includes: program counter, register contents, stack (holds local variables), memory map (contains general information about the address space), pointers to open files, user identification, etc.—altogether quite a lot of information. The information is stored within the so-called *kernel space*, a section of memory which may only be accessed by the operating system. Partly due to protection mechanisms, access to kernel space is slow.

Still assuming a sequential machine, the process mechanism is not appropriate for fine-grained inherently parallel applications, because:

- These applications contain many communications.

- Almost each communication requires a context switch, since the receiver cannot otherwise answer the message.

- Context switching is slow.

Threads were invented as a faster alternative to processes. The gain in speed is due to giving up protection between threads. In particular the following modifications are applied:

- Threads share their program code, address space, file pointers, and other resources. Hence, less information needs to be stored at a context switch.

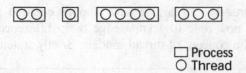

☐ Process
○ Thread

Fig. 4.2 The relationship between processes and threads: Each thread belongs to a process, and a process can contain one or several threads.

- The information is stored in *user space*. User space is the complement of kernel space, and access is faster.

Each thread belongs to a process, and a process may contain multiple threads, as shown in Fig. 4.2. The various threads of the same process can be assumed to know of each other, because they are parts of the same program.

Thread model The model considers a program as a collection of threads that cooperate in order to accomplish a common goal, or to share resources in a programmer-controlled way. The threads communicate with each other through the shared memory, as was described in the introduction.

In the thread model, multiple threads of a process share their global and dynamic (pointer-addressed) variables. They do not share their local variables, that is, each thread has its own stack. Through explicit addressing, it is possible for one thread to manipulate the local data of another, but this is not in the spirit of the model. The sharing of the program text does not contradict task parallelism, since each thread has its own program counter, and different threads can thus carry out different sections of the same code.

Application areas The design of thread models was influenced by their frequent usage in server programming. In this environment, a thread is typically created for handling a new user request, and multiple threads correspond to multiple requests. The sequence of requests cannot normally be predicted. Server threads tend to work independently of each other, except that they occasionally access a common data structure. The relationship between the threads is rather competitive than cooperative.

Other uses for threads are applications with a very large number of tasks, and applications in which the number of tasks cannot be estimated before run time. Aside from inherently parallel applications, thread models are useful for latency hiding. The principle was explained in the introduction under the name multithreading.

Implementation Thread models are typically implemented through libraries, not through language extensions. Therefore, threading aspects of programs are not normally subject to compiler optimizations.

Thread libraries are a mature technology, and several tools are available: debuggers, profilers, and static analysis tools that help to detect race conditions and deadlocks. Threaded programs are code-portable. A program that was written for a sequential machine will run on an SMP or possibly on another parallel machine without change, provided that the same library is available there.

In the following, we take a closer look at two important thread models: Pthreads and Java threads. The Pthreads library is supplied with many Unix systems, and Java threads are part of the Java language.

The Pthreads Library

Pthreads, an abbreviation for POSIX threads, designates a widely used standard for Unix thread libraries. Related thread libraries include Solaris threads and DCE threads in the context of Unix, and Win32 and OS/2 threads in the context of other operating systems. The various libraries share many central ideas. We refer to Pthreads here, but most of this section applies to the other libraries, too.

The Pthreads library defines a set of about fifty functions that can be called from a C program or, with more involved mechanisms [270], also from other languages. The main functionalities are described in the following:

Thread management The function *create* starts a thread and instructs it to carry out some user-defined function. Any thread may create an arbitrary number of other threads. There is no special relationship between a thread and its creator, that is, all threads are equal. A thread dies when it has finished its function. Alternatively, it can at any time invoke the function *exit* to stop. Finally, the thread can be killed from outside. As the set of threads is unstructured, any thread can kill any other thread, provided that it knows the thread identifier. A possible thread structure is depicted in Fig. 4.3.

Thread scheduling Since the number of threads is typically larger than the number of processors, only some of the threads are assigned to a processor at any one time. These threads are referred to as *active*. The other threads that wait for the CPU are referred to as *runnable*. Yet other threads may be blocked waiting for an outstanding synchronization event (see below); these threads are referred to as *sleeping*. In practice, things are a bit more difficult, but let us stay with this simple view here.

Each particular Pthreads implementation defines an appropriate scheduling scheme. Some implementations support time slicing, which is a periodic switching between active and runnable threads for fairness, whereas others do not. The programmer can introduce priorities to influence the scheduling. Additionally, he or she can modify the scheduling scheme itself.

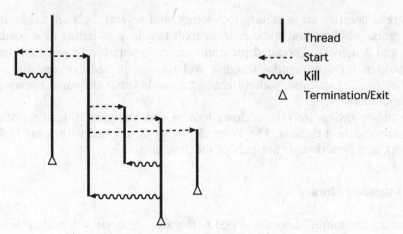

Fig. 4.3 A set of threads and their interrelationship.

With any scheduling scheme, a thread loses control if it must wait for a synchronization event. It also loses control if it is itself the cause of a synchronization event that makes a higher-priority task runnable. Further, the thread can give up control voluntarily, by calling the function *yield*. This function checks if there is another runnable thread of same priority and, if there is, transmits control to that thread.

Scheduling algorithms are especially complicated when affinity scheduling is deployed. Affinity scheduling tries to assign a thread to the same CPU on which it was run previously, to facilitate the reuse of cached data.

Synchronization   The major purpose of synchronization is the protection of shared variables and data structures. These resources are manipulated in so-called *critical sections*, which are sections of code that must be executed as a whole, and must not be interrupted by related events, to ensure correctness. A second purpose of synchronization is the avoidance of busy waiting—when a thread has nothing to do, it can set itself on idle and wait for a desired synchronization event to wake it up.

The Pthreads library supports two basic synchronization mechanisms, both of which are well known in the concurrent computing area: mutexes and condition variables. The mechanisms are described in the following. It is not necessary to understand them in every detail, but one should get a feeling for how the mechanisms work.

Both mutexes and condition variables are implemented on the basis of a hardware *test-and-set* instruction. This instruction reads a word from memory and sets it to some value, such that no interruption may occur between the reading and the writing.

A *mutex* is accessed through functions *lock* and *unlock*—*lock* is called at the beginning of a critical section, and *unlock* at the end. By calling *lock* for a particular mutex, a thread becomes the owner of that mutex. When thereafter another thread calls *lock*, the call fails and the caller is put on a waiting list. For each particular mutex, there may be several waiting threads. When the owner releases the mutex, an arbitrary one of them is awakened and calls *lock* again. The call can succeed, but is not guaranteed to succeed, since a novel thread may come in between. As an alternative to *lock*, the Pthreads library supplies a function *trylock* which, in unsuccessful cases, does not put the caller to sleep, but sets a return value to indicate failure.

Condition variables are a more general synchronization mechanism through which arbitrary conditions (not just number_of_waiting_processes = 0) can be tested. Each condition variable is associated with a mutex. To access the condition variable, a thread must first acquire ownership of the mutex. Then it evaluates the possibly complex condition, using normal C statements. If the condition evaluates to true, it continues with the computation and releases the mutex when appropriate. Otherwise, it calls a *wait* function with the condition variable as argument. In reaction, the system releases the mutex automatically and puts the thread onto a waiting list for the condition variable. When any other thread performs an action that may influence the condition, that thread will, if programmed well, notify the system. After notification, the system wakes up one of the sleeping threads, which then tests the condition again.

In addition to mutexes and condition variables, many Pthreads implementations support *semaphores*. A semaphore manages multiple resources of the same kind. At any one time, it is characterized by a value that represents the number of available resources. The semaphore is accessed via functions *post* and *wait*—the former adds a resource and the latter consumes one. To state it in more detail, a call to *post* increments the value of the semaphore and wakes up one waiting thread if there is one. A call to *wait* tests if the value of the semaphore is greater than zero. If so, the value is decremented; otherwise the calling thread goes to sleep.

In several implementations, more involved or specialized synchronization mechanisms are available. With any mechanism, the programmer is also responsible for the initialization and release of the resources that are needed by the mechanism itself.

Java Threads

The Java threads model reflects the object-oriented nature of Java. Object orientation is a topic in its own right, a substantial topic that is orthogonal to parallel and distributed computing. Although knowledge of object-orientation is not really necessary to understand this book, the following introduction to Java threads and a few other chapters occasionally refer to some basic notions.

Basic object-oriented concepts   The reader who is not familiar with object orientation may think of it in the following simplified way: In object-oriented programming, data and the functions that operate on them are put together into a *class*. A class can, for example, describe a ship, with data being position and speed, and functions being accelerate and decelerate. The data are denoted as *attributes*, and the functions are denoted as *methods*. The class describes the general concept of a ship, but not a particular ship. We can *instantiate* the class to obtain *objects*, which stand for particular ships. Different ships will have different values for position and speed, but all ships are characterized by these two quantities, and all ships can carry out the methods accelerate and decelerate.

A class can be further qualified through *inheritance*. Inheritance chiefly adds attributes and methods, and changes (overrides) the functionality of existing methods. A class that is derived by inheritance is called *subclass*. In our example, it may be a submarine with depth as an additional attribute and dive as an additional method. A submarine is a kind of ship: Like a ship, it is characterized by position and speed, and can accelerate and decelerate. As usual, particular submarines are obtained through instantiation.

In Java, a subclass may be derived from a single class only. In order to relate it to additional classes, the *interface* mechanism must be deployed. This mechanism can, for instance, express that both a submarine and a diver are able to dive. In general, an interface specifies a set of functions without implementing them. A class is said to *implement* the interface if it provides code for the functions.

The Thread class   The Java language is supplied with a large set of predefined classes. Among them is a class called *Thread*. Objects that are instantiated from this class are able to carry out the methods *start*, *run*, and *stop*, as well as several other thread methods that are surveyed later. The *run* method is empty, that is, objects that are derived by plain instantiation do not do any useful work.

Threads with an application-specific behavior are obtained via the inheritance or interface mechanisms. To outline the idea: The user declares an own class in which he or she states the relationship with *Thread* and overrides the (empty) *run* method of *Thread* with some useful code. Then the programmer instantiates the new class to declare thread objects. The threads are activated by calling their *start* method, which automatically invokes *run*.

So far, we have seen how threads are integrated into the Java language. Whereas thread creation is comparatively difficult in Java, other functionalities are more comfortable to handle than with Pthreads. In the following, we give a survey of the available methods:

Thread management   In addition to the *start* method, which was already discussed, and the *stop* method, which behaves like *exit* in Pthreads, the Java threads model provides methods to temporarily suspend a thread, and it provides thread groups. The first suspension method, *sleep*, causes a thread to sleep for a period of time, which is given as a parameter. The second method, *suspend*, causes a thread to sleep until it is woken up by another thread calling *resume*. Finally, *interrupt* sends a signal to a sleeping thread. The thread wakes up and executes some specific interruption code which may, for instance, cause it to stop.

A Java program starts as a single thread, the main thread. Afterwards, any thread may create any number of other threads, as in Pthreads. A thread may live longer than its creator; in particular it may live longer than the main thread, except if the programmer sets an option to automatically kill all threads at the end of the main thread.

Threads can be collected into thread groups, that is, the programmer can impose a hierarchical structure on the set of threads. Some Java methods are able to deal with thread groups as a whole; for instance, they can stop or resume all threads of a group at once. The major purpose of thread groups is the protection of different threads against each other's access.

Thread scheduling Thread scheduling works as with Pthreads: For example, it defines priorities and the *yield* function. As with Pthreads, the details are implementation-dependent, and time slicing may but need not be deployed. Only newer implementations of Java support physical parallelism; older implementations are restricted to time sharing on a single processor (even for multi-processor machines). The major application area of Java threads is the expression of problem-inherent parallelism. Increasingly, however, people are becoming interested in exploiting the performance potential, too.

Synchronization The main synchronization mechanism of Java is the so-called *monitor*. This mechanism is more comfortable than the synchronization mechanisms of Pthreads, but less flexible. In the simplest case, the programmer does not call any synchronization routines at all, but just marks the critical sections with the keyword *synchronized*. Java associates each object with a lock. Whenever a thread wants to enter a critical section that belongs to the object, the thread must first acquire the lock, and afterwards releases it. Lock management is hidden from the programmer, that is, Java transparently tests the lock, sends the threads to sleep, awakes them later, and so on. The *synchronized* keyword is often stated for a whole method; alternatively it can be stated for only a code section. In the case of a code section, the programmer can name the object whose lock is required; otherwise it is the present object. There is only a single lock per object, and thus a thread may block another thread even if they operate on different data. The restriction can be circumvented at the price of a larger programming effort.

The monitor concept is supplemented by the methods *wait* and *notify*. By calling *wait*, the owner of a lock voluntarily releases the lock and goes to sleep, thus giving a chance to others. A call to *notify* wakes up an arbitrary sleeping thread; *notifyAll* wakes up all sleeping threads.

The Java and Pthreads synchronization mechanisms are equivalent, although some things are easier to express in one or the other model [270]. Both models are error-prone. On one hand, the synchronization mechanisms themselves must be handled, and on the other, a large number of threads with possibly complex interactions must be coordinated. The Java threads model is widely criticized, for instance in [221, 350].

4.2 STRUCTURED SHARED-MEMORY PROGRAMMING

Thread models are biased towards applications with a large number of coarse-grained and competing tasks. They focus on task parallelism and do not explicitly support data parallelism. Although thread models can in principle be used for fine-grained parallel applications, the structured shared-memory model is a better fit.

The structured shared-memory model is exemplified by OpenMP, a recent informal but widely supported standard. OpenMP operates on a higher level than threads. Indeed, several OpenMP compilers use "C + Pthreads" as their destination language.

The flavor of OpenMP is probably closer to HPF than to thread models, although, of course, there are fundamental differences, as was noted in the introduction to this chapter. OpenMP supports both task and data parallelism, with emphasis on data parallelism and the SPMD programming style. Like HPF, OpenMP defines a set of compiler directives, as well as environment variables and library functions, which have bindings to C, C++, and Fortran. The use of compiler directives has the advantage that an OpenMP program can be translated by a sequential compiler, which just ignores the directives.

OpenMP is called a *structured* shared-memory model, because the language imposes a structure on the set of tasks. Whereas thread models allow any thread to create and kill any other thread (except if the programmer uses thread groups, but this is an add-on), OpenMP enforces a hierarchical structure. We will now look at this and other language features in more detail.

Task structure As illustrated in Fig. 4.4, a program starts execution as a single thread, called the *master thread*. Then the master thread can open a parallel region, which is a section of code that is carried out by several cooperating threads. The threads belong together and are called *children* of the master thread. At entrance into the parallel region, all children are created at once; the parallel region ends when all children have finished their work. Within the parallel region, the master thread takes the role of a child;

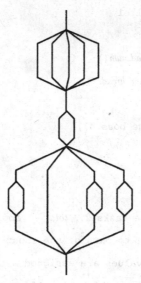

Fig. 4.4 Structure of an OpenMP program.

afterwards it turns back to its role as master thread. A program may contain multiple parallel regions, as long as the preceding region is terminated before the next region is started.

Recursively, any thread may start a parallel region and therein take the role of the master thread. An inner region will, however, always be completely enclosed by an outer one. Although the OpenMP standard permits the nesting of parallel regions, it does not prescribe that the language implementations must make use of it. Indeed, all current implementations sequentialize inner parallel regions, that is, they let the corresponding master thread carry out all the inner threads, one after another.

The programmer can control the number of threads in a parallel region with a compiler directive or by setting an environment variable for the whole program. Alternatively, the system chooses an appropriate number. Different parallel regions may work with a different number of threads, but the number remains constant throughout each individual region.

Work sharing by thread numbers   Let us now look inside a parallel region. The most basic way to specify the functionality of the threads relies on the library functions *omp_get_num_threads* and *omp_get_thread_num*, which return the total number of threads and the number of the calling thread, respectively. (The threads are numbered consecutively, starting from zero.) The programmer calls the two functions at the beginning of the parallel region, and thereafter codes the functionality of the threads in terms of their numbers.

```
#pragma omp parallel
{
    me = omp_get_thread_num();
    total = omp_get_num_threads();
    if (me==0)
        printf("I am the boss.");
    else if (me==1)
        specialTask();
    else
        /* Each of the tasks 2...total − 1 applies
           someFunction to part of the input values.
           The input values are assigned alternately to
           the tasks such that all values are dealt with.   */
        for (i = me; i < N; i+= total − 2)
            someFunction(A[i]);
}
```

Fig. 4.5 Work sharing by thread numbers.

An example is given in Fig. 4.5. The example uses the C syntax of OpenMP, in which "#pragma omp parallel" opens a parallel region. The program demonstrates the flexibility of work sharing by thread numbers: Different threads can be instructed to carry out either the same or different operations, so that both data and task parallelism can be expressed.

Work-sharing with the for construct   With the previous method, the programmer had to organize all details of work sharing. To simplify programming in common cases, two frequently used patterns are directly supported: *for* and *sections*.

The *for* directive resembles the *independent* directive of HPF in that both constructs describe parallel loops with no implicit synchronization except at the end. The constructs differ in that *for* invokes task-parallel, and *independent* invokes data-parallel tasks, according to the distinction that has been made in the introduction to this chapter. Within the loops, the difference manifests as follows:

- Accesses to shared data must be synchronized in OpenMP, whereas they are forbidden in HPF.

- Function calls must be side-effect-free in HPF, whereas they are allowed to have side effects in OpenMP.

Task scheduling As another difference, the OpenMP programmer may control the assignment of loop iterations to threads. Whereas HPF handles the assignment transparently, OpenMP lets the user choose between four scheduling schemes: static, dynamic, guided, and run-time. Consider the following example:

```
#pragma omp parallel for
    for (i = 0; i < 15; i++)
        a[i] = b[i];
```

Here, the compiler directive "pragma omp parallel for" marks the following *for*-loop as parallel. Assume that we have three threads: t_0, t_1, and t_2. *Static scheduling* assigns chunks of successive iterations to the same thread in a round-robin manner. With a chunk size of 4, for instance, it assigns iterations $0 \ldots 3$ to t_0, iterations $4 \ldots 7$ to t_1, iterations $8 \ldots 11$ to t_2, and iterations $12 \ldots 14$ to t_0 again. The user may specify the chunk size; otherwise it is chosen by the system. Static scheduling owes its name to the fact that the assignment is determined at compile time and not adjusted later.

With *dynamic scheduling*, the assignment is deferred until run time. At start of loop execution, each thread is assigned a chunk of iterations, typically with a small chunk size such as 1. The remaining iterations are kept in a task pool. Whenever a thread has finished its work, it requests the next chunk of iterations from the task pool, until the task pool is empty.

Guided scheduling works the same way as dynamic scheduling, except that the chunk size is adjusted dynamically. Execution starts with a large chunk size, and later the chunk size is reduced as appropriate.

Finally, *run-time scheduling* delays the scheduling decision until run time. Then, the choice is expressed through environment variables, which offer the same alternatives: static, dynamic, and guided.

One may have observed some analogy between the scheduling mechanisms of OpenMP and the block and cyclic data distribution mechanisms of HPF. Although these mechanisms are not really comparable, since the former refers to task scheduling and the latter to data distribution, the guidelines for the programmer are similar. Dynamic and guided scheduling are advantageous for load balancing. They are especially well suited for cases in which the load varies between iterations but successive iterations have similar computational requirements. Static scheduling, on the other hand, facilitates the exploitation of locality, and has less overhead.

Work sharing with the sections construct Whereas the *for* construct supports SPMD programming, the *sections* construct supports MPMD programming. The construct is simple: The programmer writes down a list of code sections and introduces each code section with the directive #pragma omp `sections`. Then the different code sections are carried out in parallel, each in a separate thread.

Other features of parallel regions   Multiple *for* and *sections* constructs may follow each other within the same parallel region. Normally, in between successive constructs, an implicit synchronization takes place. The synchronization can be suppressed by the programmer.

If a parallel region updates a shared variable through a commutative and associative operation, the system may be able to find a more efficient implementation than in general. The hint that a variable is subject to such a *reduction* can be expressed by the programmer in a directive.

To avoid the overhead of closing a parallel region and opening the next one, parallel regions are allowed to contain sequential sections. These sections are carried out by a single thread. The programmer can require that it be the master thread, or let the system choose a thread.

Private and shared variables   A variable is called *shared* if it is visible for all threads of a parallel region; it is called *private* if it belongs to a single thread. Whether a variable is private or shared is under programmer control. The programmer can also relate the variables inside a parallel region to their equal-named counterparts in the master thread. For instance, if a variable a is declared as private in each thread, then the programmer can request that all copies of a be initialized with the master thread's a value at the beginning of the parallel region.

Synchronization   The main synchronization construct of OpenMP is called the *critical region*. It is a label for a block of statements, usually with a name. At any one time, only a single thread may carry out a critical region with a specific name. Assume, for instance, that we have one region named A, and several regions each named B. Assume further that a thread t_0 is carrying out B at the moment. Then another thread t_1 may enter A, but it is not allowed to enter any of the B regions. Synchronization can also be achieved with the barrier collective operation, which was described in Sect. 3.4. Finally, OpenMP defines library functions for mutexes.

OpenMP implementations are allowed to buffer (delay) write accesses to shared variables. To make sure that all updates are completed physically at some point of program execution, the programmer must use the *flush* directive. Some OpenMP constructs induce an implicit *flush*.

Assessment   The structured shared-memory model supports data-parallel programming and, to some extent, task-parallel programming. Its functionality is, however, more restricted than that of HPF on one hand, and of threads on the other. In contrast to HPF, OpenMP does not provide the opportunity to specify the data distribution. Compared with threads, OpenMP imposes severe restrictions on the task structure. Both fine- and coarse-grained programs can be formulated with OpenMP, although the focus is on fine-grained programs. Shah et al. [377] describe an extended OpenMP model, in which some additional forms of task parallelism can be expressed.

OpenMP was defined in the late 1990s only. Nevertheless, several commercial and public domain compilers and tools are available already, and its practical relevance is growing rapidly. Tools include debuggers, profilers, and static analysis tools that help to ensure correctness.

An often cited advantage of OpenMP is its amenability to incremental parallelization. The advantage is partly due to the existence of a shared memory, so the sequential and parallel versions of a program can use the same data structures. In incremental parallelization, one starts from the sequential version and introduces parallelism stepwise, until the performance is satisfactory or one gives up for other reasons. At the beginning, only a few performance-relevant program parts are parallelized. Later, the parallelization proceeds with other program parts, and more sophisticated parallelization methods are deployed.

As we know, each programming model must trade off programmability and performance. The structured shared-memory model is performance-oriented, but it gives more consideration to programmability than message passing (treated in the next chapter) does.

OpenMP is targeted at SMP architectures. Although an implementation on distributed-memory architectures is in principle possible, the OpenMP standard does not define any explicit features in support of that. Nevertheless, some concrete implementations are targeted at non-SMPs. For instance, the MIPSproPower Compiler for the SGI Origin [319] supports additional directives for specifying the data distribution. An implementation on clusters of SMPs is described in Hu et al. [218]. It is reported to produce speedups that are within 7–30% of the MPI speedups, for some benchmark suite. Another implementation is targeted at workstation clusters with a dynamically changing number of processors [369]. Both of the cluster implementations translate OpenMP into TreadMarks, a distributed shared-memory system, which will be treated in the next section.

On distributed-memory architectures, message passing is often superior to OpenMP in terms of performance. Also, several applications are easier to handle with the unstructured task-parallel model of threads. To expand the OpenMP functionality in these and other cases, OpenMP facilitates the interoperability with other programming models. In particular the combination with MPI is important in practice.

4.3 DISTRIBUTED SHARED MEMORY

As stated in the introduction to this chapter, shared-memory programming has several appealing features, which motivated a large body of research into distributed shared memory (DSM). DSM stands for the realization of the shared-memory abstraction on architectures with a physically distributed memory (CC-NUMA, NCC-NUMA, NORMA, clusters, grids). DSM is not yet a mature model, although quite a lot of experience has been gained with it during the last years.

DSM systems operate on a low level and can in this respect be considered as the distributed-memory analog of the SMP threads model. The systems are used as both application programming interfaces, and destination languages for the compilation of higher-level systems such as OpenMP.

DSM can be implemented in hardware and/or software, for instance in the operating system. A basic operating-system mechanism is *virtual shared memory*. This mechanism owes its name to its resemblance to virtual-memory management in uniprocessors. In uniprocessors, programs have access to a memory that is larger than the physical memory. At any one time, only part of the virtual memory is mapped to the physical memory; the rest resides on disk. Transparent for the programmer, the operating system manages the movement of data between memory and disk. The data are moved in units of pages, which resemble large cache lines. If a program accesses data that currently reside on disk, a page miss occurs, and the operating system loads the corresponding page to memory. Since the memory capacity is limited, another page may have to be replaced, for instance the least recently used one.

Virtual shared memory generalizes the uniprocessor mechanism to parallel machines with a distributed memory. If a processor accesses a page that is currently stored at another processor, a page miss occurs. The operating system looks up the page location, sends a message to the corresponding processor, and acquires the page. Usually, the page is copied, and thus multiple copies of the same page can be around. Alternatively, the page is moved to the requesting processor, or it is kept at the old place and only the requested data are copied.

The disadvantage of virtual shared memory is a high overhead for communication, which is partially due to the large page size. Because of this size, data are moved around unnecessarily. Even worse, there is a large likelihood of *false sharing*: a single page can be modified by two or more processors that each hold a copy and access *disjoint* sections of the page. False sharing is problematic, since the operating system "thinks" in units of pages. For a write access, it registers that "the page" was modified; it does not go down to individual data. Hence, after a write access, all other processors must reload the page in order to make sure they see the right contents. If write accesses are frequent, a lot of unnecessary traffic results.

To guarantee correctness in a DSM system, all copy holders must be notified after a write access. Depending on the specific scheme, they either update the page, or mark it as invalid. If the system guarantees that any next read sees the correct values, it is said to implement *sequential consistency*.

Maintaining sequential consistency induces a high communication volume. Fortunately, it has been observed that much of the communication is actually superfluous. Many copies are not read between successive update notifications, or they are read in a false-sharing manner only. This observation has motivated weaker *consistency models*. Much of the research on DSM focuses on the design and implementation of such models. It is a large area of research. Whereas an exhaustive survey of consistency models and DSM systems is beyond our scope, we will look at a representative system in the following, and mention a few others in the final survey section.

TreadMarks One of the most influential DSM systems to date is TreadMarks. It was developed in the mid 1990s as a university project, and has been employed in several practical applications since. TreadMarks is implemented as a library, which runs on Unix and Windows NT. The library either is used by the application programmer directly, or serves as a destination "language" for compiling OpenMP and other high-level languages [218, 369, 451].

The central idea of TreadMarks is a consistency model that is called *lazy release consistency*. In this model, the notification of a copy is delayed until the information is really needed. Therefore the system makes use of the synchronization events in the program. Suppose that a thread t_0 writes to a variable a, and thereafter another thread t_1 reads a. With sequential consistency, t_1 is guaranteed to see the updated value of a in any case. If we think in terms of the underlying program, however, this looks like overkill. If the programmer is really interested in t_1 getting the updated value, then he or she must synchronize t_0 and t_1. TreadMarks exploits this observation and updates the t_1 copy only in the event of a synchronization.

Lazy release consistency reduces the communication volume as compared to sequential consistency. It does not address the case of false sharing with multiple writers, however. In that case, no single copy of the page is valid in full, since in the various copies different sections have been updated. Therefore, TreadMarks introduces a specific multiple-writers protocol. Instead of communicating the whole page after an update, it extracts the differences only. The various differences cannot conflict with each other, except if the program contains race conditions.

TreadMarks defines the following classes of functions:

- *Synchronization.* At the beginning and end of a critical region, the functions *acquire* and *release*, respectively, are called. Furthermore, TreadMarks provides barrier synchronization.

- *Task Management.* TreadMarks provides functions for thread creation and destruction. Like in thread models, the set of threads is unstructured.

- *Memory Allocation.* A specific function must be used to allocate shared memory. All other memory is private.

Weaker consistency models are still in dispute. As argued by Hill [211], some programs behave differently with sequential consistency than with release consistency. In hardware implementations of shared memory, the performance drawback of sequential consistency can be reduced with clever compilation techniques [211].

From a programmer's point of view, DSM programming has pros and cons similar to threads programming, except that the performance suffers from the gap in the access times to local and remote memory. Performance-oriented programming is therefore harder.

4.4 ONE-SIDED COMMUNICATION MODELS

This section deals with a class of shared-memory models in which the communication is explicit. The programmer must use different mechanisms to access the local and global memories, and is thus aware of the performance difference. Although one-sided communication models are usually classified as shared memory, their philosophy differs significantly from that of the other models that we have considered so far. One-sided communication models give up the objective of transparency. Therefore, part of the general assessment of shared memory given in the introduction does not apply. With respect to their pros and cons, one-sided communication models lie somewhere in between shared-memory and message passing programming.

In one-sided communication models, the shared memory must be allocated explicitly by the programmer. All other memory is private. Shared memory is allocated through a collective operation, in which the individual processes make part of their private memories available to each other. Memory can be shared among all or a subset of the processes.

After declaration, the processes access the shared memory via *put* and *get* routines. The existence of these routines is typical for the one-sided communication model, although the parameters differ between the various realizations. In the *Shmem* interface of HPVM [174], for instance, the parameters include the remote address, the local address, the name of the remote process, and the size of the data. In the one-sided communication model of MPI-2 [192], the shared memory is allocated in segments called windows, and the parameters include the name of the window and the displacement of the data from the window base address.

Several one-sided communication models facilitate the overlap between communication and computation. For this purpose, they partition *put* and *get* into two phases each, such that each phase is realized by a separate function. The first function initiates the respective operation, that is, it tells the system what it has to do. Then the first function returns, and the calling process can proceed to other work. Later on, the process invokes the second function to make sure that the operation has finished. If the operation has not finished yet, the second function either waits until completion, or returns with a value that indicates success or failure.

The one-sided communication model owes its name to the fact that only one process is involved in a communication event. Only the process that accesses a location is active, whereas the owner of the location need not do anything. In the implementation, of course, there must be a system process which sends/receives the data on behalf of the owner, but this is not visible to the programmer.

Like other shared-memory models, one-sided communication models provide synchronization mechanisms such as mutexes, barriers, and more specific mechanisms [192], as well as collective operations. Unlike other shared-memory models, however, one-sided communication models consider tasks as static or nearly static. The static view is to a certain extent inherent in the model, because each shared-memory segment is associated with a set of processes that must already exist when the memory segment is allocated.

One-sided communication models can be implemented in a library or language. Typically, they do not make up the whole system, but are defined in combination with other models. Examples are MPI-2, which is chiefly a message-passing system, and BSP, which is a message-passing-related system. Both MPI-2 and BSP will be treated in later chapters of this book.

4.5 MORE ON THIS TOPIC

Although the concept of shared-memory programming is closely associated with the notion of threads, communication via a shared memory is also possible for processes. The Unix operating system [401] provides functions through which processes can agree to share part of their address spaces. Synchronization mechanisms are available, as are functions for creating and terminating processes. Therefore, the same functionality as with Pthreads can be realized with processes, too, although the coding is harder and the performance is worse [270].

The Ada 95 programming language [75, 419] supports communication through shared variables. In Ada, shared variables coexist with other parallel models, which are treated in later chapters of this book. Ada provides a monitor-like construct for synchronization, similar to that of Java.

We have restricted structured shared-memory programming to OpenMP, since it is the only widely used and portable system. Prior to OpenMP, several proprietary systems prevailed, which have similar programming models.

DSM research is diverse. Besides TreadMarks, many other systems were suggested, for instance: CVM [246], Brazos [397], Rthreads [137], Millipede [227, 228], SciOS [253], SMiLE [245], Proteus [420], Shasta [368], and Sirocco [371]. Some interesting aspects of particular systems include: explicit support for clusters of SMPs, integration with SCI hardware, task migration, and data sharing in smaller units than pages.

In *object-based DSM systems*, data are shared in units of objects which, as usual, consist of data and methods to access the data. Thus, object-based DSM systems impose a structure onto the shared memory, and the granularity of the data-sharing units is chosen in an application-specific way. Objects are transparently migrated and replicated. Unlike other object-based approaches, object-based DSM systems consider objects as primarily a type of storage through which processes exchange information. Further information can be found in Tanenbaum [408] and on the Web page [132]. An exemplary language in this context is Orca [36].

Several systems that are treated in later chapters of this book could alternatively be put under the heading of shared memory. In particular Linda (see Ch. 8) defines a shared-memory model. Unlike the shared-memory models of this chapter, the Linda model imposes a structure on the shared memory, so the memory is accessed in application-specific units instead of in pages. Other related models are treated in the context of transparent migration (Sect. 7.4) and graph-based abstract models (Sect. 11.6).

The *put/get* model of one-sided communication is used in the languages Split-C [122] and Titanium [450]. Split-C was introduced in the early 1990s and supports data-parallel, shared-memory, and message-passing programming. As in HPF, the user can specify the data distribution, although the concrete mechanism is different. The *put/get* model allows the programmer to work with pointers, which can be either local or remote. Titanium is a Java-related language that adopts a similar programming model to Split-C. Titanium is currently under development [414].

BIBLIOGRAPHICAL REMARKS

Shared-memory programming is covered in several textbooks, such as Hwang and Xu [220] and Pfister [338]. A very readable introduction to threads, with focus on Pthreads, is Lewis and Berg [270]. Other useful resources on Pthreads include Tanenbaum [408] and Kleiman et al. [250]. Java threads are covered by the Java specification [183], and are also described in several Java textbooks, such as Niemeyer and Peck [307] and Farley [146]. An in-depth treatment is given in Oaks and Wong [308]. The description of OpenMP draws on the C/C++ standard [318] and on other information from the OpenMP homepage [320]. In particular the FAQ, the tutorial on OpenMP [141], and vendor information (Kuck&Associates, Inc.; Silicon Graphics, Inc.) were used. The virtual-shared-memory concept is explained in Tanenbaum [408]. DSM issues are surveyed in Judge et al. [239]. A large collection of links to DSM projects can be found at the Web page [132].

5

Message Passing

The model to be discussed in this chapter supports task parallelism as well, but it deploys a fundamentally different intertask communication mechanism. The chapter is structured slightly differently from the previous ones, since it does not distinguish between submodels. Instead, the various sections are devoted to different aspects of the same model. The introduction is comparatively long, since from the previous chapters we have now two closely related models to compare the present one with. As usual, let us start with a definition.

> In the message-passing model, several processes run in parallel and communicate with one another by sending and receiving messages. The processes do not have access to a shared memory.

Hence, in message passing, the processes operate on disjoint address spaces, and all communication is accomplished through explicit message exchange, as depicted in Fig. 5.1. The central communication routines are *send* and *receive*. In order for two processes to exchange information, one of them must invoke a *send*, and the other must invoke a matching *receive*. It is always exactly two processes that are involved in such a communication. The functions *send* and *receive* exist in several variants, and practical message-passing systems add further functions, as we will see later. Nevertheless, the notion of message passing is closely associated with *send* and *receive*.

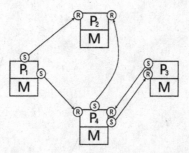

Fig. 5.1   The message-passing model. S stands for *send* and R stands for *receive*.

Message exchange may serve different purposes. The most obvious purpose is the exchange of data between a sender and a receiver that know each other and whose interaction was planned in detail by the programmer. A second purpose is the establishment of a connection between a sender and a receiver whose interaction was not planned in advance. A connection can only be established if the receiver is prepared for an eventual request: it must have posted an anonymous *receive*, and it must occasionally check whether a message has arrived. An eventual sender will use the initial message to transmit to the receiver details about the desired transaction. For instance, it can state the length of a message to be sent or the location of requested data. A third purpose of message exchange is *synchronization*. A process may send a message in order to indicate that it has reached a certain point of program execution.

Note that synchronization is just a special case of communication. Separate synchronization routines as in shared-memory programming are not needed, since each communication implicitly induces a synchronization between sender and receiver.

In the *send* and *receive* routines, the programmer must specify low-level details such as the number (identity) of the receiver process, the address and size of a source or destination buffer, and the length of the message. Section 5.1 describes the send/receive routines in more detail.

In this book, the notion of message passing is restricted to models that are based on *send* and *receive*. Often, the notion is used in a wider sense, and covers all systems in which the processes run in private address spaces and cooperate through explicit communication routines. We refer to message passing in the wider sense as *message exchange*. It includes one-sided communication, RPC, sockets, and other models that we treat in later chapters.

Relation to data parallelism and task parallelism   Message passing supports both SPMD and MPMD programming, with focus on SPMD. The typical application domain is performance-oriented scientific computing, in which message passing is currently the prevailing model. There seem to be two major reasons for the focus on SPMD:

- Many scientific applications are naturally data-parallel.

- Programs are easier to write, maintain, and debug, since the programmer must deal with a single program text only.

Although the message-passing model is often used for the coding of data-parallel applications, there are fundamental differences between the data-parallel and message-passing models. First, data-parallel models operate on a much higher level. In message passing, the programmer must handle details that are committed to the compiler in the data-parallel case. Second, message passing adopts a localized view. The programmer thinks in terms of the individual processes, whereas the data-parallel model encourages a global view.

Message passing supports task parallelism, but to a varying degree. Whereas some task-parallel patterns are well supported and frequently deployed, others are not. In a message-passing program, the set of processes is typically static or nearly static. Although several message-passing systems provide functions for the creation and termination of processes, these functions are used infrequently. A reason is the binding of communications to processes: In order to send a message, a sender must know the identity of the receiver. Although process numbers may be communicated, the communication induces overhead, and it is easier for the programmer to think in terms of a static structure. A second reason is the overhead for task creation. This overhead is high, because tasks are normally implemented as processes and not as threads.

Assessment of the Model

The message-passing model closely follows the architecture of distributed-memory machines. Therefore it is easy to implement, but operates on a low level. Indeed, message passing is sometimes called the assembler language of parallel programming. The low-level approach has the following consequences:

Programmability   Message passing imposes a heavy burden on the programmer, who is responsible for managing all details of data distribution and task scheduling, as well as of the communication between tasks. Particular responsibilities include load balancing, data replication, and the maintenance of coherency. Message passing is therefore time-consuming and error-prone, and the programs are hard to maintain and debug. Compared with shared-memory programming, message passing has nevertheless some programmability advantages, which will be discussed in the next subsection.

Efficiency   The primary argument for message passing is efficiency. Since everything is under the programmer's control, the programmer can achieve close to optimum performance if he or she just spends enough time in performance tuning. The programmer manages the communication in an application-specific way. He or she can, for instance, distribute and redistribute the data and processes with any pattern, replicate the data in variable-size units, and aggregate communications. Efficiency is the major reason for the predominance of message passing in compute-intensive application domains. In these domains, people are often willing to spend much time in program development and performance tuning. Nevertheless, in several applications and on several architectures, shared-memory programming is superior.

Portability   A second argument for message passing is code portability. This argument is not really inherent in the model, but more a consequence of the development in the past. Because message passing became popular quite early, it was also early that the first standards were established. Although message passing focuses on distributed-memory architectures, the model is also implemented on SMPs, clusters of SMPs, and sequential architectures. As usual, code portability does not imply performance portability. On SMPs, shared-memory models are normally superior, since their communication mechanism induces less overhead. On clusters of SMPs, the performance suffers from unnecessary communication overhead within the individual SMP nodes. Even among distributed-memory machines, there is no guarantee of performance portability. If the performance was tuned for one architecture, it will not normally transfer to another, at least not to the same degree.

Comparison with Shared-Memory Programming

It is a matter of debate whether and in which cases either of the two models is more appropriate. Here are some arguments:

- The shared-memory model has a certain advantage in *programmability*, because the data structures need not be divided up between processes. This advantage helps in particular with large irregular data structures that are implemented with pointers.

- The shared-memory model is more similar to the familiar *sequential* programming model, and hence the transition is easier for programmers.

- The shared-memory model is more amenable to *incremental parallelization*. Transforming a sequential program into a message-passing one is a more abrupt break, since the data structures must be divided up. One can nevertheless start from the sequential program and put more or less effort into the parallelization project. A step-by-step approach is, however, less suitable, since intermediate programs are not much use.

- In *performance-oriented* shared-memory programming, the programmer must take the distribution of data and computations into account. Hence, the first advantage from this list is weakened. In the message-passing model, the programmer can directly state his or her intentions, whereas in the shared-memory model, the programmer must second-guess the compiler's transformations.

- Message passing tends to be superior with respect to *performance*, but we must differentiate between the various architectures, applications, and programming systems. In general, message passing takes longer for the individual communication operation, but it avoids superfluous communications, and thus the whole program often runs faster.

- In message passing, the performance is more *predictable*, since the program text says when a communication is taking place. Also, data distribution and task scheduling are known to the programmer.

- Message passing requires the consideration of low-level *details* in communication, and shared-memory programming requires the detailed organization of synchronization. Many people think that shared-memory programming is nevertheless simpler, but this is a matter of debate. Whether there is an advantage and how large the advantage is depends on the application, the background of the programmer, the concrete system, and other factors.

- In message passing, *synchronization errors* seem to be less likely. Although race conditions and deadlocks can occur, the errors are less subtle, because the interfaces between the processes are well defined, and the programmer is thus aware of the fact that communication takes place. The programmer cannot forget to protect shared variables, as there are none. Message-passing errors are of a different nature, and include sends without a matching receive, and receives that match another send than intended.

Systems

The notion of message passing is closely associated with two systems: the Message Passing Interface (MPI) and the Parallel Virtual Machine (PVM). These systems are very popular; indeed, Gannon and Grimshaw [171, p. 230] estimate that "the vast majority of parallel applications written today use MPI or PVM".

Both MPI and PVM follow the library approach, and are thus easy to implement. The libraries are defined for C, C++, and Fortran; extensions to Java have been suggested and are mentioned in the final survey section. Many tools, for instance debuggers and performance visualization tools, are available.

MPI is actually not a system but a standard. It was defined by the MPI Forum, a group of hardware vendors, research institutions, universities, and industrial users. The first version of the standard, MPI-1, appeared in 1994. It is implemented in various commercial and public-domain systems. An enhanced standard, MPI-2, was released in 1997. This standard is a superset of MPI-1 and much more involved. Therefore, MPI-2 implementations are still rare. Most systems support MPI-1 and a subset of the MPI-2 functionality.

PVM was developed in the early 1990s in a university project. Although PVM is being replaced by MPI in many cases, PVM has a large code base and some specific strengths, for which it is still widely used. PVM contains less functions than MPI and tends to be slower, but it gives more attention to heterogeneity, interoperability, and fault-tolerance issues. Whereas MPI must be embedded in an implementation-specific environment, PVM is self-contained.

Although the foci of MPI and PVM differ slightly, their basic philosophy is the same. The following sections are devoted to various aspects of the systems, except for Sect. 5.4, which handles another submodel.

5.1 INTERPROCESS COMMUNICATION

This section describes the *send* and *receive* routines in more detail. While the basic mechanism is conceptually simple, the MPI standard defines a multitude of variants. We briefly survey the variants as well, to give an impression of the variety. The section refers to MPI-1, but the same functionalities are also available in MPI-2, and PVM implements a subset.

The basic *send* and *receive* routines   The following example shows a simple but typical MPI program[1]:

```
char msg[20];
int me, total, tag=99;
MPI_Status status;
...
MPI_Comm_rank( MPI_COMM_WORLD, &me );
MPI_Comm_size( MPI_COMM_WORLD, &total ); /* can be omitted */
if (me == 0)
  strcpy( msg, "Hello there");
  MPI_Send( msg, strlen(msg)+1, MPI_CHAR, 1, tag, MPI_COMM_WORLD);
else if (me == 1)
  MPI_Recv( msg, 20, MPI_CHAR, 0, tag, MPI_COMM_WORLD, &status);
```

---

[1]Adapted, by permission, from M. Snir et al., *MPI: The Complete Reference*, [394, p. 16]. © 1996 Massachusetts Institute of Technology.

In the example, two processes, numbered 0 and 1, are working in parallel. Process 0 sends a message to process 1, and process 1 receives the message. The example follows the SPMD coding style. All processes work with the same program text, but different processes carry out different sections of the text. The work sharing between the processes is specified as in OpenMP: At the beginning, the programmer calls the functions *MPI_Comm_rank* and *MPI_Comm_size*, which yield the number of the caller and the total number of processes, respectively. Thereafter, the functionality of the processes is coded in terms of their numbers. In MPI, work sharing must always be specified through process numbers. There is no such alternative as the *for* and *sections* constructs of OpenMP.

The example program shows the usage of *MPI_Send* and *MPI_Recv*, and demonstrates the low-level nature of these routines. *MPI_Send* has the following parameters (in this order):

- *Address of the Send Buffer*. The send buffer must be allocated by the programmer, within the sender's address space.

- *Number of Data to Be Sent*. The number must be stated explicitly, in units of the datatype sent.

- *Datatype*. This is the type of the data sent. We come back to MPI datatypes in Sect. 5.3.

- *Destination Process*. The sender must always state the number of the receiver.

- *Message Tag*. This is an application-defined label for the message. The receiver can use the label to distinguish different messages from the same sender by their contents.

- *Communicator*. Communicators are treated in Sect. 5.2. Roughly speaking, a communicator is a group of processes to which both the sender and the receiver belong. MPI_COMM_WORLD is the group of all processes in the system.

The meaning of the parameters in *MPI_Recv* is similar:

- *Address of the Receive Buffer*. The buffer must be allocated within the receiver's address space. Note that this requirement is fulfilled in the example, because sender and receiver work independently, and thus use different instances of the variable *msg*.

- *Maximal Number of Data*. This is an upper bound on the size of a message. The receiver states that it is prepared to accept up to that number of data.

- *Datatype*. As above.

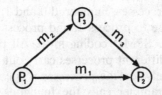

Fig. 5.2 A possible race condition.

- *Source Process*. The receiver may, but need not, state a concrete number here. If it does, only messages from that particular source are accepted. Otherwise, messages from any source are accepted.

- *Message Tag*. As before, the receiver may, but need not, state a concrete value.

- *Communicator*. As above.

- *Status*. Through the status variable, *MPI_Recv* informs the calling process about the received message. The status contains the number of the source process, the tag, and the actual length of the received message. Technically, the status variable is a kind of pointer to a set of return values. It must be declared by the programmer.

For a communication between sender and receiver to be successful, the message must match with the parameters of *MPI_Recv*. Therefore, it must agree in the following parameters: sender, tag, communicator, and datatype.

If the sender and/or tag are not specified, race conditions can occur. MPI guarantees that messages from the same sender to the same receiver are nonovertaking. If an intermediate process is involved, however, no assumption can be made about the relative progress. In the example of Fig. 5.2, process p_1 first sends message m_1 to p_2, and later m_2 to p_3. Process p_3 sends message m_3 only after having received m_2. Nevertheless, m_3 may overtake m_1, that is, either m_1 or m_3 may be received first.

Variants of send and receive   The variants differ chiefly in that they return at different times. The major distinction is between blocking and nonblocking communication. With *blocking* communication, a send routine returns when the sending has been completed at least to the point that the process may reuse the send buffer. With *nonblocking* communication, the send returns immediately after having registered the desired message transfer with the system. While the transfer is performed in the background, the process can continue with other useful work. The principle is the same as in the two-phase *put* and *get* routines of Sect. 4.4, and, likewise, the send must be completed by a separate function call. There are two variants of the second function: one that waits until completion, and another that returns immediately and yields a value that indicates success or failure. Blocking and nonblocking communications are also defined at the receiver side. In general, non-blocking communications complicate programs, but they tend to improve the performance (since they overlap computation and communication).

Both the blocking and the nonblocking sends can be further distinguished as standard, buffered, and synchronous mode. The modes differ in how they handle the case that a matching receive has not been posted yet. In *synchronous* mode, the system waits for the posting of a receive before it starts transferring the message. In *buffered* mode, the system copies the message from the send buffer to a system buffer and lets the sender process proceed. In *standard* mode, the system is free to buffer the message or not, depending on the available resources.

Another group of send and receive routines is specific to the case that the same pair of sender and receiver exchanges information periodically. Yet other communication routines are available, for instance, for inspecting a message before receiving it, and for canceling an outstanding communication request.

In addition to the pairwise communication routines, both MPI and PVM define *collective operations*. MPI defines a large number of them. Like send and receive, collective operations operate on a low level.

5.2 TASK MANAGEMENT

The most elementary functions of task management are the creation and termination of processes. These functions are not defined in MPI-1. Instead, the MPI-1 standard assumes that a set of running processes is given a priori. The approach has two consequences: On one hand, the number of processes is fixed throughout a program—a severe restriction of task parallelism. On the other hand, MPI-1 implementations need to supplement facilities for the creation and termination of processes at the beginning and end of a program run. Since these facilities are not covered by the standard, they are not portable.

PVM takes a different approach and considers task management as an integral part of the system. PVM provides functions for process creation and termination, which work similarly to their counterparts in thread models. Furthermore, PVM is supplied with a PVM console, which is a system management tool through which the user can at run time create and terminate processes. PVM is targeted at clusters. Through the PVM console, the user can at any time add and delete hosts, query the binding of processes to hosts, and create processes on specific hosts. The set of hosts that take part in a computation is called *virtual machine*, giving PVM its name. To support heterogeneity, PVM addresses the compilation of programs for different hosts. PVM also provides functions to support fault recovery after a node crash.

MPI-2 expands the MPI task management functionality towards that of PVM, but it is still more restricted than PVM. The MPI-2 standard defines functions for process creation, but it does not define an equivalent of the PVM console.

Process groups A different aspect of task management is the organization of processes into groups. The group mechanism is more expressive in MPI than in PVM, and hence we look at MPI in the following. Process groups serve two purposes: describing the set of participants in a collective operation, and structuring a program.

The concept of process groups is intertwined with that of communicators. Although MPI makes a difference between the two notions, we equate them for the purposes of this overview. Roughly speaking, a process group is a set of processes that cooperate in the solution of a subtask. A process group is created through an explicit function call, which is collectively invoked by all future members of the group. At any time, several process groups may exist, and they may overlap or contain each other.

In any call to a communication routine, the process group must be stated. Communication typically takes place within a process group, but MPI also defines the concept of *intercommunicators*, which are communication channels between disjoint groups. The management of process groups raises specific difficulties when processes are created dynamically. MPI-2 addresses this issue, too.

A novel feature of MPI-2 is the opportunity to connect process groups that have been created independently of each other, for instance by different users. This feature falls under the heading of client/server computing and is handled in Ch. 6.

Task-parallel patterns A frequently deployed pattern in message passing is *master/slave*. This pattern resembles the OpenMP *for* construct with the dynamic scheduling option, except that the programmer organizes the work sharing by hand. As illustrated in Fig. 5.3, we have one master and multiple slaves. The master maintains a pool of tasks, which are independent and typically of about the same size. Initially, the master assigns a task to each slave. Whenever a slave has finished its assignment, it sends the result back to the master and in return gets a next assignment. The final result is generated by the master, which combines the partial results into an overall solution.

The *divide-and-conquer* pattern, which was described in Sect. 3.3, can be interpreted as a generalization of master/slave. In this generalization, each slave internally functions as a master: It divides its task up into independent subtasks, and assigns the subtasks to subordinate slaves. The scheme is illustrated in Fig. 5.4.

In addition to the dynamic scheduling option of OpenMP, the static and guided options can be expressed as well, as can many application-specific patterns of task parallelism. Compared with OpenMP, the MPI mechanism is more flexible but less convenient.

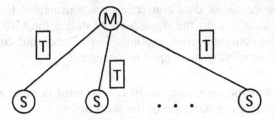

Fig. 5.3 The master/slave paradigm. M stands for master, S stands for slave, and T stands for task.

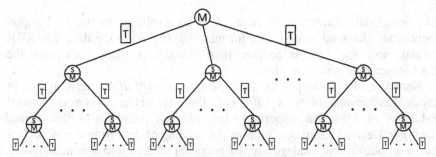

Fig. 5.4 The divide-and-conquer paradigm. M stands for master, S stands for slave, and T stands for task. Each slave takes the role of a master internally.

5.3 INTEROPERABILITY

As noted in Sect. 5.1, *MPI_Send* and *MPI_Recv* require a datatype parameter. This parameter supports heterogeneous environments, in which the sender and receiver of a message work with different representations of the same datatype. The representations may, for instance, use a different precision, deploy a different encoding scheme, or store the bytes in a different order. Thus, the data formats must be converted in a communication.

Data conversion is not specific to message passing. It is required with any programming model that addresses heterogeneous systems. Indeed, the topic is often discussed in the context of the remote-procedure-call model (Sect. 6.3).

Data conversion is based on a common data format that must be supported by all hosts in the system. A widely supported data format is the *external data representation* (XDR). Conversion into this format and from this format back into a machine-specific representation is accomplished through operating system libraries. MPI-2 defines a data format that is designated external32. Each MPI-2 implementation must support this format in read and write routines to files.

Although the details of data conversion are transparent to the programmer, he or she must request the conversion by stating the MPI datatype as a parameter in the communication routines. For a successful communication, the following compatibility rules must be observed:

- The MPI datatype parameter in *MPI_Send* must be compatible with the C, C++, or Fortran datatype of the send buffer.

- The MPI datatype parameters of *MPI_Send* and *MPI_Recv* must be compatible with each other.

- The MPI datatype parameter in *MPI_Recv* must be compatible with the datatype of the receive buffer.

The actual data conversion, if required, is accomplished by the MPI implementation: The send routine can, for instance, transform the data into XDR format, and the receive routine then transforms them back into the machine-specific representation.

Normally, the datatypes of *MPI_Send* and *MPI_Recv* must agree. In saying that compatibility is sufficient, the rule refers to several special datatypes of MPI. An important class of such datatypes is the *derived datatypes*. Derived datatypes, support the sending of data from a noncontiguous send buffer, and analogously the receiving of data into a noncontiguous receive buffer. Derived datatypes can be used, for instance, to send a column of a matrix that is stored row–wise.

In PVM, the programmer can choose between XDR encoding and "no encoding", with the latter option speeding up programs in homogeneous environments. Both MPI-2 and PVM address the issue of interoperability between different programming languages.

Another aspect of interoperability is addressed by the recent Interoperable MPI (IMPI) proposal, which is an extension of the MPI-2 standard. IMPI primarily addresses metacomputing environments, in which several parallel machines are interconnected through a slower TCP/IP connection. Whereas MPI covers communication within a single parallel machine, IMPI is concerned with cooperation across machine boundaries. In particular, IMPI addresses interoperability between MPI implementations from different vendors.

5.4   VERY LOW-LEVEL MODELS

This section differs from the previous ones in that it is devoted to a different submodel, not just to a different aspect of message passing. The submodel has already been mentioned in Sect. 2.5; it is the programming model that underlies lightweight protocols. This model does not really fit under the heading of message passing, because it is not based on a send/receive mechanism. The model is, nevertheless, handled in this chapter because, like message passing, lightweight protocols adopt a low-level view and focus on a symmetric message exchange between parallel (as opposed to distributed) processes.

Lightweight protocols make most of the hardware performance accessible to the programmer, but require the consideration of too many details. Therefore, they should not normally be used by the application programmer, but are better suited as compilation targets for higher-level models such as MPI, PVM, DSM, sockets, and RMI (described in later chapters).

The low-level protocols are implemented as libraries. Major representatives include Active Messages (AM, AM-2) and Fast Messages (FM, FM-2). The basic idea of these and other low-level protocols, as compared with message passing, is the replacement of receive by a *message handler*. The message handler is a user-written routine that is part of the receiver's program text, and hence shares global variables with the receiver. Before a handler can be used, the receiver must register it with the system, by calling a certain library function. A receiver may register multiple handlers.

A send must specify the receiver process, and it must specify a handler that should process the message. Upon message receipt, the handler is activated in an implementation-specific way. Ideally, the handler is notified and immediately scheduled to a CPU. The handler receives and processes the message as coded in the user routine. In a simple case, for instance, it may just print a string on the screen, saying that a message has arrived. Frequently, the handler writes the message to a data structure within the receiver's address space. The handler can also set a flag to inform the receiver about the message receipt.

A major reason for the efficiency of AM, FM, and related protocols is the avoidance of message copying. Since the messages are immediately written to user space, copy operations at the receiver side are avoided. The mechanism also supports the overlapping of computation and communication, and reduces the role of the operating system.

The very low-level protocols are targeted at distributed-memory parallel computers and clusters. Compared with loosely coupled distributed systems, these architectures have a lower rate of transmission failures, and a reduced need for protection. These properties are exploited by efficient protocol implementations.

Another source of efficiency is a *streaming mode* that exists in part of the protocols. In this mode, messages are sent piecewise so that the head of a message may have reached the destination while the tail has not even been sent yet (as in wormhole routing; see Sect. 2.5). Streaming mode demonstrates the low-level nature of the protocols: In order to accomplish a single send, an FM-2 programmer must invoke a sequence of function calls. The first call initiates the send, each of the intermediate calls transmits a piece of the message, and the last call finishes the transfer.

FM-2 places particular emphasis on making its performance accessible to higher-level programming models. FM-2 guarantees that there is no message loss, and that messages from the same sender to the same receiver cannot overtake each other. The higher-level systems need not reimplement this functionality, and thus gain performance.

Many lightweight protocols are restricted to SPMD programming, since the sender must know the handler address. AM-2 generalizes the handler mechanism to MPMD programming. In AM-2, the system maintains a lookup table that translates between handler names and addresses. The system also supports tags so that different process groups can cooperate without confusing their messages. Furthermore, AM-2 combines the lightweight protocol model with threads. Threads are used, for instance, to run a message handler in parallel with its main program.

Very low-level models adopt a minimalist view. They implement only the most basic functionalities that cannot be composed from others. Collective operations, for instance, are not supported.

Although lightweight protocols have an efficiency advantage, good implementations of higher-level models retain much of it. Lightweight protocols are not only tedious to handle, they are also less portable.

5.5 MORE ON THIS TOPIC

Prior to the standardization of MPI, parallel programming was chiefly based on proprietary message-passing libraries. Indeed, MPI originates from these libraries [394]. Meanwhile, the proprietary libraries have been largely replaced by vendor implementations of MPI. At the very beginning, parallel programming was based on architecture-specific systems, in which the programmer had to think in terms of the physical interconnection network [375].

Bulk-synchronous parallelism (BSP) can be considered as a different submodel of message passing. Although several BSP implementations exist, the model was originally proposed as an abstract model, and is therefore handled in Ch. 11.

Whereas the MPI standard is restricted to C, C++, and Fortran—the traditional languages of scientific computing—the focus of attention is more and more shifting towards Java. The Java Grande Forum [232] coordinates several activities that are directed at improving the parallel-processing capabilities of Java. One activity has been the definition of a Java binding for MPI, called mpiJava. Descriptions of mpiJava and related proposals can be found in [34, 87, 237, 238, 304].

A few research projects in the context of message passing deal with the development of graphical tools for the design of MPI or PVM programs, for example PVMbuilder [333]. Other projects combine advantages of shared-memory and message-passing programming in an integrated approach [360,

396]. Another subject of research is the programming of SMP clusters, for which none of the existing programming models seems to be sufficient [372]. One approach is the combination of OpenMP with message passing [201, 372, 396]. In this combined model, fine-grained parallelism within an SMP node is handled by OpenMP threads, and coarse-grained parallelism between different SMP nodes is handled by MPI processes.

Prior to IMPI, related systems were proposed, for example the PACX-MPI library [167].

BIBLIOGRAPHICAL REMARKS

The primary references on MPI-1, MPI-2, and PVM are the books by Snir et al. [394], Gropp et al. [192], and Geist et al. [172], respectively. Of course there are also the standard documents on MPI-1 [292] and MPI-2 [293]. Further information is available from the home pages of the MPI Forum [291], the LAM implementation of MPI [259], and the PVM project [351]. A comparison and survey of MPI and PVM is also given by Pramanick [347]. The relationship between message-passing and shared-memory programming is discussed throughout the literature. Detailed treatments include Culler et al. [124] and Shan and Singh [378]. XDR is, for example, described in an online book from Sun [402], in Coulouris et al. [119], and in Singh [386]. For further information on the emerging IMPI standard see [223, 224].

The AM protocol was introduced in von Eicken et al. [434]. Other references on AM and AM-2 include von Eicken et al. [435], Mainwaring and Culler [278], and Parab and Raghvendran [331]. The FM protocol is described in Pakin et al. [327], and in Lauria et al. [263]. A brief introduction can also be found on the Web [326].

6

Client/Server Computing

Whereas the previous chapters have considered parallel models, we are now moving into the distributed-computing domain. As noted in the introduction, distributed computing deals with multiple processes that use different resources at different locations. In contrast to parallel processes, distributed processes are specialized to their resources, and therefore the programs are typically MPMD.

Client/server is the most common paradigm of distributed computing at present. The paradigm describes an asymmetric relationship between two processes, of which one is the client, and the other is the server. Almost all applications involve multiple clients, and many applications involve multiple servers, but let us look at just two processes for now.

The first process, the *server*, manages some resource, for instance a database. It offers a *service*, which can be used by other processes. In the example, the service is access to the database. The server, once started, runs permanently over a long period of time. It is passive in that it does nothing but wait for a client request.

The *client* is a process that needs the service in order to accomplish its work. Therefore it sends a request to the server, in which it asks for the execution of a concrete task that is covered by the service. In our example, the client may want to retrieve a particular entry from the database. Upon receiving the request, the server becomes active, carries out the task, and sends the result back to the client. Thereafter the server becomes passive again and waits for the next task. In summary:

> In the client/server paradigm, a server process offers a service that is used by client processes. Client and server typically run at different locations.

Client/server computing does not imply parallelism. While the server is processing the request, the client is passively waiting for the answer. Hence, the paradigm does not necessarily contribute to efficiency, but is primarily a method for structuring programs and for integrating different resources.

Particularly *large applications* are often organized along client/server lines. In these applications, the separation between client and server is frequently a separation between different programs that are developed by different programmers or even by different companies. The client/server pattern contributes to a clear interface between the programs. This aspect is very important in practice, but it is outside the scope of this book.

Although client/server computing does not imply parallelism, neither does it preclude it. The client site may deploy *multithreading*, and it may thus switch to another task while the client itself is waiting for an outstanding request. Other sources of parallelism will be mentioned later on.

Client and server may reside on the same machine. More frequently, however, and this is the case we are interested in, they reside on different machines. The typical architectural basis is a *loosely coupled distributed system*, either a LAN or a WAN. Because of this architectural focus, client/server computing gives much more attention to security, fault tolerance, heterogeneity, and interoperability than parallel models do.

Another difference from most of the parallel models is the *dynamic* nature of client/server. Whereas in parallel computing, a programmer starts from the specification of the whole program and partitions it into processes, the term "whole program" does not usually make sense in client/server computing. In contrast to parallel computing, the programmer does not start from a single, well-defined "task to be solved". Instead, a programmer who codes a server knows the interface that the server should implement, but he or she does not know the number of clients, nor the complete set of applications that will later use the service. Moreover, the clients themselves often do not know each other. For these reasons, client/server computing is by far not as predictable as parallel computing.

Client/server programming is typically MPMD, but multiple clients can run the same code. The client and server programs run in *separate address spaces* and communicate by exchanging messages. The concrete mechanisms are different from send/receive and will be described later.

Besides the passive waiting on the client side, there is another waste of resources on the *server side*: While the server is waiting for incoming requests, it does not carry out useful work. On the other hand, the server must be designed to accommodate periods of high load. The waste of server resources can be reduced if the machine switches to another application during idle time.

Note that client/server is a *paradigm* as opposed to a model. Section 6.1 describes the paradigm in more detail. Furthermore it surveys various concrete forms of the paradigm and outlines application domains. The next two sections of this chapter are devoted to two programming *models* that support the paradigm: sockets (Sect. 6.2), and remote procedure calls (Sect. 6.3). As usual, the chapter finishes with a survey of related approaches and with bibliographical remarks.

6.1 THE CLIENT/SERVER PARADIGM

Client/server computing matured in the late 1980s. The paradigm is now ubiquitous and has large commercial relevance. As noted before, client/server describes a pattern of work sharing. The server's task is managing a resource and offering a service through which the resource can be accessed by others. The client's task is providing a user interface. The application as such can be run by either the client or the server, giving rise to variants of the basic paradigm, which will be described later. Typical resources include file systems, printers, databases, and complex programs. Normally, the server resides at the same location as the resource, or close to it. A simple client can, for instance, translate a user request into an appropriate format, transfer the request to the server, and present the server results in a user-friendly format. Another client can carry out a complex computation on its own, and thereby occasionally contact the server.

The relationship between client and server is rarely one-to-one. As already noted, most servers cooperate with multiple clients. Vice versa, a single client can cooperate with multiple servers during its lifetime. Finally, a server can internally utilize the services of another server.

In the elementary case of a single server with multiple clients, the server can be *iterative* or *concurrent*. An iterative server deals with one client at a time. While the server is busy with processing one request, it is not able to respond to the next. A concurrent server is internally multithreaded and processes each incoming request in a separate thread. Concurrent servers are a good match with SMPs and other parallel machines.

To avoid overloading a server machine, the same service can be offered by multiple servers. The collection of servers is then accessed through a dispatcher program, which directs the incoming requests to the individual servers. The dispatcher can consider server specialization, task priorities, and load balancing when choosing a particular server.

A buzzword in the context of client/server computing is *middleware*. The term does not have an agreed-upon definition and stands for more or less all software that glues together independently developed software components, including client and server programs. Middleware is positioned in the middle between hardware/operating-system and application programs. The notion is thus related to our concept of parallel/distributed models, although a model describes a programmer interface, whereas middleware denotes the software that realizes this interface. The notion of middleware is typically used in the context of involved high-level systems, such as object-oriented systems (see Ch. 9). Advanced middleware not only transfers messages, but additionally includes directory, authentication, and other services.

Assessment   It is difficult to assess the paradigm, since we do not yet have a competitor for comparison. Nevertheless, we outline here some appealing features.

The most important advantage has already been noted: The client/server paradigm improves the structure of programs, and thus supports collaborative software development. A related advantage is *flexibility*: The client and server programs can be updated or replaced separately, as long as the interface is not changed.

Moving from the software technology to the parallelism/distribution point of view, client/server computing supports *specialization*: Each subtask can be run on the most appropriate machine of the system. Furthermore, the paradigm supports *scalability* in various forms:

- Clients can be added without changing the overall program structure.

- An overloaded server can be moved to a more powerful machine.

- An overloaded server can be replicated onto multiple machines.

Relationship with parallel computing   As noted above, the client/server paradigm can be combined with parallelism to improve the performance. There are at least three opportunities:

- use of multithreading in the client program,

- sharing of the server machine between different applications, and

- use of a concurrent server.

The client/server paradigm itself cannot really be compared with parallel models, since it is targeted at the exploitation of distribution as opposed to parallelism. Nevertheless, there are similarities. Client/server computing is most similar to message passing, because both approaches work with disjoint address spaces. Indeed, the client/server paradigm can be implemented in the message-passing model, although the sockets and RPC models are a better fit. In client/server computing, as in message passing, the programmer (or system administrator) is responsible for data distribution, task scheduling, and replication issues. Client/server programs are typically more coarse-grained than message-passing ones, since they assume a slower network.

The client/server paradigm bears a certain resemblance to the master/slave pattern, which was introduced in Sect. 5.2. Indeed, this pattern can be expressed in a client/server program that uses one client and multiple servers. The client takes over the role of the master, and schedules the work onto the servers. The servers carry out the actual computations, as usual. Code mobility is helpful for instructing the servers; we come back to this issue in Sect. 7.1. Conversely, not all client/server patterns can be realized by a master/slave program, because master/slave assumes the set of tasks to be static.

The client/server approach is in a sense opposite to multithreading: In multithreading, there is one process with multiple threads of control, whereas in client/server computing, there is one thread of control, but the control switches between two processes.

The two- and multitier variants   Client/server is a buzzword, and means different things to different people [322]. In the classical meaning, a client/server system consists of a powerful server machine and several less powerful client machines such that the roles are fixed once and for all. In other systems, any machine can function as both a client and a server, with respect to different tasks. Let us now look at some common arrangements in more detail. The arrangements are also illustrated in Fig. 6.1.

The basic arrangement is that of a static *two-tier* system. As the name says, such a system consists of two tiers:

- A server tier, in which one or several servers reside, and

- A client tier, in which the clients reside.

The server tier provides access to the resource, and the client tier realizes the user interface. If the application program resides on the client side, then we speak of a *fat-client* system; otherwise we speak of a *thin-client* system. Intermediate variants are used, too.

Many newer systems split the server tier up so that a total of *three tiers* arises:

- A back-end server tier (for instance a database server),

- A middle tier, in which the application runs, and

- A client tier.

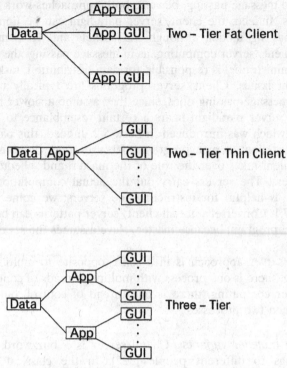

Fig. 6.1 Two- and three-tier systems. GUI stands for graphical user interface, App stands for application program, and Data stands for data access.

Three-tier systems are thin-client, since the application resides in the additional middle tier. Typically, a system consists of one or a few back-end servers, multiple servers in the middle tier, and many clients. Compared with two-tier systems, three-tier systems scale better, since one can independently adjust the number of back-end servers, the number of middle-tier servers, and the number of clients.

Both fat- and thin-client systems are deployed in practice, although there is some tendency towards thin-client. The two cases compare as follows:

- Thin-client systems are easier to maintain, since many system updates are local to the server, and the server is often under direct control of a system administrator. In a fat-client system, an updated version of the application program must be distributed to all clients.

- Thin-client systems tend to require less network bandwidth, since they only need to send a single message in order to initiate a possibly complex computation on the server. Fat-client systems, in contrast, may have to send several messages.

- Fat-client systems put less load on the server. The reduced load can be advantageous and lead to, for instance, more stable response times.

- Fat-client systems can be extended more easily. In particular, one can incorporate a new client with a different functionality, and need not change the server.

Application areas   Classical application areas are *databases* and *transaction processing*. A transaction is a sequence of statements that is executed either completely or not at all. Transaction processing is deployed in booking systems such as flight reservation. If the reservation of an outward flight was successful but a matching return flight could not be found, then the reservation is undone. Transaction-processing is a good fit with a three-tier system: The middle tier accommodates the actual transaction processing functionality and schedules the requests to back-end servers; the back-end server tier provides access to one or more databases; and the client tier implements the user interface.

Other application areas include print servers, name servers, and file servers. A well-known *file server*, for instance, is the Network File System NFS [386, 408], which facilitates the sharing of files between multiple machines. In NFS, each machine can function as both a server and a client, that is, it can both export local files and import remote ones.

The largest client/server application today is the *web*. In the web, any machine can take over the role of both the client and the server. Even at the same time, it can function as a client for one application, and as a server for another. Apart from this additional flexibility, many web applications follow a two-tier pattern. In web surfing, the servers offer access to web pages, and the clients load and graphically represent the pages on behalf of their users.

Other web applications follow a three- or multitier pattern, in which the web server invokes an application program, which in turn uses a back-end server. A typical example is the processing of forms. A *form* is a web page into which the user inserts information, such as details on a desired flight, and submits it to the web server. The application program is often invoked through the Common Gateway Interface (CGI) protocol. With this protocol, the web server accepts user requests as in the two-tier setting. If a request refers to a program instead of a page, then the server locates and activates the program and passes on user parameters to it. The parameter-passing mechanism of CGI is elaborate and slow [322], partially because the server runs in a different address space than the application and must thus buffer and resend the parameters. Improved mechanisms exist, for instance *servlets* [219, 322].

An example of a client/server system in the context of *numerical computing* is NetSolve [93]. This system offers access to numerical library routines, which are executed on remote servers. The servers may differ in their power and specialization; a scheduler forwards each incoming request to an appropriate server.

Fox and others [35, 93, 161] encourage the use of client/server techniques in the context of *grid* computation. They suggest a three-tier system, in which the first tier accommodates the user interface; the second tier accommodates scheduling, transparency, and other management functionalities; and the third tier accommodates the actual computing power, for instance in the form of supercomputers. A prototype system along these lines, WebFlow, has already been built. Another related system is Javelin [108, 306].

6.2 SOCKETS

Sockets are a low-level programming model that supports the client/server paradigm. Essentially, sockets are an interface through which the programmer can access the functionality of TCP, UDP, and other protocols. The interface introduces little performance overhead, and therefore sockets are fast (as fast as a TCP/UDP-based mechanism can be).

Sockets are implemented as libraries, and normally supplied with the operating system. Seemingly each operating system today supports sockets. We refer to a widely used Unix implementation here, Berkeley sockets, which has been around since the early 1980s. The second part of this section is devoted to a language realization: Java sockets.

Berkeley Sockets

The sockets model is restricted to pairwise communications; that is, exactly two processes communicate with each other. The processes are called client and server, and use different communication functions. Client and server may reside on the same machine; we assume here that they reside on different machines. The term sockets is used in plural to denote the model, and in singular to denote one of the communication endpoints (client or server).

The following sub-subsections give a brief introduction to sockets programming. It will be clear that sockets operate on a low level, and that the programmer must deal with many details.

Addressing In order to communicate with a server, the client must know the address, which is composed of a host address and a port number. The host address is a 32-bit number, which is obtained by calling a conversion function and giving as argument the host name in dotted-decimal notation (such as 123.45.67.89). This host name must be known to the programmer; it can be easily determined for a given machine.

A *port* can be thought of as being one out of many entrances into a computer. Each server is connected to a particular port and receives only those messages that come in through that entrance. The port number is assigned when the server registers itself with the system (see below). Which particular port number is assigned depends on the application. For specific services such as ftp, there are predefined port numbers. For other services, the programmer chooses the number more or less arbitrarily from a certain permitted range.

Server initialization   The programmer first registers the server with the system, by calling the functions *socket* and *bind*. These functions have several parameters, through which the server passes the port number, selects a protocol (e.g. TCP), and states whether it is willing to accept connections from anywhere or only from a selected set of hosts.

Now the server starts its lifetime by calling *listen* if it is a connection-oriented (TCP) server, or *recvfrom* if it is a connectionless (UDP) server. The function *listen* takes as parameter the number of messages that the system shall buffer when the server does not immediately respond to a request.

Accepting requests   A *connection-oriented* server accesses the next incoming request by calling *accept*. This function returns the client address, as well as a handle for the socket connection. Thereafter, client and server can exchange messages back and forth, possibly in a separate thread. The communication is accomplished through *read* and *write* functions, which take the handle as an argument. The read and write functions work in a similar way to the receive and send functions in message passing, except that the source and destination addresses are encoded in the handle and not given explicitly. As in message passing, several variants of the functions exist that, for instance, transfer data from or to noncontiguous memory buffers. The connection is finally closed from either side.

A *connectionless* server accesses the next incoming request by calling *recvfrom*. This function returns the client address and the actual message contents. The server processes the request and returns an answer to the client. Thereafter the message exchange is finished, and the server can post a new *recvfrom* to receive the next request from any client.

All communication routines, including *accept* and *recvfrom*, are blocking. Therefore, the server is idle while it is waiting for a request, and analogously the client is idle while it is waiting for an answer. Although nonblocking variants of the communication routines exist, their semantics is different from that in MPI. If a request cannot be fulfilled immediately, a nonblocking routine returns with an error code and does not carry out the desired function.

Client side   Although the concrete sequence of function calls is different on the client side, their flavor is the same. A client must first do some initializations, which include the specification of the desired protocol. Then it issues a *connect* if it uses a connection-oriented, or a *sendto* if it uses a connectionless, protocol. In either case, it is the client that initiates the message exchange. Connection establishment is summarized in Figs 6.2 and 6.3.

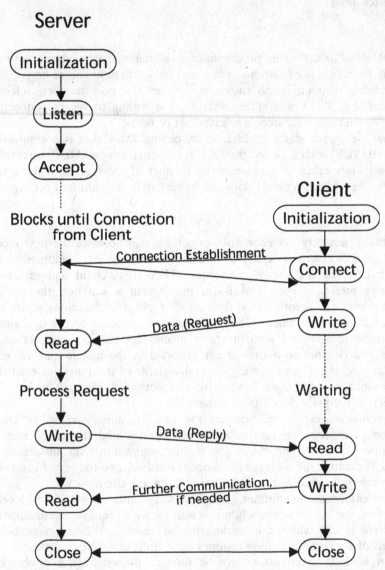

Fig. 6.2 A connection-oriented message exchange. Adapted from *Unix Network Programming* by W. Richard Stevens, © 1990. Reprinted by permission of Prentice-Hall, Inc., Upper Saddle River, NJ.

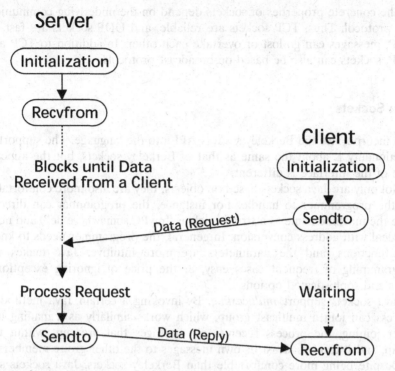

Fig. 6.3 A connectionless message exchange. Adapted from *Unix Network Programming* by W. Richard Stevens, © 1990. Reprinted by permission of Prentice-Hall, Inc., Upper Saddle River, NJ.

Other programmer responsibilities Additional responsibilities include data conversion in heterogeneous environments, and the provision of additional buffer space in case more than the standard amount is required. The operating system supports these and other activities with a rich set of functions, but it is the programmer's responsibility to invoke the functions at appropriate places and with the right parameters.

Assessment A definite plus of sockets is portability. Sockets are available on seemingly any machine and can deal with heterogeneous environments. Obvious drawbacks are their low-level nature and their reliance on the relatively slow TCP and UDP protocols. Because of the high programming and performance overhead, sockets are not, in general, suited for parallel programming.

Nevertheless, several PVM and MPI systems are implemented on top of sockets. Although these systems have limited performance, their portability is excellent, and they are useful for program development and teaching. Higher-level distributed models are implemented on top of sockets, too, as will be noted later.

The concrete properties of sockets depend on the underlying communication protocol. Thus, TCP sockets are reliable, and UDP sockets are fast. In UDP, messages can go lost or overtake each other. In addition to TCP and UDP, sockets can also be based on broadcast protocols.

Java Sockets

Java incorporates the Berkeley sockets API into the language. The supported functionality is about the same as that of Berkeley sockets, but the appearance of the interface is different.

Not only are Java sockets based on objects; they are also more comfortable for the programmer to handle. For instance, the programmer can directly state the machine name as a string (such as "myPC.somewhere.de") and need not deal with address conversion. In general, the programmer needs to know less functions, and the parameters are more intuitive. Java makes the programming of frequent cases easy, at the price of ignoring exceptional cases and sophisticated options.

Java sockets support *multicasting*. By invoking a certain Java method, a process can join a multicast group, which works similarly as a mailing list. After joining, the process receives all messages that are sent within the group, and it can broadcast its own messages to the other group members.

Despite being more comfortable than Berkeley sockets, Java sockets still operate on a low level. The Java system considers messages as plain byte streams. In order to understand each other's messages, client and server must agree on a (possibly application-specific) protocol. If a conversion of data formats is necessary, the programmer is responsible for invoking the corresponding routines.

In Java, it is possible to exchange objects over a sockets connection, which include program code. This aspect is elaborated upon in Ch. 7.

6.3 REMOTE PROCEDURE CALLS

A remote procedure call (RPC) is an interprocess communication mechanism that resembles a normal procedure call. As usual, a procedure is a piece of code that receives several parameters, carries out a function, and maybe finally returns results. In a normal procedure call, all this happens within one process, whereas in an RPC, caller and called procedure belong to different processes.

An RPC is a client/server communication mechanism, in which the called procedure takes the role of the server, and the caller takes the role of the client. Despite its similar appearance, an RPC is different from a normal procedure call. The RPC mechanism is illustrated in Fig. 6.4.

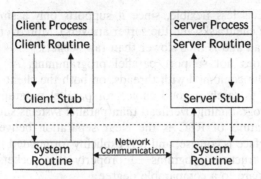

Fig. 6.4 Realization of an RPC.

Figure 6.4 shows local representatives for the remote program parts—the *stubs*. A stub is a local procedure that manages the communication on behalf of its client or server. Thus the client or server communicates with the stub, and not directly with the other side. When the client invokes a remote procedure, only a local procedure call to the client stub is issued internally. While the client stub is then doing the actual work, the client itself sits idle.

So what has the stub to do? Well, it must first transmit the request to the server using lower-level communication mechanisms such as sockets. Then it waits for the server's reply, and finally it returns to the client. In order to use the underlying communication mechanism, the stub must pack the input parameters into one or several messages, and unpack the output parameters afterwards. These packaging activities, which may require conversion to another data format and flattening pointer-based data structures, are referred to as *marshaling* and *unmarshaling*, respectively.

On the server side, the mechanism is similar. The incoming reply is received by the stub, which unmarshals the parameters and invokes the actual server procedure through a local procedure call. Upon return of the procedure, the stub marshals the results and transmits them back to the client.

The stubs need not be programmed explicitly. For stub generation, the programmer describes the server procedures in a specific *interface definition language* (IDL), puts the description into a file, and invokes a kind of compiler. Both the IDL and its compiler are system-dependent. In general, the programmer must state the name of each remote procedure, as well as the types of the parameters. It is a good idea to put comments into the specification file, but the IDL deals solely with syntax.

Assessment Compared with sockets, the advantage of RPC is its higher-level nature. The programmer need not consider network details. To him or her, RPC looks almost like a normal procedure call, albeit a slow one. On the other side, RPC is less flexible, since it supports only a single pattern of cooperation (the client asks and the server answers). Moreover, RPC induces a certain overhead and is thus slower than raw sockets.

RPC itself does not support parallel programming. As noted before, however, it can be combined with threads, on both the client and the server sides. Yet, RPC is rarely a good choice for parallel programming, since it induces more programming overhead than parallel systems such as MPI.

A striking feature of RPC is the clear separation between client and server. The interface is concise, and it is explicitly formulated in IDL. Hence, RPC helps to structure programs—a property that sockets and parallel models do not share to a comparable degree.

The transparency of RPC is limited, because RPC has a high probability of error. In particular, transmission errors can occur, or a server may be switched off at the time it is contacted by a client. The programmer must be prepared for possible failures, and thus should be aware of a procedure call's remote nature.

Implementations   Various implementations of RPC are around. Each of them defines a concrete protocol for the message exchange between client and server. For instance, it prescribes data formats, and decides whether the RPC is implemented on top of a connection-oriented or a connectionless sockets mechanism. The implementation also supplies an IDL compiler. Moreover, it addresses some questions that the general RPC mechanism leaves open: How does the client locate an appropriate server? How are network errors and other exceptions handled? Can parameters be passed by address, and if so, how?

An example of an implementation is ONC RPC. The abbreviation ONC stands for Open Network Computing, which is a middleware system from Sun. ONC RPC is built on top of TCP or UDP sockets and uses the already mentioned XDR format for data exchange. With ONC RPC, a programmer writes the client and server programs and generates the stubs, as described before. Upon activation, the server registers itself at a local binder, called the *port mapper*, which keeps track of the assignment between program names and ports. A client thus only needs to know the host name and the name of the server program, not the port number. ONC also supports a system-wide naming scheme that helps in locating the host.

Another example is DCE RPC. The abbreviation DCE stands for Distributed Computing Environment, which is a widely used middleware system. DCE supports heterogeneous environments and interoperability between clients and servers that have been written in different languages. In addition to the RPC model, DCE supports threads, and comprises a file management facility, a directory service, and other components. The components are integrated with each other, and thus a remote procedure call can use the directory service to locate a desired server at whatever location in the network.

With both ONC and DCE RPC, the interface of the remote procedure must already be known during the compilation of the client stub. Because of this requirement, the RPC mechanism is described as *static*. A dynamic mechanism will be treated in Sect. 9.1. If multiple servers with the desired interface are registered, the binder may select one of them, for instance on the basis of load-balancing considerations.

6.4 MORE ON THIS TOPIC

Client/server computing is a large area, and we have only scratched the surface. Many developments are specific to a particular application domain, such as databases or the Web, and not covered here. The following paragraph mentions some additional activities that are either of a general nature, or related to parallel computing.

Besides Berkeley sockets, there are some related systems, for instance WinSock [352] and the Transport Layer Interface (TLI) [401]. Yau and Lam [448] describe a sockets implementation that supports QoS. Whereas the performance of sockets is normally limited by that of the underlying TCP and UDP protocols, some high-performance implementations simulate the sockets API on top of lightweight protocols [139, 327, 361]. The resulting performance gain can also be exploited by RPC systems that are implemented on top of the sockets.

Another way to speed up RPC is the use of asynchrony. In asynchronous RPC [214, 273], as in nonblocking message passing, the caller returns immediately after having issued the request. Later it invokes a second function to complete the call. A different programming model along similar lines is messaging-oriented middleware. We treat this model, in which the client is uncoupled from the server, in Sect. 8.3.

An RPC-like mechanism is the *rendezvous* of Ada 95 [75]. Like an RPC, a rendezvous takes place if at the same time both a server has posted a *wait_for_requests* and a client has posted a matching request. If only one of the partners has posted its part, then the other side is blocked and waits for the partner. Since both partners must be ready before the communication starts, the rendezvous is a form of synchronous communication. The rendezvous mechanism differs from that in an RPC in that it is built into the Ada language and not provided through libraries. Since Ada is not specifically targeted at distributed-memory architectures, stubs are not needed for a rendezvous. In Ada, the client and the server belong to the same program. The server contains a mix of operations, only part of which are *wait_for_requests*. The server may thus accomplish its own task and use the rendezvous mechanism as a means for communicating with others. As a last difference, the concrete functions to be invoked on the client and server sides are different in a rendezvous than in an RPC.

RPC is normally used with C and other procedural languages. More elaborate variants of RPC have been developed in the object-oriented domain; they will be treated in Ch. 9.

The performance of client/server applications partially depends on the scheduling algorithm that manages multiple incoming client requests on the server side. If there are multiple servers, for instance, the assignment of requests can take the source of the messages into account so that locality is exploited [325]. A survey of scheduling strategies is given by Graham and Majumdar [186].

The client/server and message-passing paradigms supplement each other. Message passing enables high performance for programs with a predictable structure, whereas client/server computing can handle dynamic structures. To combine the respective strengths, MPI-2 introduces a specific client/server model. This model allows independent MPI-2 programs to come into contact with each other. The relationship between the programs need not follow the client/server pattern. Instead it can be symmetric, and is then denoted as *peer-to-peer*. Nevertheless, one of the processes is selected as the client and the other as the server. As with sockets, the server attaches itself to a port, and the client connects to the server by sending a request to that port. Alternatively, the server may register itself with a name server so that the client can provide the service name instead of the port number. The MPI-2 client/server routines share some resemblance with sockets, except that the MPI communicator mechanism comes into play.

BIBLIOGRAPHICAL REMARKS

An in-depth treatment of client/server computing is provided by Orfali et al. [322]. Introductions are also given by Singh [386], Coulouris et al. [119], Lewandowski [269], Crichlow [120], Kirtland [249], and El-Rewini and Lewis [142]. NFS is described in [386, 408].

Stevens [401] contains a chapter on Berkeley sockets, whereas Java sockets are described in Farley [146], Niemeyer and Peck [307], and other Java books. Another useful reference on sockets is Orfali and Harkey [321]. Stevens [401] gives a concise introduction to RPC. Other useful references on RPC and concrete RPC systems include Tanenbaum [408], Orfali et al. [322], Singh [386], and the ONC+ Developer's Guide from Sun [402].

7

Code Mobility

This chapter investigates the observation that not only data but also code can be moved around during the execution of a program. To be more precise, code mobility is not so much concerned with the *moving around* of code, as with its *execution* at remote locations. Code mobility is neither a paradigm nor a model. It is an opportunity that gives rise to several models, which are the contents of this chapter. Most of the models focus on distributed computing.

Code mobility allows for a different approach to communication. In the traditional models, each process is bound to a fixed location throughout its lifetime. When the processes cooperate, they stay at their respective locations and send messages. Mobile processes, in contrast, can meet each other in a common place and accomplish the communication locally. Taking another viewpoint, traditional models put all the control into stationary components and allow only passive messages to be mobile. Models based on code mobility, in contrast, put part or all of the control into mobile components. In the extreme, the stationary components are merely passive execution units.

Most people consider code mobility as not a substitute for, but a supplement to traditional parallel and distributed models. Code mobility can lead to higher performance and better programmability in some cases, whereas it is inferior in other cases.

The choice between moving code and moving data has an analogy in human interaction. In order to cooperate, we can either call or email each other, or meet in person. Depending on the particular situation, we prefer

TABLE 7.1 Criteria for the use of mobility in human interaction and process interaction.

Human interaction	Process interaction
Travel expense (money, time)	Costs of exchanging code in comparison with costs of communicating data
Amount of information that is exchanged	Message size
Frequency of interaction	Granularity of application
Willingness to adapt to a new environment, for instance in a foreign country	Ability of a process to work in a heterogeneous environment, which may involve other operating systems, libraries, etc.
Hostility of the other side	Degree of support for visiting processes and their specific requirements
Binding to home	Importance of local resources
Opportunity to travel with family	Opportunity to move or copy resources together with the process
Attractiveness of the remote place	Amount of remote resources that are valuable for the process
Security level at the remote place and on the way	Security level at the remote place and on the way

either one or the other opportunity. The decision is based on criteria that have counterparts in the parallel- and distributed-computing field. Table 7.1 lists such criteria.

Code mobility is a simple and striking idea, but it gives rise to many questions and concerns, for instance how to protect remote machines from malicious code (and vice versa visiting code from being manipulated by remote machines), and how to charge for the use of remote computing time and resources. Although code mobility is already deployed in some simple forms and in specific application areas, the field as such cannot yet be considered as mature. Advanced forms of code mobility are currently addressed in various academic and commercial projects.

The term code mobility refers to software in motion. A related term is *mobile computing*, which refers to nonstationary hardware such as laptops, cell phones, and PDAs. Mobile computing introduces specific requirements, such as dealing with limited bandwidth and interruptions in connectivity [335]. Mobile computing and code mobility are related insofar as the latter is a means to address the specific requirements of the former. Mobile computing is not a programming model, and therefore is not further discussed.

This chapter is organized into four sections, each of which considers one of the following four classes of mobile code models:

- Enhanced client/server computing
- Mobile agents
- Parallel mobile code
- Transparent migration

The models are discussed separately, since they have widely differing characteristics. Before we start, the rest of this introduction deals with general issues: mechanisms for code migration, and alternative classification schemes.

Code Migration Mechanisms

Since, at a low level, program code is represented as a sequence of bits, it can be easily sent around, provided that the participating computers have agreed on some common format. More difficult, however, is the execution of the code on the remote machine, especially if the remote machine has a different architecture and instruction set. The following principal options exist:

- Compile the code in advance for each architecture in the system, and then send the respective version of the executable code.
- Send the source code, and compile it on the remote site.
- Send the source code, and interpret it on the remote site.
- Compile the program to an intermediate language prior to sending. At the remote machine, either compile or interpret the intermediate language.

The last approach is the most popular one. It reflects the philosophy of Java, in which the intermediate language is called *bytecode*. Closely related is the concept of the *Java Virtual Machine* (JVM), which is an abstract architecture that is able to directly execute bytecode instructions. The JVM is not a real machine, but it is implemented in software on each participating computer. Technically, the JVM is realized by a bytecode interpreter. It can be supplemented by a bytecode translator that optimizes the bytecode.

The use of an intermediate language such as bytecode represents a compromise between portability and speed. Since the code is partially compiled, it has reasonable performance. Since it is *only* partially compiled, the performance is worse than that of completely compiled code. If a bytecode translator is used, the additional optimization expense nevertheless causes an increase in running time. A specific advantage of bytecode is its compactness and correspondingly low communication expense.

The ability of Java to send code around is supplemented by a facility called *object serialization*. With this facility, the current state of an object can be transferred. A programmer deploys object serialization by invoking a pair of methods on a particular object. These pack the values of all attributes into a message, and restore them on the receiving site. If an object contains references to other objects, the attributes of the referenced objects are included as well, recursively. In addition to the attributes, references to the object code are sent, so that the receiver can later load the code as needed.

Another achievement of Java is a security concept. Java gives visiting code access to the virtual machine, but it does not allow the code to use any other functionalities or resources of the host (e.g. file access). The security is weakened in that some visiting processes need access to sensitive resources in order to do their work. Therefore, the user (owner of the machine) must be able to relax the access restrictions for particular processes. Despite the usefulness of this scheme, security is still not guaranteed, since the user can make mistakes or trust faulty software.

Because of its built-in support for mobility, the Java language is used in the majority of mobile-code systems. Nevertheless, some systems deploy other—often specifically developed—languages, or support multiple languages by means of multiple interpreters on each machine.

Code mobility can refer to either code or processes. In the former case, "lifeless" program code is moved around and invoked elsewhere. In the latter case, a running process is interrupted, transferred to another machine, and continued or restarted there. For the movement of a process, it is not sufficient to transfer the code; one must also transfer the *state* of the process. The state includes the values of local and global variables, register contents, program counter, file pointers, etc.

A migration mechanism is called *strong* if it transfers the complete state, in particular the program counter, along with a process; otherwise it is called *weak*. In a system with weak migration, variable values and other parts of the state can be transferred by hand. Nevertheless, strong migration is superior with respect to programmability. Unfortunately, strong migration is harder to implement, especially in Java, where the JVM does not give the implementor access to the internal state [166]

Classification Schemes

As is often the case with a new research direction, mobile-code research is characterized by variety. Our classification into enhanced client/server computing, mobile agents, parallel mobile code, and transparent migration is original and by no means the only way to organize the topic. To give an impression of the variety, some alternative classification criteria are listed in

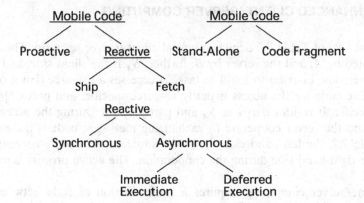

Fig. 7.1 Classification criteria for mobile code.

the following. They are not really orthogonal to the section topics, and thus we will see examples later. Some of the terms are used with various meanings in the literature. A survey of the classification criteria is given in Fig. 7.1.

First, the migration of *stand-alone code* can be distinguished from the migration of a *code fragment*. Stand-alone code is a complete program, which can be started as a separate process by the operating system. A code fragment is a piece of code, such as a function or an object, which is incorporated into a running process.

Next, there is the question of who initiates the transfer. We call code movement *proactive* if the migrating code itself decides to move, and otherwise *reactive*. Reactive code movement can, for instance, be initiated by the operating system or by surrounding code, and is further classified into *code shipping* and *code fetching*. In the first case, it is the sender that initiates the transfer; in the second case the receiver.

Reactive code movement can also be classified as *synchronous* or *asynchronous*, depending on whether the initiator waits for the execution (result) of the moved code or not. In the asynchronous case, the code can be executed *immediately*, or the execution is *deferred*.

We have already noted the difference between transferring code and processes. A process transfer is either a *migration* or a *cloning*. A migration *moves* the code from source to destination, whereas a cloning *copies* it. Thus, after migration, the process ceases to exist at the source, whereas after cloning, two or more instances of the process run in parallel, independently of each other.

A final distinction can be made between homogeneous and heterogeneous systems. Fuggetta et al. [163] present a comprehensive classification framework, in which they separate the models along three dimensions: technology, design paradigm, and application domain.

7.1 ENHANCED CLIENT/SERVER COMPUTING

The first row of Table 7.2 depicts a typical client/server scenario. The client is denoted by A, and the server by B; further, S_A is the client side, and S_B is the server side. In order to fulfill its task, A accesses a resource that is owned by B. The code for the access is partly resource-specific, and partly application-specific. It resides partly at S_A and partly at S_B. During the access, the client and the server cooperate by exchanging messages; code is not moved. In Table 7.2, the left-hand side shows the situation before the cooperation, and the right-hand side during the cooperation. The active process is printed in bold.

Client/server computing requires a static division of code between the client and the server sides. Each particular division has pros and cons, which were noted previously. To restate some arguments, fat-server systems are not able to adapt to changing client requirements. It is not possible to add a new client functionality when the server is already in use; otherwise the client becomes fat. The drawback of fat clients is high communication volume.

Enhanced paradigms Code mobility is a means to overcome these deficiencies. Under the heading of enhanced client/server computing, code mobility takes two forms: *remote evaluation* and *code on demand*. Both forms are illustrated in Table 7.2.

TABLE 7.2 Comparison between client/server, remote evaluation, code-on-demand, and mobile agents. Adapted, by permission, from A. Fuggetta et al. [163] © 1998 IEEE.

	Content			
	Before		After	
Paradigm	S_A	S_B	S_A	S_B
Client/server	Part of code A	Part of code resource B	Part of code A	Part of code resource **B**
Remote evaluation	Code A	Resource B	A	Code Resource **B**
Code on demand	Resource A	Code B	Resource Code **A**	B
Mobile agent	Code A	Resource	—	Code Resource **A**

> Remote evaluation is a modification of the client/server paradigm, in which code is moved from the client to the server at run time.

This modification overcomes the problem that fat servers cannot adapt to changing client requirements. Remote evaluation dynamically enhances the server functionality, that is, it makes the server (temporarily) fatter. In all other respects, the paradigm works just like client/server. Therefore, an interaction starts with the sending of data and code. It is code fragments that are sent, not standalone programs. Then the server incorporates the code into a base program and runs this program. Finally, the server returns and sends back the results to the client.

In some contexts, remote evaluation is referred to as function shipping. The remote evaluation paradigm is useful if

- The client functionality is compute-intensive, and it is therefore more efficient to run the code at a powerful server,

- The client functionality is communication-intensive, and it is therefore more efficient to transfer the code instead of many data, or

- The connection between client and server is error-prone or nonpermanent, as in mobile computing.

The decision whether a particular piece of code is executed locally or remotely is taken by the programmer, who must therefore estimate the relative costs.

> Code on demand is a modification of the client/server paradigm, in which the server maintains a code base, and the clients load the code as needed.

Thus, code on demand is a kind of opposite approach to remote evaluation. The paradigm enhances the client functionality, that is, it makes the client fatter. The paradigm is well suited for a set of similar clients that must potentially be able to support many functionalities, although only a small percentage of them are really needed. A typical example is a web browser, which should be able to support many media and formats, although any particular user encounters only a fraction thereof.

A related application area is maintenance. With code on demand, updated or novel code need not be distributed to all clients. Instead, only the interested clients download the code as needed. The use of code on demand can furthermore improve the performance. If it turns out that a code needs many client data, then it can be advantageous to migrate it to the client.

Many code-on-demand interactions are accomplished in one step: the client loads the code, executes the code on its data, and finishes. Alternatively, a large program can be organized into multiple code sections. The client first loads and executes an initial section. Depending on the outcome, it then requests the next section, executes it, and so on. The reloading approach saves bandwidth if only part of the code is needed.

Summarizing so far, remote evaluation and code on demand are modifications of the client/server paradigm through which the code division can be adjusted at run time. Remote evaluation makes the server fatter, and code on demand the client. Sometimes it can be useful to execute the same piece of code on the client side in one invocation and on the server side in another, based on, for instance, the current load.

In terms of the classification scheme above, remote evaluation is a form of code shipping, and code on demand is a form of code fetching. Remote evaluation can be synchronous or asynchronous. Code on demand is asynchronous, since it does not require a final reply.

Applications A practical realization of code on demand is Java *applets*. Applets are Java programs that are embedded in a web page, often for the purpose of adding attractive effects to it. The client downloads the applet together with the page; and the web browser invokes the applet automatically.

A practical realization of remote evaluation is *volunteer computing*. In this paradigm, a user, let us call it M, solves a compute-intensive task with the help of other users $V_1, \ldots, V_k$, which may be situated anywhere in the Internet. These users, called volunteers, put part of their computing power at M's disposal. M organizes the computation according to the master/slave paradigm so that M is the master and $V_1, \ldots, V_k$ are the slaves. (Volunteer, slave, and server are synonyms in this context.)

In order to take part in the computation, a volunteer first registers itself with M. In return, it receives a task, which consists of program code and data. V_i performs the task, sends the results back to M, gets a next task, and so on, as in the master/slave paradigm. Volunteer computing differs from master/slave in that a volunteer can at any time stop cooperation. Also, the volunteers can register at different times. From M's point of view, the volunteers come and go in an unpredictable manner.

Volunteer systems are often implemented through applets. In this approach, each V_i runs a web browser. V_i registers with M by directing the browser at M's web page. In return, it is assigned a task in the form of an applet, which is automatically invoked by the web browser. Coded in the task, the results are finally returned to M, and the next task is assigned, as usual. V_i can stop the cooperation by redirecting the browser to another page, or by stopping the browser altogether.

Another example for remote evaluation is the Javelin system [108, 306], which was mentioned in Sect. 6.1. Javelin is a three-tier client/server system in which the middle tier fulfills two purposes. On one hand, it is a broker that mediates between client requests and server functionalities. On the other hand, it provides caches for the storage of frequently accessed client code. Since a server can download the client code from cache instead from the client, the performance is improved, especially if the connection to the client is slow or nonpermanent.

An important application is the emerging *Jini* technology [27, 235, 437]. Jini is a network infrastructure, into which Jini-enabled devices of whatever kind (not just computers) can be plugged and start running instantaneously. No configuration or setup is required, and thus networks can be built by the unexperienced user. A related system is Universal Plug and Play from Microsoft [42]. It exhibits a similar functionality, but is implemented differently.

Jini deploys Java and the JavaSpaces model (see Ch. 8). When a device is plugged into the network, it registers itself automatically at a lookup server. The device informs the lookup server about details of its functionality. In particular, it publishes descriptions of its own services, if it offers any. A client device that needs a certain service asks the lookup server for help. If a device with a matching service is registered, then the lookup server assists in establishing the connection. Thereafter, the client and the server devices start to cooperate as usual.

Code mobility comes into play as the potential clients may need specific code in order to cooperate with a server device (e.g., they may need a printer driver). The Jini system assists in moving the code to the client. Additionally, Jini supports remote evaluation: If a device does not implement the JVM, it can send code to another device for evaluation.

7.2 MOBILE AGENTS

The mobile-agents model represents a stronger turning away from the traditional client/server organization. A mobile agent is a program, including data, that is able to migrate to other machines during its lifetime. The typical agent makes a round trip that involves several machines. In each migration, the agent stops execution at the present machine, and continues after having been transferred to the next machine. The agent decides autonomously when and where it will migrate. Indeed, proactive code movement is a defining characteristic of agents. In summary:

> A mobile agent is a program that operates autonomously on behalf of a user. In order to fulfill its task, the agent proactively moves around in the network and uses several resources on the way.

The new model makes the division of labor as manifested by the client/server organization disappear. Instead, it considers the distributed system as a set of equal machines with possibly different specializations and resources. Such an organization is denoted as *peer-to-peer*, as was mentioned before.

In Table 7.2, the mobile-agents model is contrasted with client/server and enhanced client/server computing. As the table shows, a mobile-agent program is moved as a whole to the other side, whereas remote evaluation ships only a particular piece of code. With mobile agents, not only the code is moved, but the whole running process. After migration, the mobile agent completely disappears from the source platform. Table 7.2 avoids the notions of client and server, since they are not meaningful in the conceptual framework of mobile agents.

Applications   Mobile agents have the same advantages as remote evaluation, together with some new ones. Notably the following scenarios can be tackled:

- *Mobile Computations*. The user uploads his or her agents to the net and then disconnects. The agents operate independently, thereby possibly carrying out extensive computations and roaming the network. After having done their work, the agents return home to a base machine. At a later time, the user reconnects and picks up the results. The same scenario is also useful for networks with a fast backbone but slow or unreliable end-user connections.

- *Computations That Would Otherwise Require a Lot of Interaction Between Client and Server*. The argument is essentially the same as in remote evaluation: Instead of communicating a large number of data, it is more economical to transfer the program. Mobile agents differ from remote evaluation in that they apply the idea repeatedly. An agent moves from host to host without coming back to the source in between.

- *Remote Events That Need Immediate Response*. The agent is placed directly at a critical location, such as in an electronic marketplace. At this location, it can react instantaneously to interesting events such as special offers. The response time is reduced because of the elimination of network delay.

- *Flexible Choice of Platform*. Mobile agents can survive machine crashes, since they can escape to another platform. Due to their loose platform binding, mobile agents can also avoid overloaded hosts.

Limitations As argued by Chess et al. [104], mobile agents do not have a "killer application". Everything that can be done with mobile agents can also be done in a more traditional way. Nevertheless, mobile agents are sometimes the more natural, easier, or more efficient approach. The model and its usefulness are still a matter of debate [299].

The single most severe problem of mobile agents is security. Questions such as how to protect a mobile agent from a malicious platform are still partially unsolved [428]. Security is a pressing issue, even more as mobile agents are intended to be used in e-commerce. It is mainly the lack of security mechanisms that has so far prevented the wide application of mobile agents in practice.

Although the use of mobile agents can improve the performance, it can also degrade it. Whether it is more efficient to transfer the data or the code must be decided case by case, as discussed in the introduction to this chapter. The decision may depend on the concrete program and the dynamic situation in the network. It can be taken by either the programmer or the system. If the programmer has coded a migration, for instance, a system may decide to transparently replace it by an RPC [70].

Implementation The use of mobile agents presupposes an underlying infrastructure in each participating machine in the network. The infrastructure, called the *agent system*, is a middleware run-time environment that provides functionalities to start, stop, migrate, and otherwise support agents. A programmer who codes an agent typically writes down a simple function call such as *go(destination)* in order to request migration. All the required packaging and communication with the destination platform, as well as the restart of the agent there, are handled transparently by the system.

The system is also responsible for converting formats in heterogeneous environments. Furthermore, it manages the movement of resources that are needed by the agent, but are not available at the destination platform. For instance, it may copy libraries. Agent systems can be based on weak or strong migration. While strong migration is desirable, weak migration is still more frequently used.

Agent abilities Mobile agents have their roots in distributed-systems research, but also in artificial intelligence. Programs that autonomously carry out tasks on behalf of their users are a long-standing concern for artificial intelligence. These agents are often stationary instead of mobile, and thus security and other issues are less important. Stationary agents are already deployed in many practical applications [251]. Because of their origin in artificial intelligence, mobile agents are not normally considered as just moving code, but are also associated with properties such as intelligence and adaptivity.

On their way through the network, mobile agents make use of remote resources, which are often databases. In some implementations, the agents may modify their own behavior by incorporating novel code that they encounter on the way. Mobile agents may coexist with stationary agents, which may, for instance, manage the resources.

Interagent communication   Agents can cooperate with other agents that they meet by chance or intentionally. Interagent communication is a topic of research, especially in artificial intelligence. Specialized agent communication languages have been developed, for instance the Knowledge Interchange Format (KIF) [252] and the Knowledge Query and Manipulation Language (KQML) [258]. Technically, any inter-task communication mechanism can be used, although some mechanisms are better suited than others [80].

Frequently used mechanisms include *mutual procedure calls*, *blackboards*, and *messaging*. In mutual procedure calls, as in RPC, one agent invokes the procedures of another. Blackboards are shared memories like the tuple-based model that will be introduced in Ch. 8. Messaging is a model for asynchronous message exchange, and will also be introduced in Ch. 8.

Assessment and general properties   Because of the support by the agent system, agent programming is comparatively high-level. Since agents encapsulate both computation and communication, the programmer has an integrated view of these activities. This approach to programmability, in which the programmer has explicit control over the sequence of locations, is in a sense opposite to that of large client/server systems, which focus on location transparency. In the mobile-agents paradigm, the programmer need not necessarily think in terms of the low-level network organization, because the agent system can be coupled with a name server that translates between machine names and higher-level service descriptions. Furthermore, the infrastructure can support visiting agents by suggesting an appropriate host for their next task.

Mobile agents are primarily a distributed (as opposed to a parallel) model. Although multiple agents can cooperate in the execution of a single task, it is more typical that the various agents in a system are unrelated and belong to different users. There is no central control, and the overall activity of the agent community cannot be planned statically. Nevertheless, the model exploits the performance potential of parallelism, since multiple agents can run in parallel.

The mobile-agents model is envisioned to be deployed on a large scale. If and when the security problems are solved, mobile agents should be well suited for use in WANs (such as the Internet) and grids. Meanwhile, many applications are restricted to an intranet scale.

Systems   Mobile agents are currently a research subject with first applications; they are not yet a mature technology [299]. Several concrete systems have been implemented, both research prototypes and commercial systems. Well-known examples include Telescript [251], D'Agents [189], Grasshopper [187], Voyager [312], Aglets [260], and Mole [303]. A survey is given in Fuggetta et al. [163]. The commercial interest in mobile agents manifests itself in the emergence of industry standards: OMG MASIF, which stands for Mobile Agent System Interoperability Facility [298], and FIPA, which stands for Foundation for Intelligent Physical Agents [160].

7.3   PARALLEL MOBILE CODE

Many mobile-agent systems allow the cloning of agents so that multiple streams of control work in parallel on the solution of a single task. This opportunity is not really characteristic of the model, however. Instead, the term mobile agent is typically used for a single process that moves around.

In another, less well-known research area, the parallelism aspect is of central importance. We use the term *parallel mobile code* for this area, which is currently shaped by three major systems: MESSENGERS [165], self-migrating threads [405], and WAVE [365]. Although these systems differ in implementation, language, and other details, their overall philosophy is the same:

> The parallel-mobile-code model uses proactive migration to exploit the combined computational power of multiple computers in a network.

Like mobile agents, processes in parallel-mobile-code systems deploy proactive migration. The processes are started independently by users or other processes. Thereafter, they operate autonomously, without central control. Whereas mobile agents deploy migration for the purpose of using *specialized* resources at remote locations, parallel mobile code as well deploys migration to incorporate *additional* resources into the computation.

Description of the model   An important concept of parallel-mobile-code systems is the logical or *knowledge network*, which is a distributed data structure. The knowledge network stores knowledge or intermediate results that have been accumulated so far. The knowledge network is both built up and explored by the application. Sapaty [365] gives a useful analogy, in which he compares the execution of a parallel-mobile-code application with the building of a house. The house corresponds to the knowledge network. It is the emerging result, and is constructed in a step-by-step process. At any one time, the (incomplete) house represents both the result of previous steps and the basis for future ones.

The building of the house is accomplished by cooperating workers, who correspond to parallel processes. The house has a certain spatial extent, which corresponds to a distribution of data among multiple locations. Typically, an individual worker operates on a single part of the house at a time. Later, he or she proceeds with another part, and for that purpose moves to the new location physically. Likewise, the processes move between different locations to work with different data.

The knowledge network is implemented on top of an infrastructure that is similar to that of mobile-agent systems, the *daemon network*. This network realizes the receiving, running, and transferring of processes, as well as their access to local resources and their communication with one another. Whereas the knowledge network is created dynamically by the application, the daemon network is configured by the user prior to the start of the application. Altogether, parallel-mobile-code systems comprise three layers: physical network, daemon network, and knowledge network. The correspondence between the physical and the daemon network is not necessarily one-to-one. For instance, multiple daemons may run at one physical node.

The knowledge network is a graph of arbitrary topology. Its nodes and arcs are labeled with application-specific information, which is often data, but can also be code. The knowledge network is built up by the parallel processes. Through special language constructs, the processes create and destroy nodes and arcs, or store information there. The processes can specify the assignment of knowledge network nodes to daemon network nodes; otherwise the nodes are assigned automatically.

When roaming the network, processes can use both the daemon network and the knowledge network for *navigation*. In the former case, they state the name of the destination node(s) explicitly. In the latter case, they formulate an expression that depends on information that is stored in the current node and in incident arcs. The expression describes a set of destinations and may be complex. When a process moves to multiple destinations, it is cloned.

While residing in a node, a process may use local resources. For instance, it may invoke a local function. The function is then carried out within the calling process, or a new process is created and run in parallel with the original process. In Fukuda et al. [165], mobile processes are interpreted as coordinators of local activities. We come back to this viewpoint in Sect. 8.3.

Of course, while residing in a node, the mobile processes can also carry out computational statements, and they can stop themselves or other processes. In the MESSENGERS system, the processes are moreover able to incorporate novel code so that they can change their own behavior dynamically.

Mobile processes communicate with one another by reading/writing from/to the knowledge network. If a process wants to read data that have been written by another process, it must visit the same node. As in shared-memory programming (the knowledge network is shared), the reader may have to synchronize with the writer, to make sure that it gets the correct value. Reader and writer can visit the node at the same or at different times. They can also be the same process, that is, the writer can store data for its own later use. In the knowledge network, data can live longer than the writer.

Implementation and applications   In summary, mobile programs contain computational statements, function invocations, navigational statements, and synchronization statements. The code can be compiled or interpreted. As parallel-mobile-code systems are targeted at high-performance computing, there is some bias towards compilation [405]. Navigational statements are implemented through lower-level mechanisms such as sockets.

So far, the parallel activities have been denoted as processes. This is not fully correct, as the various systems differ in this respect. For example, the self-migrating threads system works with threads for efficiency. WAVE adopts a two-level structure, in which closely related activities are collected into processes called waves. There is parallelism both within a wave and among different waves.

The parallel-mobile-code paradigm can be implemented in both WANs and LANs, although the characteristics differ. In WANs, process migration is expensive, and thus the model supports only coarse- to medium-grained applications. In LANs, the performance potential of threads can be exploited to run more fine-grained applications [405].

The three parallel-mobile-code systems are currently in the stage of research prototypes. They are available in the public domain and have been tested on several toy problems and real applications.

Typical application areas of parallel mobile code include graph problems and simulation tasks. In particular, individual-based simulations [165], in which the system behavior is determined by the activities of interacting individuals or particles [165], can profit from the approach. Individual-based simulations are deployed, for instance, in particle-level simulations in physics, traffic modeling, and biomedicine.

For these and other application areas, the parallel-mobile-code model seems to be a natural fit. Since the programming model is close to the structure of the applications, the programmability is good. Preliminary performance measurements in [405] look promising, too. Another advantage of the model is its amenability to load balancing and other performance optimizations. Since both the processes and the nodes of the knowledge network can be relocated, applications can adapt to dynamically changing environments.

Relationship to parallelism In addition to the application-internal parallelism, the model can exploit parallelism between multiple applications, which possibly belong to different users. Multiple applications may share all or part of the knowledge network.

Fukuda et al. [164] compare the parallel-mobile-code model with message passing. In message passing, messages are passive, whereas in the parallel-mobile-code model they contain much of an application's functionality. Parallel-mobile-code systems involve a daemon network, whereas message-passing systems do not. Thus, message-passing processes always need a partner process to access remote resources, whereas mobile processes can cooperate with the daemon.

7.4 TRANSPARENT MIGRATION

With the topic of this section, we are moving backwards in history. Transparent migration has been used at least since the late 1980s. The concept can be described as follows:

> A transparent migration system moves processes or threads to another location during their execution, in order to improve load balancing, locality exploitation, dependability, or similar issues. The migration is initiated and managed transparently by the system.

Here, "system" stands for operating system, run-time system, or middleware. In terms of our classification scheme, transparent migration is reactive. Since the migration is hidden from the programmer, we are actually dealing with not a programming model, but an implementation strategy. Yet, the fact that the system may reschedule computations should be considered by the programmer, if he or she is concerned about performance.

Transparent migration is especially common with shared-memory models; here the threads can be migrated without moving the data. It is also used in the implementation of object-oriented languages, where the units of movement are objects.

In distributed-memory architectures, transparent migration can be used as a complement to data redistribution. Both techniques address the case that the processes access varying data sets during their execution. Whereas data redistribution improves the locality by moving the data to the computations, transparent migration instead moves the computations to the data. If some data are needed by multiple processes at a time, either the data are replicated, or the processes migrate to the data's location.

Sometimes, transparent migration systems clone code instead of moving it. Code cloning improves fault tolerance, and can also improve performance. Some systems relax the transparency concept and give the user a certain amount of control over the code location. In COOL [97], for instance, the user is allowed to annotate the program with hints for appropriate code placement.

Transparent migration systems and mechanisms are described in a large number of papers. Some representative references include: Antoniu et al. [22], Artsy and Finkel [28], Chandra et al. [97], Chang et al. [101], Douglis and Ousterhout [136], Tan et al. [407], Jenks and Gaudiot [234], and Thitikamol and Keleher [413].

7.5 MORE ON THIS TOPIC

Since specific references have already been given in the first four sections of this chapter, not much remains to be said here. A topic that does not fit into any of the four sections is *active networks*. This research topic follows the idea that the network itself should be made programmable. In the active-networks model, a message includes not only data, destination address, and related information, but also a program that is executed by routers and other devices along the way. The program can, for instance, cause the routers to multicast or encrypt the message, or it can request encryption for the messages that follow. The active networks model is studied by several research groups, but it is still in its infancy. Further information can be found in Ortiz [323].

The IceT project [188, 222] follows an approach that is in between the transparent migration and mobile-agent models. IceT assumes a heterogeneous metacomputing environment. Process migration is transparent, but the purpose of process migration is the use of specialized remote resources.

Code mobility is also deployed in several object-oriented and higher-level models that are described in later chapters of this book.

BIBLIOGRAPHICAL REMARKS

The contents and presentation of the introduction have been inspired by several papers: Fuggetta et al. [163], Bic et al. [48, 49], Fukuda et al. [164], and Cardelli [85]. Particularly the subsection on the classification of mobile code systems draws on material from Fuggetta et al. [163].

Applets are a feature of Java, and as such are described in many Java books. For further information on volunteer computing see, for example, Sarmenta [366] and Silva et al. [384].

A comprehensive reference on mobile agents is the book by Knapik and Johnson [251]. Other useful resources include Chess et al. [104] and Fuggetta et al. [163]. Interesting reading is a collection of interviews [299], which contrasts several opinions.

Parallel mobile-code systems are described in Sapaty [365], Bic et al. [50], Fukuda et al. [165], and Suzuki et al. [405].

8

Coordination Models

Coordination models separate the computation activities that are performed within a single process from the cooperation activities that are performed between the processes. The concept was introduced in the late 1980s by Carriero and Gelernter, who define coordination as the process of "building programs by gluing together active pieces" [90].

In our context, the "active pieces" are tasks (processes, threads, mobile agents) that carry out computations. In a wider context, the pieces can also be users, devices, or other autonomous entities.

"Gluing together" refers to the communication and synchronization between tasks, as well as to task creation, destruction, and scheduling. Coordination has a spatial and a temporal aspect; it refers both to processes that run at different locations, and to processes that run at different times. Characteristic for the coordination concept is an uncoupling of tasks, that is, the sender and the receiver of a message do not need to know each other. The coordination concept is very general and goes beyond parallel and distributed computing. To restate the essential idea:

> A coordination model describes the interaction between autonomous tasks and deals with communication, synchronization, and task management. The term coordination focuses on approaches in which the computation and interaction aspects are strictly separated, and in which the cooperating tasks are anonymous to each other.

The coordination approach has several advantages:

- The separation between computation and coordination helps in structuring programs. As in client/server computing, the structure supports collaborative software development, verification, and maintenance, as well as the reuse of both computation and coordination components.

- The separation between computation and coordination supports heterogeneity and interoperability. Since the coordination components of a program have a black-box view of the processes, it does not matter if the processes are implemented in different languages and on different architectures.

- Anonymity supports dynamic applications, in which the tasks do not know each other before run time.

- Anonymity supports code mobility and mobile computing, because it facilitates integration into a novel environment.

Whereas coordination models describe the principles of a coordination approach, *coordination languages* are programming languages or sets of programming-language constructs through which the programmer expresses the coordination aspects of an algorithm. Thus coordination languages complement conventional languages. The programmer expresses the computation aspects of an algorithm in a conventional language, and the coordination aspects in a coordination language.

From our model-oriented perspective, it is difficult to draw a clear line between coordination and other parallel and distributed models. It can be argued that many models presented in this book are coordination models to some extent, if only for the reason that the notion of models has been restricted to parallelism/distribution aspects. Things look different from a language-oriented or program analysis perspective. Yet, from our perspective, coordination stands more for a different viewpoint than for a different class of models.

This chapter has nevertheless been included, to cover those models that are commonly put under the heading of coordination: tuple-based coordination models (Sect. 8.1) and channel-based coordination models (Sect. 8.2). As usual, the section finishes with a survey of related approaches.

8.1 TUPLE-BASED COORDINATION

In this model, the processes are glued together by a shared datastructure, as in the parallel-mobile-code model. In contrast to that model, the implementation of the datastructure is hidden from the programmer. Although the datastructure can be distributed, many implementations provide location transparency so that the datastructure looks to the programmer like a single

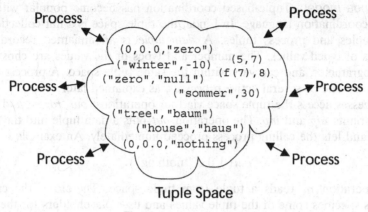

Fig. 8.1 A tuple space.

homogeneous resource. As another difference, tuple-based coordination can, but need not, be combined with code mobility.

The term *data*structure should not be taken literally: in addition to passive data, the datastructure may hold active processes. The datastructure can represent an emerging result, as does the house in the house-building analogy of Sect. 7.3. More often, it is a kind of box into which processes put information that other processes take out later. Multiple processes can access the datastructure at the same time.

The datastructure takes the form of an associative memory called *tuple space*. A *tuple* is an ordered collection of information, such as (0, 0.0, "nothing"). The tuple space contains a set or multiset of tuples, as illustrated in Fig. 8.1. It is an associative memory, and thus the tuples are identified by their contents, not by their position. In other words, unlike with arrays, one does not access the 1st, 2nd, 3rd, etc. tuple, but one specifies part of the contents and obtains the rest. The tuple-space concept is explained in more detail below, for the Linda submodel.

Tuple-based coordination decouples the cooperating processes. Thus, one process writes to the tuple space, and any other process can, independently and at a different time, take out the written value later. In other words, the receiver is anonymous to the sender and vice versa, except, of course, if they encode the respective identity in the value written. Tuple-based coordination is sometimes described as *generative*, since each write operation generates a new tuple.

The tuple-based coordination model shares some resemblance with distributed shared memory (Sect. 4.3) in that the communication is accomplished through a shared medium that is managed transparently. In contrast to DSM systems, tuple-based models impose an internal structure onto the memory. They consider the memory as a collection of tuples instead of as a low-level sequence of pages.

The Linda model   Tuple-based coordination has become popular with the Linda coordination language. In Linda, the tuple space is a flat collection of data tuples and process tuples. A *data tuple* is an unnamed record that consists of typed values. The number and types of the values are chosen by the programmer, and can vary within the same tuple space. A process tuple represents one or several active processes, as explained later.

Processes access the tuple space via four operations: *out*, *rd*, *in*, and *eval*; with variants *rdp* and *inp*. The operation *out* puts a data tuple into the tuple space, and lets the calling process proceed immediately. An example is

$$out(0, 0.0, \text{``nothing''}).$$

The operation *rd* reads a tuple from tuple space. Therefore, the calling process specifies some of the tuple values and uses placeholders for the rest. A tuple with placeholders is called a *template*. The placeholders are names of local variables in the calling process. A call to *rd* assigns to them concrete values. For instance, the call

$$rd(0, 0.0, ?s)$$

starts a search for a tuple that consists of three values: the first must be 0, the second must be 0.0, and the third may be any string (assuming that s is declared as a string). If there are multiple matching tuples, one of them is chosen arbitrarily. Consequently, in the example of Fig. 8.1, s is set arbitrarily to either "nothing" or "zero". The operation *rd* is blocking, that is, if there is no matching tuple in the tuple space, then the calling process blocks until there is one. Thus, *rd* implies an implicit synchronization between the writing and the reading process. *rdp* is a nonblocking variant that returns immediately with a value that indicates success or failure.

The operation *in* and its nonblocking variant *inp* work the same way as *rd* and *rdp*, except that they not only read a tuple but additionally remove it from tuple space.

Finally, the operation *eval* starts other processes. At first sight, *eval* is similar to *out* in that it writes a tuple to tuple space. Unlike *out*, however, *eval* writes a *process tuple*, in which one or several positions are function calls instead of values. For each such position, *eval* creates a new process that evaluates the respective function. When a process has finished its work, the corresponding function call is replaced by the result, and thus the process tuple turns into a data tuple. If another process tries to read a process tuple before its evaluation has finished, that process is blocked until the result is available. The functions and their parameters must be declared in the process that calls *eval*. An example is

$$eval(3, \text{sqrt}(3), \text{my\_function}(x, y))$$

This call generates two processes, which evaluate sqrt(3) and my_function(x, y), respectively. The identifiers x, y and my_function must be declared in the calling process.

Despite its simplicity, the tuple space model allows for the expression of many parallel and distributed patterns and constructs (for example master/slave and semaphores), as well as of common datastructures (for example arrays and lists). To give a concrete example, the tuple ("A", 2, 5) may express that the value of $A[2]$ is 5, and the operation *in* ("A", 2, ?k) may assign the value of $A[2]$ to the variable k.

Assessment of the Linda model   In addition to the general advantages of coordination models, specific strengths of Linda include its simplicity and relatively high-level nature. Therefore, Linda has inspired a lot of research in the theoretical domain. Like distributed shared-memory systems, Linda manages data and process distribution transparently (with the usual consequences for programmability and performance), and the programmer is responsible for avoiding race conditions and deadlocks.

Various Linda implementations have been developed, including commercial implementations. Each concrete system combines Linda with one or several base languages (for instance C, Fortran, or Prolog) in which the programmer expresses the computations of a program. Linda has been implemented on several parallel architectures, including clusters. Many implementations follow the library approach and supply the Linda operations through library routines. In other implementations, the compiler translates both coordination and computation statements.

Originally, Linda was developed in the parallel computing domain. Despite considerable success, it has never been widely adopted in this domain (at least not as widely as message passing). At present, there is a growing interest in the Linda approach in the distributed domain. As has been discussed in the introduction to this chapter, the clear separation between computation and coordination is especially appealing in a distributed environment, since it supports openness, heterogeneity, and dynamic behavior. We will see examples of distributed Linda systems below.

Related Models

Over the years, a large variety of Linda dialects and modified tuple-space models have been suggested. Surveys are given in Papadopoulos and Arbab [330], Ciancarini et al. [111], and Ciancarini [110]. While many models are research proposals with little practical significance, commercial tuple-space models include TSpaces from IBM [447], Paradise from SCIENTIFIC [373], and JavaSpaces from Sun (explained later).

The modifications address several weaknesses of the base Linda model, first of all the restriction to a flat tuple space. Linda-related models such as Bauhaus Linda [92], PoliS [109], and MobiS [281] structure the tuple space into multiple subspaces such that each tuple belongs to a particular subspace. The subspaces can be arranged as a hierarchy. Like process groups in MPI, separate subspaces improve the modularity of a program, and thus support large-scale software development. Further variants of the tuple-based coordination model consider, for example, the following extensions:

- Replication of tuple spaces [66],

- Collective read operations [362],

- Nonblocking (two-phase) communications [362],

- Dynamic extensions of the operation set [447],

- Tuple spaces for the publication of service offerings [415],

- Support for fault tolerance and scavenging in clusters [72],

- Support for mobile environments [343], and

- Secure access operations [73].

Several tuple-based models have been developed in the context of web computing, especially for the communication between mobile agents. A survey is given in Ciancarini et al. [111]. These models typically support multiple tuple spaces. In a distributed setting, multiple tuple spaces have the additional advantage of improving the performance, since they allow for the exploitation of locality. To state it in more detail, subspaces are often shared by groups of agents that reside on the same node. Consequently the subspaces can be implemented locally and have faster access. Ciancarini et al. [11] distinguish the following approaches to the management of multiple tuple spaces:

- The location of the tuple spaces is *transparent* to the programmer, and each agent can access each tuple space. In this approach, the system may be allowed to migrate the tuple spaces transparently to another location [362].

- Each agent is *implicitly* assigned to a single tuple space at its current location, and may access that tuple space only. If an agent wants to access a different tuple space, it must first migrate there [79, 343].

- The programmer is aware of the tuple space locations and may *explicitly* access both local and remote tuple spaces [315].

To give an example, the *tuple centers spread over networks* model TuCSoN [315, 316] addresses the communication in a mobile-agents environment. TuCSoN uses multiple tuple spaces called tuple centers, which can be accessed locally or remotely. In TuCSoN, the behavior of the individual tuple spaces can be programmed so that the standard Linda functionality is enhanced. An enhanced tuple space is still accessed via the standard operations, but these operations can, in addition to their normal functionality, modify the tuple space. For instance, they may delete related tuples if a new tuple is inserted.

Another example is the already mentioned JavaSpaces system from Sun [162, 233]. In JavaSpaces, tuples, as well as the entries in the tuples, are objects instead of simple data values. The tuples are written to the tuple space with the help of the object serialization facility of Java (see Ch. 7). JavaSpaces implements the Linda operations *in*, *out*, and *rd* (under different names), but it does not implement *eval*. JavaSpaces introduces a new operation, *notify*. This operation takes as a parameter a template, and instructs the tuple space to send a signal to the caller when a matching tuple is inserted. As another modification, the tuples are held in the tuple space for a limited amount of time only. JavaSpaces works with multiple tuple spaces, which are managed transparently. Typically, the tuple spaces reside in the middle tier of a client/server system. In JavaSpaces, the elementary operations can be grouped into transactions, which are executed completely or not at all. A single transaction may access multiple tuple spaces. The practical importance of JavaSpaces is chiefly due to its use with the Jini technology (see Sect. 7.1).

8.2 CHANNEL-BASED COORDINATION

The subject of this section is quite different from that of the previous one. Whereas tuple-based coordination resembles shared-memory programming, channel-based coordination resembles message passing.

The channel-based model considers processes as black-box computational activities that are characterized by their input/output behavior. The processes are coordinated by considering the outputs of one process to be the inputs of another. Channel-based coordination models are sometimes put under the heading of message passing. We classify the models as coordination models, since they clearly separate computation activities and coordination activities, and since several channel-based models place emphasis on this aspect.

Channel-based coordination is an old concept that goes back to the development of the *communicating sequential processes* (CSP) model by Hoare in the late 1970s. CSP is not only the first notable such model; it is also the most influential one.

The CSP model According to the general concept of channel-based coordination, CSP considers a parallel program as a collection of sequential processes that are glued together by input/output activities. The model can be described as follows:

- Processes are created and destroyed in a structured way. CSP defines a construct called *par* that is comparable to the parallel-regions construct of OpenMP. Thus, at the beginning of a parallel region, a set of processes is created, which then run in parallel until termination. Only when all the spawned processes have finished does the computation proceed with the next statement after the parallel region. The number of parallel processes must be fixed in the program text. Parallel regions may be nested.

- All interprocess communication is accomplished through input and output operations; there is no shared memory. Only pairwise communications are supported. The output (*write*) and input (*read*) operations correspond to, respectively, send and receive in message passing. Unlike the message-passing routines, *write* and *read* have simple parameters: the data (explicit value or name of a variable) and the destination/ source. The original CSP definition requires sender and receiver to name each other explicitly. In a newer version [213], local port names are used instead, and we refer to this modification in what follows.

- The concept of *ports* is different in CSP than in client/server computing. Whereas in client/server computing a port is an entrance into a machine and can be used by multiple processes, a CSP port is an entrance into a process and is used by only one partner process. CSP communication uses *channels*, which one can think of as being tubes that connect two ports, and thus exactly two processes, with each other. Data are filled into the tube at one end (*write*), and taken out at the other (*read*). Other processes cannot look inside the tube. Channels are unidirectional, that is, a port is either an input port or an output port. The channel concept is illustrated in Fig. 8.2.

- Communications are always blocking and *synchronous*. As in MPI, a synchronous communication starts only when both the sender and the receiver are ready. Thus, each communication implies a synchronization.

- Nondeterministic control structures can be expressed through *guarded commands*. A guarded command is a group of statements, of which only one is selected for execution. Each statement in the group is preceded

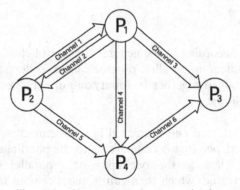

Fig. 8.2 Channel-based communication.

by a conditional, called a *guard*, as in the following example

$$x \geq 0 \rightarrow y := x$$
$$[]x < 0 \rightarrow y := -x$$
$$[]x = 7 \rightarrow y := random$$

At run time, the various guards are evaluated, and the successful statement is chosen nondeterministically from those statements whose guard evaluates to true. In the example, if $x = 7$, then either $y := x$ or $y := random$ is executed. Often, the guards are *read*s instead of conditionals, and a guard evaluates to true if a matching *write* has been posted.

CSP serves both as a basis for the definition of parallel programming languages, and as a mathematical model in which one can describe programs and reason about their behavior. We restrict ourselves to the first aspect here, but the second aspect is at least equally important in general. With the help of the mathematical model, one may, for instance, be able to prove that a certain program is deadlock-free.

Occam Closely based on the CSP model, the programming language Occam was developed in the early 1980s [236, 399]. Occam is a comparatively primitive language. For instance, it does not support recursive functions, and uses indentation to mark blocks of statements. The major language constructs of Occam are parallel regions (PAR), sequential regions (SEQ), and guarded commands (ALT). The keywords indicate that the next (indented) statements should be executed in parallel, in sequence, or as guarded alternatives. Occam also supports variants of PAR and ALT in which the statements are assigned priorities according to their textual order. An example Occam program is outlined in Fig. 8.3.

```
CHAN OF INT com:

PAR

    INT x:

    SEQ
    :

        com!x          Output Statement

    INT x:

    SEQ
    :

        com?x          Input Statement
```

Fig. 8.3 An example Occam program.

Occam had a certain practical significance until several years back. Now it has been largely replaced by other languages. Occam is closely tied to a specific class of parallel architectures: transputer networks. These are distributed-memory parallel machines in which each node is directly connected to at most four neighbors. In Occam, all aspects of parallelism must be handled by the programmer. The programmer must place the processes onto processors, declare channels, and even assign the ports to one of the four physical processor links.

Related Models

While Occam is mainly interesting for historical reasons, the CSP model lives on. In recent projects [121, 208, 231], CSP has been combined with Java. The motivation for this work is the strength of CSP in ensuring program correctness. CSP programming is less error-prone than programming in the standard Java threads model, and verification tools for CSP are available.

The guarded-commands mechanism of CSP is also supported by the language Ada [75], where it is used in connection with the rendezvous (Sect. 6.4). By invoking a guarded command, called *select* in Ada, a server can wait for one out of several possible requests. If multiple requests arrive at the same time, one of them is chosen arbitrarily. The willingness to accept a certain request can be made conditional on some guard. Except for guarded commands, Ada is fundamentally different from Occam: It supports a dynamic number of processes and has a complex concurrency model (see Sects. 4.5, 6.4).

An especially clean realization of the coordination concept is embodied in the *idealized-worker idealized-manager* model IWIM [24] and the related coordination language Manifold [25, 279]. IWIM distinguishes between computation (worker) and coordination (manager) processes. A worker process receives data through input ports, performs computations on the data, and writes results to output ports. A worker process does not know anything about its environment. In particular, it does not know the identity of the partner processes to which it is connected through the input and output ports. All coordination aspects are handled by managers. The managers connect and disconnect the channels dynamically at run time. They may also plug a channel endpoint into a different process than before; this change is transparent to the worker processes. Moreover, the managers create and destroy worker processes and other manager processes. The manager processes are organized into a hierarchy, in which the lower-level managers are considered as workers by the higher-level managers. Normally, a channel connects exactly two ports; the model can be extended to multiple incoming or multiple outgoing connections per port. Manifold is a research proposal, which has been tested on only a few real applications so far. It is supplemented by a graphical environment called Visifold [67], which helps in constructing, debugging and optimizing programs. A related language is JavaPorts [168].

Further channel-based coordination models are surveyed in Papadopoulos and Arbab [330].

8.3 MORE ON THIS TOPIC

Parallel mobile code As was noted before, the parallel-mobile-code and *tuple-based* coordination models are closely related. In Fukuda et al. [165], the MESSENGERS parallel-mobile-code model is furthermore interpreted as a kind of *channel-based* coordination model. As explained in Sect. 7.3, processes in MESSENGERS are mobile and invoke local functions in the nodes they visit. The local functions can be considered as computations whose execution is coordinated by the mobile processes. In particular, the mobile processes determine the order of function invocations, and they transfer the input and output data between the functions. Thus, there is a strict separation between computation and communication, and the various functions are anonymous to each other.

Messaging This paradigm describes a group of middleware systems for client/server or peer-to-peer computing, and is also called message-oriented middleware (MOM) [322]. Messaging is related to tuple-based coordination in that the processes communicate by reading/writing information to a shared datastructure. The organization of the datastructure is different, however.

Unlike other client/server models, such as sockets and RPC, messaging uncouples the processes in space and time. Therefore, the client and server processes need not be ready at the same time. This feature is especially appealing in mobile computing. In general, it leads to a different style of programming, which may or may not be appropriate for a certain application. MOM has a large and probably growing commercial significance. It is standardized in the Java Message Service API [198], and many products are available. The importance of MOM is not so much based on its role in distributed computing as on its role in software technology. Messaging focuses on coarse-grained programs, and helps in structuring large applications.

Messaging can be classified into two submodels: message queuing, and publish-and-subscribe. The concept of *message queuing* is quite old; for example, the Unix operating system [401] has used message queuing for many years. In message queuing, the shared datastructure takes the form of one or several queues. Each process can write to or read from any queue. A process can access both local and remote queues, provided that it knows the address of the queue, and that the queue is not protected by security mechanisms. The internal organization of a message queue can, but need not, strictly follow the first-in, first-out scheme. When writing to a queue, a process typically assigns a priority to its message, and states a timeout after which the message can be deleted. A reading process inspects or browses the messages in the queue, and takes out specific messages. Queues are typically shared between multiple processes. In a client/server system, for instance, they are shared between multiple clients and multiple servers. The clients are writing requests to the queue, and the servers are taking them out according to an application-specific load-balancing or work-sharing scheme.

The *publish-and-subscribe* paradigm distinguishes between producers (publishers) and consumers (subscribers) of information. Whereas in message queues messages are typically written by one process and taken out by another, publish-and-subscribe focuses on multicasting. The shared datastructure is divided into substructures called *topics*, which correspond to application-specific real-world topics. Publishers write messages to specific topics, and subscribers register for one or several topics they are interested in. When a message is published, it is then automatically forwarded to all subscribers, as in a mailing list. Often, the topics are organized into a hierarchy, and a subscriber may register for a topic together with all subtopics.

Grid middleware To a certain extent, the term coordination can also be applied to middleware systems through which application processes access the functionality of a grid (see Sect. 2.7). A well-known system in this context is Globus [157, 180]. This system provides a uniform set of services for resource management, resource location, multicasting, security, and other purposes. It is built upon heterogeneous low-level protocols and systems, and can be used by higher-level systems such as MPI and CORBA. Globus differs from other grid middleware in that it does not make any assumptions on the internal structure and programming model of the application programs. Therefore we classify it as a coordination model. Other grid middleware systems are handled in Ch. 9.

As noted before, many more models can be put under the heading of coordination. In particular the skeleton and compositional models (see Ch. 10) are closely related.

BIBLIOGRAPHICAL REMARKS

The concept of coordination has been suggested and advocated by Carriero and Gelernter, for example in [90, 91]. Originally, the term was coined for tuple-based models. Nevertheless, many authors classify channel-based models as coordination models, too [330]. A quite recent survey of coordination languages is provided by Papadopoulos and Arbab [330]. Other useful resources include Arbab et al. [25], Omicini [314], and talk slides by Ciancarini [110].

The Linda model has been described by Carriero and Gelernter, for example in [89, 90]. For a discussion of Linda implementations see Fenwick and Pollock [150]. The original source on CSP is Hoare [212]. Messaging is, for example, treated in Orfali et al. [322] and in Singh [386].

9
Object-Oriented Models

Another clear separation between program parts is provided by object orientation. As explained in Sect. 4.1, an object encompasses attributes and methods. Thus it can be considered as a black box that internally implements computations. The various objects coordinate their activities through mutual method calls. We have already seen several programming models of object-oriented languages before. This section concentrates on approaches in which the parallelism/distribution model is closely integrated with the concept of objects. We can summarize our focus as follows:

> In object-oriented models, a typically large number of autonomous objects with different functionalities are available in a distributed system. The objects run in disjoint address spaces. Through explicit communication routines, they invoke and use each other's functionalities.

Thus, we include among object-oriented models only certain of the models that incorporate parallelism/distribution into object-oriented languages, namely, those that closely integrate the concepts as described above. Object-oriented models address general forms of task parallelism. They consider a distributed application as a collection of functionally specialized objects that exist independently of each other.

According to the characteristics of object orientation, each object has an internal state, which is described by the values of its attributes. The object is accessed from the outside through methods which may represent services for use by others and/or modify the state. Object-oriented models are chiefly targeted at large-scale coarse-grained applications in the distributed domain, although there are also applications in medium-grained parallel computing.

Especially in the 1990s, there has been a lot of interest in combining object orientation and parallel/distributed computing. The interest was mainly motivated by the general advantages of object orientation for the engineering of large software systems, such as:

- *Encapsulation.* There are clear interfaces between the objects. Only methods (and possibly a few attributes) are accessible from the outside, whereas the implementation of the methods is hidden within the boundaries of a single object. Such a modular program design facilitates collaborative software development, debugging, and maintenance. Moreover, object implementations can be replaced without changing the overall system, and objects may be coded in different languages.

- *Inheritance.* Related objects can share part of their code, as was explained with the submarine example in Sect. 4.1. Code reuse improves the productivity of software development and helps in structuring programs.

Since distributed systems tend to be complex, these advantages are especially relevant to them. Another argument for the combination is that objects are self-contained, so that they suggest themselves as units of distribution. Technically, we can distinguish between three approaches for combining object orientation and parallelism/distribution:

- Parallelism/distribution is hidden within the boundaries of individual objects. This approach has already been covered in the context of data parallelism in Sect. 3.4.

- Processes exist independently of objects, and thus a process carries out methods of different objects during its lifetime. Several approaches allow multiple methods of the same object to be active at the same time, and therefore require synchronization mechanisms. An example of this approach is the Java threads model (Sect. 4.1).

- Each object is associated with one or several processes that execute the accesses to the object. Only this approach is referred to by our notion of object-oriented models.

Over time, a huge number of experimental languages have been suggested for all three approaches. The variety is partially due to the existence of fundamental problems in integrating object orientation and parallelism/ distribution. Most importantly, the *inheritance anomaly* states that the (minor) modification of a subclass may induce the need for significant changes to the overall synchronization structure [285]. Another problem is the existence of class variables, which provide a kind of shared memory between objects and thus weaken the principle of encapsulation.

Object-oriented models are naturally amenable to location transparency because, even in sequential computing, objects conceptually operate in disjoint address spaces and communicate by passing messages. Thus it does not really matter for the semantics of a program whether the objects are stored locally or remotely. Transparency has pros and cons. On the positive side, it improves the programmability, since the programmer need not deal with distribution details. Moreover, the system can transparently migrate and possibly replicate objects to improve locality and load balancing. On the negative side, the programmer is not aware of important issues and thus loses control: communication is not reliable, remote nodes can fail independently of each other, security must be provided for, and remote communication is slow.

In this section, we consider two classes of object-oriented models: distributed objects and active objects. The concept of distributed objects is realized in popular middleware systems such as CORBA, Java RMI, and DCOM. Section 9.1 explains the concept mainly with the example of CORBA. The concept of active objects is closely associated with the actor model. Section 9.2 describes the base version of this model and outlines some extensions. In the final survey section we treat, among other topics, object-oriented grid middleware.

9.1 DISTRIBUTED OBJECTS

In distributed-object models, objects are the units of distribution. Objects are typically coarse-grained. In fact, they can be very coarse-grained, to the extent of representing a complete product that is sold as a unit by a company. To distinguish these powerful objects from ordinary small-scale objects of object-oriented languages, the powerful objects are often called *components*. The terms object and component are used with varying meanings in the literature. In general, "object" is more a programming-language term, and "component" is more a software technology term. Both objects and components are software entities with well-defined interfaces. The term object emphasizes the encapsulation of data and code, and the term component emphasizes the opportunity to compose the entities into large applications. The term object is frequently used for the entities within a single program, whereas the term component implies an independent existence, that is, components can interoperate across program boundaries. We use the term "object" in the following, but our objects could be called components as well.

Distributed objects are both a distributed-programming model and an approach for organizing programs. In particular, large applications are often organized as *open* software systems. In such systems, objects can be added, updated, and withdrawn while the rest of the system is already running.

Systems such as CORBA and DCOM come with a rich set of facilities that help build large applications. Buzzwords in this domain include frameworks, design patterns, business objects, and beans. The facilities support specific application requirements. Since we restrict ourselves to the middle levels of the model hierarchy (Sect. 1.4), the facilities are not elaborated upon here, even though they make up much of the CORBA and DCOM functionality.

From the parallelism/distribution point of view, distributed objects are a third model for the realization of the client/server paradigm, besides sockets and RPC. Like those, distributed objects are task-parallel and MPMD. Each individual interaction between objects follows the client/server pattern. Nevertheless, the overall structure of many distributed-object systems is peer-to-peer, that is, the roles of clients and servers can change over time. Collective operations may be provided through higher-level facilities as described, for example, in [148].

If we relate distributed objects to the client/server paradigm, methods correspond to services. Each distributed object is bound to a process called a server, which carries out the operations of the object. Note the difference from Java threads. Whereas a Java thread carries out code of different objects during its lifetime, distributed-object models bind each process to a particular object (or group of objects; see below). Therefore, a client process cannot execute the code of a service method directly, but must ask a server process to do so.

The difference reflects the fact that Java threads are a shared-memory model and distributed objects are a distributed-memory model. The Java threads approach cannot be realized in a distributed system because the server object is stored in a different address space and the code is thus not visible for the client. In homogeneous systems, the client could download the code for execution, but code mobility is not part of the distributed-objects model. Nevertheless, code mobility and distributed objects are frequently combined; we will see examples later.

The communication mechanism between client and server is called *remote method invocation* (RMI). It is an adaptation of the remote procedure call mechanism to object-oriented computing. Although, conceptually, RMI and RPC are quite similar, realizations of RMI tend to be more elaborate than realizations of RPC. There are at least two reasons for this difference: First, RMI is a successor of RPC and thus reflects recent progress. Second, RMI follows the ambitious goal of object orientation to support large-scale software development. A conceptual difference between RMI and RPC can be seen in the fact that objects have a state. Thus, different invocations of the same method with the same parameters can lead to different results in the case of RMI. An RPC call, in contrast, will always return the same result, except, of course, if the server internally accesses a database or global variables and is thus comparable to an object.

CORBA The next paragraphs exemplify the distributed objects approach with the *common object request broker architecture* (CORBA). The related DCOM and Java RMI models are briefly outlined thereafter. CORBA is a standard that has been established by the Object Management Group (OMG), an organization that comprises over 800 companies. Correspondingly, the CORBA standard is supported by a large number of mature implementations, extensions, and tools, and has large commercial significance. In the following, we describe basic features of the CORBA programming model. We refer to CORBA 2.0, the present version of the standard, but most of the features are defined the same way in CORBA 3.0, the already announced successor version.

Interfaces A characteristic feature of CORBA is support for heterogeneous environments. CORBA enables interoperability between both programs that are written in different languages, and between programs that run on different machines. Interoperability is achieved through a clear separation between interface and implementation of a service. Any program, existing or new, can be transformed into a CORBA object by describing its interface in an interface definition language (IDL). The interface comprises the names of the services with parameters, a name for the object itself, and possibly attributes and exceptions. The interface is the sole basis for the handling of the object by CORBA. The actual implementation is not referred to, except that CORBA must know whether it exists and where it is located.

Objects need not be implemented in object-oriented languages; it suffices that the interfaces *look* objectlike. In any case, CORBA must support the particular language, because the implementation must be able to call CORBA functions. If an object-oriented language is used, a distinction is made between CORBA objects, for which an IDL interface is defined, and ordinary language objects, for which it is not. When we speak of objects in this section, only CORBA objects are meant.

IDL supports an inheritance mechanism to help organize objects. This mechanism applies to interfaces only. Inheritance within the implementation must be formulated separately by means of the implementation language (if it provides corresponding constructs).

Location transparency. As the name suggests, a central component of CORBA is the *object request broker* (ORB). Its purpose is mediating the communication between client and server objects in a location-transparent way. Transparency is achieved as follows: When a client accesses a server, it gives as address an *object reference*. This is a system-wide unique identifier for the object, which is automatically assigned when the object is created. The client does not normally know the physical location of the server and therefore cannot send its request to the server directly. Instead, it hands over the request to the ORB, which looks up the location and passes on the request. A client can obtain the object reference as follows:

- Upon object creation, the creator obtains the reference from the CORBA system and can communicate the reference to potential clients.

- The creator registers the object with a *name server*. For that purpose it chooses an arbitrary string as the name of the object. Clients can then contact the name server and obtain the reference belonging to a given name. They may know the name, since it is coded in the (server) program.

- A "comfortable" name server called a *trader* can be used. The trader maintains service descriptions instead of plain names and is contacted by clients who do not know the name.

Remote method invocation CORBA supports two basic variants of RMI: static invocation and dynamic invocation. These variants are supported by different modules of CORBA; the overall structure is depicted in Fig. 9.1.

Programming *static invocations* is similar to programming an RPC: The programmer first describes the server interface in IDL and puts this description into a file. Then the file is translated with a precompiler, to produce stubs for the client and server sides. If client and server are coded in different languages, then different precompilers must be used (or the precompiler be invoked with different options). The server-side stub is called the

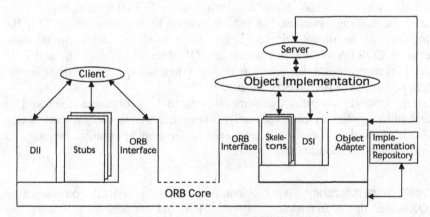

Fig. 9.1 Structure of a CORBA system.

skeleton in CORBA; the client-side stub is called the *stub*. A remote method invocation consists of the following steps:

1. The client calls the stub.

2. The stub marshals the parameters and sends the request to the ORB.

3. The ORB locates the server and passes on the request. More accurately, the ORB does not send the request directly to the server, but to an *object adapter* (explained later).

4. The object adapter invokes the skeleton.

5. The skeleton unmarshals the parameters and invokes the service method.

6. When the service method has finished its work, the results are returned to the client, which normally has been waiting passively in the meantime.

Dynamic method invocation is more involved. This mode supports open software systems; in particular, it allows a client to use services that did not exist yet at the time the client was written. To use dynamic invocation, a client, as usual, needs an object reference. It obtains the reference from other objects, or from a name server or trader. CORBA maintains an *interface repository* in which all interfaces are stored. Using this repository, the client can find out details of the server object, in particular the names and parameters of services. Despite this knowledge, the client cannot invoke the methods as usual, since it lacks a stub. In a homogeneous environment with code mobility, the client could load the stub, but in a general heterogeneous environment, it cannot. Therefore, CORBA defines a facility called the *dynamic invocation interface* (DII), which is a kind of "general-purpose stub". Like a normal stub, it accepts requests from a client, marshals the parameters, and passes the request on.

Dynamic method invocation is flexible, but it requires more programming effort than static invocation and is slower. Dynamic method invocation is also different in that it uses a nonblocking two-phase protocol, as in MPI. In this protocol, the client hands over the request to the DII and proceeds to other work. Later it calls a second function to explicitly wait for completion. The default that static invocation is blocking and dynamic invocation is nonblocking can be changed

Another feature of CORBA is a mode called *oneway*. By using this mode, a client assures that it does not need an answer. The client may thus proceed immediately, but has no guarantee that the service is executed successfully.

At the server side, the *dynamic skeleton interface* (DSI) allows a server implementation to dynamically discover its own interface. DSI is out of our scope.

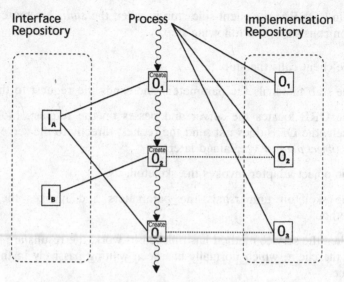

Fig. 9.2 The relationship between objects, interfaces, and processes. I stands for interface, and O stands for object.

Object activation Many distributed-object systems contain a large number of objects that are accessed infrequently. In these systems, it would be wasteful if not impossible to always have all server processes running. Therefore the processes are activated by need; activation and deactivation are managed by the already mentioned object adapter.

To avoid confusion at this point, it is probably useful to look at Fig. 9.2, which compares the notions object, interface, and process with each other. As noted before, an *interface* is an abstract description of a piece of code. The same interface can be realized by multiple *objects*. Each object has a different object reference. Objects are created by *processes*. The process that has created an object is called its *server*. This process is responsible for the object throughout the object's lifetime.

CORBA maintains an *implementation repository* (different from the interface repository mentioned above), into which each object is entered when it is created. The implementation repository stores information about the responsible server process, in particular the address of the executable server code and the (operating system) command to reactivate the server. When a client accesses an object through RMI, the object adapter checks if the responsible server is running, and otherwise starts it. So the client is given the illusion that the server has always been running.

A server can accommodate one or several objects. After activation or reactivation, the server creates the objects and reports their existence to the CORBA system. A server can run forever (that is, until the next system crash), for a certain period of time, or for the execution of a single method only. The choice is taken by the programmer who must code each server specifically. Between successive server activations, the state of an object is normally lost. Objects can be made persistent; then the state is saved to permanent memory whenever the server is deactivated, and restored when it is activated again.

Object creation Normally, objects are created by servers, independent of prospective clients. For more flexibility, CORBA supports the concept of object *factories* [169], which are objects that are able to create other objects on behalf of a client. By using an object factory, a client can create its personal instance from an interface, which is an object that maintains a client-specific state.

Implementation CORBA is used on both the intranet and internet scales. Due to a standardized underlying protocol called Internet Inter-ORB Protocol (IIOP), different CORBA implementations are able to interoperate. IIOP runs on top of TCP/IP. The CORBA standard also defines a common data format comparable to XDR, called Common Data Representation (CDR).

Combination with other models Much of the CORBA functionality is supplied by higher-level extensions. Part of these extensions incorporate ideas from other parallel/distributed models into CORBA. An example is *event* channels: Objects can register their interest in certain events and are then informed appropriately, as in publish-and-subscribe (Sect. 8.3). Another example is *beans*, which are pre-built components that can be composed into programs by appropriate tools. The beans model resembles channel-based coordination in that the output of one bean is taken as the input of another.

Combination with Java Frequently, CORBA objects are implemented in Java, which has important advantages:

- The Java virtual machine provides a kind of portable operating system that hides the heterogeneity of architectures.

- Java adds code mobility to CORBA. Objects can thus be moved both at the programmer's will (enhanced client/server computing) and transparently.

- Object implementations can use the rich languages features of Java, such as the threads model.

Likewise, CORBA extends the Java programming model by support for the interoperability between languages, as well as by remote communication mechanisms, location transparency, and a comprehensive set of facilities for distributed programming. The combination of Java and CORBA is useful for web programming; it is then called *object web*. The object web is an alternative to CGI, which has better programmability and higher performance [321].

Assessment of the model The strengths of CORBA clearly lie in its support for interoperability, openness, and scalability. Especially when coupled with Java, CORBA systems are a powerful tool for the development of distributed programs from a variety of application areas. The CORBA model places emphasis on portability, heterogeneity, and programmability; performance is given less consideration. Although the various CORBA implementations differ in their consideration of performance, there are general limitations. In particular, all communication is mediated by the ORB, which induces a certain overhead.

The claim that CORBA has good programmability is mainly based on its support for higher-level models such as frameworks, beans, etc. Low-level programming of distributed objects is not really easy, as discussed for the related Java RMI case in [342]. Nevertheless, even for low-level programming, a certain degree of programmability is achieved through location transparency. As usual, location transparency comes at a price: Since a programmer does not normally know whether a CORBA object runs on the same or on a different node, the programmer must conservatively assume that all CORBA objects are remote and may thus raise exceptions for transmission faults etc. On the positive side, CORBA implementations may exploit transparency to replicate and migrate objects for performance and fault tolerance. Despite this opportunity, locality optimization is given little consideration in most CORBA implementations.

Distributed objects are clearly a distributed-programming model. Nevertheless, parallelism can be incorporated, as has been discussed in Ch. 6. As noted there, the servers can be internally multithreaded, and multiple objects can be instantiated from the same interface to solve subtasks according to the master/slave paradigm. The parallel creation of multiple objects is supported by object factories. Especially in connection with parallelism, deadlocks can occur, and it is the programmer's responsibility to avoid them.

DCOM The Distributed Component Object Model (DCOM) is a competitor of CORBA that has been developed by Microsoft. The functionality of DCOM is comparable to that of CORBA, but its technical realization and conceptual framework are different. Especially in the last years, interoperability between CORBA and DCOM has become possible. Further information on DCOM and related technologies (e.g. ActiveX, COM+) can be found in Kirtland [249], Orfali et al. [322], and Singh [386], as well as on the Web page [295]. Comparisons between CORBA and DCOM are given by Lewandowski [269] and Yee [449], and in several papers collected at the Web page [309].

Java RMI Besides CORBA and DCOM, a third popular system is Java RMI. This system is supplied as part of the Java API and does not support interoperability with other languages (at least not directly). Heterogeneity is nevertheless supported, because of the JVM concept. Java RMI is closely integrated with Java and exploits the opportunities of code mobility. It does not define a separate interface definition language, but relies on Java syntax. Distributed objects must implement a certain interface, and are thus distinguished from ordinary Java objects. Remote method invocation works like static invocation in CORBA—with stubs, skeletons, object references, and a name server called registry.

Both distributed and ordinary objects can be used as parameters in remote method invocations. In the former case, as in CORBA, objects are passed by reference, that is, the object reference is sent along with the request, and the receiver can later access the object remotely. Since Java RMI supports code mobility, the required stub can be sent dynamically too, so that a DII facility is not needed. Ordinary Java objects are passed by value, that is, they are copied and transferred with the help of the object serialization facility of Java. Except for this novel opportunity, Java RMI has a more restricted functionality than CORBA and DCOM. Further information can be found in Java books such as Farley [146], Orfali and Harkey [321], and Niemeyer and Peck [307].

9.2 ACTIVE OBJECTS

Conceptually, active objects differ from distributed objects mainly in that they focus on asynchronous as opposed to synchronous communication. The real gap between the two approaches is, however, much larger, because they are worked upon in different communities. Whereas the development of distributed-object models is largely driven by software engineering considerations and commercial needs, active objects are a research field. As such, they belong to the more general area of concurrent object-oriented programming, which investigates the conceptual integration of object orientation and concurrency/distribution in a largely theoretical way.

As another difference from distributed objects, active objects are targeted not only at distributed, but also at parallel computing. Although active objects can implement the client/server paradigm, the individual communications do not follow this pattern. Instead, the objects are considered as peers that coordinate their activities by exchanging messages. Although the purpose of message exchange can be the use of remote services, the model does not explicitly associate communication with service use. Active objects have two key characteristics:

1. In addition to data and methods, they encapsulate one or several processes, and

2. They communicate by asynchronous message exchange.

The concept of active objects originates with the actor model, a fairly old proposal that goes back to Hewitt [203]. We refer to a somewhat newer version of the model that was introduced in 1986 by Agha [9]. In the first part of the section, we describe and discuss the actor model. In the second part, we outline extensions and modifications.

The actor model   As in distributed object models, a computation is carried out by a community of *actors* that cooperate with each other. Each actor is an autonomous entity that is characterized by a *behavior*, a *mail queue*, and a *mail address*. Since the original definition of the model did not refer to object orientation, the terminology differs. According to the original definition, the behavior is a description of the functionality of the actor. In object-oriented terms, it corresponds to a set of values for the attributes together with a set of methods that the actor is able to execute.

Actors are reactive. Like servers in client/server computing, they passively wait for requests, carry out the requests, and become passive again. The requests are called *messages*. As illustrated in Fig. 9.3, messages are stored in a mail queue, and the actor processes them in order. Depending on the contents of the message and its own behavior, the actor responds to a message with one or several of the following actions:

- It sends messages to other actors.
- It creates other actors.
- It replaces its own behavior.

Message exchange is a one-sided activity. As in the AM and FM protocols from Sect. 5.4, the sender specifies the receiver address and the message contents. The receiver does not post a matching receive, but the message is automatically appended to its mail queue. Message exchange is nonblocking, that is, the sender can proceed immediately after having sent off the message. The model supposes that messages are eventually delivered. Nevertheless messages may be subject to delay, and they may overtake each other. The message content depends on the destination actor; typically it is the name of a method to be invoked and parameters to that method.

A sender must know the mail address of the receiver. A mail address is comparable to an object reference in distributed-object models. As such, it is not a physical address but a reference that is translated into a physical address by the actor runtime system. The mail address is assigned by the system when an actor is created, and it is told to the creator at that time. Mail addresses may be communicated, and consequently dynamic process structures can be built up. Input/output is accomplished through mail addresses, too. At the beginning, a few actor addresses are known to the environment for input, and some addresses in the environment are known to

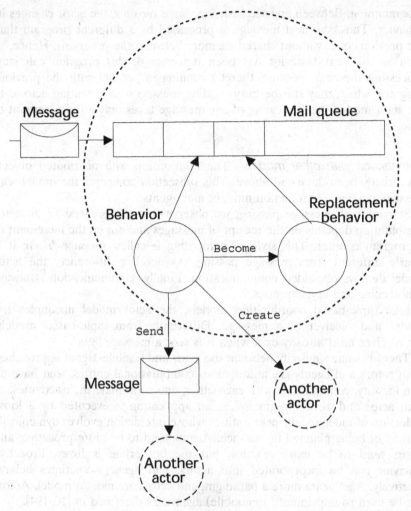

Fig. 9.3 The actor model. Reprinted, by permission, from D. Kafura and J.-P. Briot [243]. © 1998 IEEE.

the actor system for output. The addresses may be communicated and new addresses be added dynamically as well.

The actor model supports parallelism in two forms: *Inter-actor* parallelism is exhibited by different actors that run in parallel on the same or on different nodes of a distributed system. *Intra-actor* parallelism is exhibited by multiple threads of control that run in parallel within a single actor. In object-oriented programming, intraobject parallelism is difficult to achieve, since, as in shared-memory programming, concurrent accesses to the state must be synchronized [340]. The (theoretical) actor model circumvents this problem in a peculiar way that reflects the origin of the model in functional programming: Between any successive message receipts, the actor changes its behavior. Thus, the next message is processed by a different program than the previous one, without shared memory between the programs. Hence, as soon as the next behavior has been determined, this program can start processing the next message, thereby running in parallel with the previous program, which may still be busy sending messages and creating actors. In the actor model, the processing of any message takes only a finite amount of time.

Comparison with other models The relationship with distributed objects has already been discussed above. This subsection compares the model with message passing, coordination models, and agents.

Starting with message passing, we observe that the progress of an actor computation depends on the receipt of messages and not on the increment of a program counter. This style of computing is called *message-driven*; it is clearly different from message passing. As another difference, the actor model deploys one-sided communication. Finally, communication is always nonblocking and asynchronous.

Like tuple-based coordination models, the actor model uncouples the sender and receiver of a message. Differently from tuple-based models, the receiver must already exist when it is sent a message [89].

There is some similarity between the actor and (mobile-)agent approaches. Both actors and agents are autonomous computational entities that have an own identity, communicate with each other, and coordinate their activities. In both actor and agent programming, an application is executed by a loose collection of independent peer entities whose interaction evolves dynamically instead of being planned in advance. Agents tend to be more proactive, and actors tend to be more reactive, but the borderline is fuzzy. Proactive behavior can be incorporated into actors, and agents sometimes behave reactively. Agents are more a paradigm, and actors are more a model. Actors can be used to implement (nonmobile) agents, as described in [10, 194].

Assessment of the model The actor model supports parallel, as well as distributed, and mobile computing, although the concrete implementations differ [11]. The model allows for the expression of general forms of task parallelism, since actors can be created and their mail addresses be communicated dynamically. The performance potential of parallelism is exploited through inter-actor and intra-actor parallelism, and also through overlapping communication and computation in asynchronous message exchange. Since multiple actors may run on the same node, another actor can be scheduled to the CPU if an actor is out of messages. The actor model supposes fair scheduling schemes, and thus each actor is guaranteed to obtain the CPU after a finite amount of time. The performance of actor programs can be predicted under some simplifying assumptions, as explained in Agha and Kim [11].

Because of its dynamic features, the actor model supports open architectures in which nodes are added and replaced at run time. Since actors can be compiled independently, the model also supports heterogeneity to a certain degree. Location transparency is achieved through location-independent mail addresses. Since actors are self-contained, code mobility and replication are supported as well.

The actor model is a good fit for applications that are naturally described as a system of independent interacting entities. Unfortunately, actor programming is low-level because the programmer has to think in terms of the individual actors and messages. Moreover, the restriction to asynchronous message exchange complicates programming in cases in which the receiver needs a response. Therefore, higher-level extensions have been suggested, for instance synchronous message transfer and data-parallel constructs [8].

Extensions and implementations of the model   The actor model has been suggested in a theoretical context and is supported by a large body of theoretical work. In addition to serving as a programming model, it is used for describing and reasoning about distributed systems. Proposed early, the actor model has substantially influenced the development of concurrent object-oriented languages, many of which follow the model more or less closely.

The proposed actor languages extend the original model chiefly by a variety of higher-level constructs. An example is synchronization constraints, which specify a set of object states under which a particular method may be invoked by a message [8]. Another example is the ActorSpace model [82], in which actors (or groups of actors) are selected through pattern matching instead of through low-level mail addresses. In yet another extension [427], the actors are hierarchically organized into groups and each group is represented by a director.

The actor model is not only implemented in new languages, but also in libraries that can be called from existing languages. An example is the recent Actor Foundry proposal [2], a class library for Java. In Actor Foundry, a program is a collection of user-defined actor classes that are derived through inheritance from a particular library class called *actor*. Actor objects are instantiated from the user-defined classes, that is, those classes describe possible behaviors. At program start, some actors are started explicitly. Later, new actors are created by other actors. In communications, the sender includes the name of the method that it wants to be executed, and the parameters of that method. Actor Foundry provides explicit support for both synchronous and asynchronous communication. The actors can use service offerings such as traders to locate an actor with a desired behavior. Also, they can request their own migration. Actors and ordinary Java objects can be mixed in applications. Actor Foundry was developed in a university research project and is available in the public domain.

9.3 MORE ON THIS TOPIC

Both within and outside the actor approach, a huge number of concurrent object-oriented languages have been proposed. Most of the languages are experimental; only a few languages have been used in real applications so far. A comprehensive survey is given by Philippsen [340], who overviews a total of 111 languages. Another survey is given by Briot et al. [71], who distinguish between the library, integrative, and reflective approaches. Roughly speaking, the library approach corresponds to the models that we have treated in previous chapters, and the integrative approach subsumes active objects and distributed objects.

The reflective approach has not been covered so far. Its basic idea is a separation between the actual functionality of an application and parallelism/distribution management. Therefore the approach makes use of metaobjects in which the programmer describes strategies for scheduling, buffering, migration, etc. [71].

Although a detailed survey of concurrent object-oriented languages is out of our scope, some additional classification criteria and language features are mentioned in the following. Further information can be found in [71, 340].

- *Degree of Concurrency*. Languages differ in whether they allow intra-object parallelism.

- *Synchronization Mechanism*. If intraobject parallelism is allowed, then languages differ in their synchronization mechanisms. Many synchronization mechanisms have been adapted from shared-memory programming.

- *Message Selection*. In several languages, object code may express constraints on the set of messages that an object is willing to process. The constraints can be expressed through, for instance, guards.

- *Support for Data Parallelism*. Several languages provide constructs for creating multiple objects at once.

- *Locality*. Several languages provide constructs for the explicit placement and migration of objects. The placement may be described relative to the physical processor arrangement, or to a virtual one. The constructs are less comfortable to handle than the block and cyclic assertions in HPF, but they are able to deal with dynamic process structures. Other languages support transparent migration and replication. An interesting approach is taken by Mentat; here the programmer indicates that certain objects should be placed together on the same node. Many languages do not address the issue of locality at all.

The rest of this section is devoted to object-oriented approaches in high-performance and grid computing.

High-Performance C++   This language combines several parallel and distributed models [170, 216]. It has been developed in a large-scale project that involves several universities, industry, and government laboratories. HPC++ adopts a two-level programming model. The first level deals with shared-memory programming. It provides class libraries for threads programming (similar to Java threads), parallel loops (similar to HPF loops), and collective operations.

The second level addresses distributed-memory architectures: parallel machines, clusters, distributed systems, and grids. Combining the first and second levels, a program can consist of multiple processes each of which is internally multithreaded. HPC++ focuses on SPMD programming, but it is in principle possible to write MPMD programs. At the second level, HPC++ introduces global pointers, through which a program can easily access remote variables of simple types. Furthermore, HPC++ defines an RMI mechanism. To use it, objects must register themselves as being remotely accessible. Processes can be started at the beginning of a program execution, as well as dynamically. Independently started processes can come into contact with each other through a client/server-like mechanism as in MPI-2.

Details of the communication mechanisms depend on the underlying run-time system, which somewhat restricts code portability. Three run-time systems are available, each for a different class of architectures. Heterogeneous systems, for instance, use the already mentioned Globus run-time system (Sect. 8.3). HPC++ can interoperate with Java; interoperability with CORBA and DCOM is planned.

JavaParty   Distributed-object systems are targeted at wide-area networks, and therefore they give the programmer much control over network details such as the handling of transmission errors. In more reliable cluster environments, these opportunities are overkill, and JavaParty [342] has been suggested as a simpler alternative. JavaParty programs look almost identical to Java threads programs, except that some of the objects are marked with the keyword *remote*. These objects are subject to transparent placement and migration by the underlying run-time system.

JavaParty is implemented on top of Java RMI. Before compilation, a preprocessor automatically inserts calls to Java RMI routines that are needed to access the objects marked as *remote*. Since communication, addressing, and networking exceptions are handled transparently, the programmability is much better than that of distributed-object systems. The price is usually a small performance overhead [342]. A major objective of the JavaParty project is the investigation of object placement and migration strategies. By improving the locality, these strategies may speedup programs as compared to the conventional RMI case.

Other high-performance approaches   Phillipsen et al. [341] describe a fast implementation of RMI that is especially useful for fast networks and high-performance computing.

A medium-scale academic project called Common Component Architecture (CCA) investigates the use of components in high-performance computing [26]. The aim of the project is defining a standard that enables interoperability among scientific components. Such a standard would facilitate the reuse of, for instance, simulation and numerical software.

A working group within the OMG [206] considers CORBA extensions for high-performance computing. Several proposals in response to a request for information have been collected [310]. The proposals address, besides other issues, the integration of internally parallel MPI servers into CORBA environments.

Object-oriented grid middleware   Legion [171, 191, 266] is a distributed-object system for metacomputing environments. It can be considered as a "wide-area operating system" and is concerned with the seamless integration of distributed resources. Legion follows the object-oriented approach consistently: Every system component, both software and hardware, is modeled as an object. The objects are described in an IDL and communicate with each other through an asynchronous variant of RMI. Each object is associated with a process that carries out the object methods. Groups of Legion objects are managed by a group-specific programmable class manager, which is responsible for object creation, scheduling, and activation/deactivation. Despite a certain resemblance to CORBA, Legion differs in its focus on resource management and high-performance computing. Legion is relevant for parallel programming, because parallel-programming languages and libraries (HPC++, MPI) can be implemented on top of it, and because parallel programs can be encapsulated within Legion objects. At present, Legion is deployed in a metacomputing testbed that involves several supercomputers.

Other experimental metacomputing systems include Manta [425] and Globe [426]. Manta is a pure Java system and uses a fast implementation of Java RMI. Globe places much emphasis on object replication as a means for performance improvement.

BIBLIOGRAPHICAL REMARKS

General surveys of object-oriented models and languages are provided by Wilson and Lu [442], Briot et al. [71], and Philippsen [340]. Whether object-oriented models should provide transparency is discussed in Guerraoui and Fayad [193], and Waldo et al. [438]. These authors argue that full transparency is impossible to achieve.

CORBA and other distributed object models are described in Orfali and Harkey [321], Orfali et al. [322], and Lewandowski [269]. For the preparation of this chapter, I have additionally used Redlich [356]. The new standard, CORBA 3.0, is outlined in [382]. Further information can be obtained from the home page of the OMG [311]. For a broad survey of actor-based research see Agha and Kim [11].

10

High-Level Programming Models

This chapter describes several models that are the subject of research. Although most of them are not yet widely used at present, their importance may grow. All models treated in this chapter operate at a high level of abstraction, so the programmer is not concerned with architectural details. Furthermore, all of them focus on parallel as opposed to distributed computing. The following models are discussed: automatic parallelization, skeletons, compositional models, functional programming models, and logic programming models.

10.1 AUTOMATIC PARALLELIZATION

Dealing with parallelism introduces a certain programming overhead, no matter which particular model is used. From a programmer's perspective, it would be desirable to commit all parallelization responsibilities (identification of parallel tasks, data distribution, task scheduling, etc.) to tools. Especially when parallelism is not part of the application, such tools would free the programmer from dealing with implementation details, and allow him or her to concentrate on the application at hand.

The good news is that such tools exist, in the form of *parallelizing compilers*; the bad news is that their performance and range of applicability are still far from satisfactory. A parallelizing compiler starts from a sequential program and transforms it into a parallel one that follows any of the

177

previously treated programming models. The sequential programming language is often Fortran, less frequently C, C++, or Java. The notion of parallelizing compilers is typically associated with imperative languages or object-oriented languages. Automatic parallelization is also investigated in functional programming; we come back to this topic in Sect. 10.4. Parallelizing compiler design faces fundamental problems:

- Devising an efficient parallel algorithm for a given problem is challenging even for a human algorithm designer. Parallel algorithms differ significantly from their sequential counterparts. Since they require novel ideas and innovative approaches, parallel algorithms are still being developed within research projects, and it appears unlikely that this activity can be automatized within the foreseeable future.

- Unlike programmers, parallelizing compilers do not start from a high-level description of the problem, but from a sequential solution in which information about the problem is intermixed with details of the sequential execution. Bernstein's theorem ([45], as cited in [220]) states that it is in general undecidable whether two operations of an imperative sequential program can be executed in parallel.

- Parallelizing compilers do not know the values of the input parameters. A human programmer, in contrast, can often estimate the parameters, because he or she knows the application.

- There are several intractable (NP) problems (see Sect. 1.3).

Despite these problems, several parallelizing compilers exist. Their objectives are, however, more modest: Existing compilers do not try to replace the whole algorithm, nor do they try to achieve optimum performance. Instead, they are based on a bunch of useful techniques and try to apply these techniques wherever possible. Depending on the particular program, this approach can lead to optimal performance, achieve no improvement at all, or end up with any intermediate result.

At present, parallelizing compilers work comparatively well for regular applications, but they handle only a few patterns of irregularity. The focus of research has been on loop restructuring, that is, on exploiting data parallelism by transforming sequential *for* loops into parallel loops. In summary, we define the model as follows:

> Automatic parallelization transforms an imperative sequential input program into a parallel program automatically. At present, chiefly data parallelism is exploited. It is introduced by restructuring and parallelizing the sequential loops.

Techniques   Some loops can be trivially parallelized because the loop iterations operate on disjoint data, as in the following example:

for $i = 0$ *to N do*   *for* $i = 0$ *to N do parallel*

    A[i] = 2*B[i] + 3 ; $\longrightarrow$ A[i] = 2*B[i] + 3 ;

end   *end*

Other loops can not be parallelized so easily. The next program computes in A[i] the sum of the original values A[0],...,A[i]:

for $i = 0$ *to N do*

    A[i] = A[i] + A[i-1]

    end

If the loop were parallelized as in the previous example, then A[i] would be set to A[i]+A[i-1], or even to an indefinite value if lockstep synchronization is not available. In other words, a parallel execution would change the semantics of the program and is therefore not permitted. In general, a transformation should only be applied to a program if

1. The semantics of the program is not changed, and

2. The transformed program has better performance than the original one.

Let us now look at these requirements in more detail. For the first requirement, the compiler must check whether the transformation violates *data dependences*. A data dependence occurs if one loop iteration writes a variable and a later iteration reads the variable, as in the example above. A data dependence also occurs if the first access is a read and the second a write, or if both accesses are writes. (The precise definition of data dependences is slightly different, but let us stay with this simple view here.) If there is a data dependence, then the order of the corresponding accesses must not be changed. Therefore, the loops can not be parallelized, except if the compiler inserts additional communications, or applies other restructurings treated below.

Detecting data dependences is a major concern of parallelizing compilers. For loops over arrays, a compiler must check whether two index expressions may evaluate to the same value. For instance, A[2*i+11] in iteration 1 accesses the same array element as A[5*i-2] in iteration 3, namely A[13]. The problem has been shown to be NP-complete, even in the simple case that the index expressions are linear functions in the index variables of the surrounding loops. The problem is, in practice, even harder if the index expressions contain function calls or indirect accesses, or if the program uses pointers. Therefore, the compiler often cannot determine with certainty whether a data dependence exists. To guarantee correctness, it must conservatively assume that there is one, and thus wastes parallelism potential. Dependence analysis is an ongoing research topic.

The second requirement, that the transformed program have better performance, is a research issue, too. Even if parallelism can be identified in a program, it is not always useful to exploit it. Indeed, the overhead for creating the parallel tasks may outweigh the advantages of parallelism. Moreover, a transformation that improves the parallelism may degrade the locality, and may thus slow down the program. Yet more tradeoffs exist. In general, whether or not a transformation is useful depends on the input parameters, as well as on details of the architecture. It is thus difficult to anticipate whether the transformation is profitable.

An example of a transformation technique is *loop distribution*. It replaces a single multistatement loop by multiple single-statement loops, as in the following example:

for i = 0 to N do

   `A[i] = 2*B[i]+3;`

   `A[i] = A[i]+A[i-1];`

end

$\longrightarrow$

for i = 0 to N do

   `A[i] = 2*B[i]+3;`

end;

for i = 0 to N do

   `A[i] = A[i]+A[i-1];`

end

The transformation is semantics-preserving in the example, even though this may not be obvious on first view. Due to the dependence in the second statement, the loop on the left side cannot be parallelized. The first loop on the right side, in contrast, can.

The second loop on the right side cannot be parallelized either, at least not in the usual way. Fortunately, its structure corresponds to a pattern called *scan*, which frequently occurs in scientific computing. A scan determines for each i the sum (or other function) of `A[0],...,A[i]` and can be parallelized as sketched in Fig. 10.1. Since the parallel implementation reorders the operations, numerical phenomena may modify the overall result. Several parallelizing compilers are able to recognize and replace frequent patterns such as the scan. Usually the user can indicate whether operation reordering is permitted.

Going back to standard transformations, loop distribution is only one out of many techniques. Other program restructuring techniques include data privatization and loop permutation. The techniques are described in the

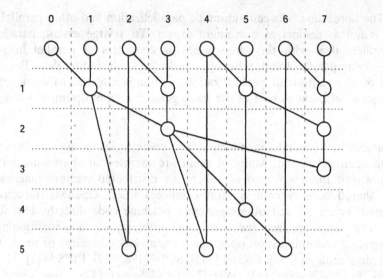

Fig. 10.1 Parallel implementation of a scan. The circles in the top row represent input data A[0],...,A[7]. The remaining circles stand for intermediate results obtained by adding the marked data. In the example, five parallel steps are needed instead of seven sequential ones. Although here this improvement is minor if observable at all, the transformation is useful for large arrays.

compiler literature; see the references section. Although many useful techniques have been devised, it is not yet fully understood how to combine them. Since a transformation can enable or prevent other transformations, the immediate performance improvement is only a vague indicator of a transformation's usefulness. Whereas the interplay between transformations has been understood for classes of transformations [443], it is still tackled with heuristics in the general case.

Assessment of the model Parallelizing compilers are useful for the parallelization of legacy codes, and also for software projects in which one is not willing to spend much time in program development. In the approach, the tradeoff between programmability and performance clearly favors programmability. Portability is supported as well, because the programmer only needs to recompile (but not to rewrite) the program when moving to another architecture.

Most of the transformation techniques developed to date refer to sequential *for* loops, although, especially during the last years, progress has also been made in compiling *while* loops [268], pointer-based data structures [21, 364], and other forms of irregularity [147, 272, 363], as well as in recognizing and replacing algorithmic patterns [280]. Development in the parallelizing-compiler area is going on, and the number of program constructs that can be handled successfully is growing steadily.

The borderline between automatic parallelization and other parallel models is not as distinct as one might expect. To a large extent, parallelizing compilers deal with the same issues as compilers of parallel languages: identifying parallel loops, scheduling tasks, and distributing data. Because of this overlap, automatic parallelization is often considered as not a separate research field, but as part of the more general area of optimizing compilers.

Realizations Several experimental and commercial parallelizing compilers have been developed. Many of them are targeted at shared-memory machines, but there are also compilers for distributed-memory machines. In the shared-memory case, several compilers insert OpenMP directives or related directives, and others generate machine code directly. Distributed-memory compilers face the additional problems of data partitioning and generating communication operations. Exemplary compilers or related tools include Paradigm [332], Polaris [345], SUIF [196, 412], PIPS [411], MIPSpro [153], FORGExplorer [23], PGF77/PGCC Server [339], and Visual KAP [430].

To improve the quality of the results, several compilers (e.g. CAPtools [84]) allow the user to influence the parallelization process interactively. There are also tools that, unlike a compiler, do not generate code at all, but produce suggestions for the parallelization that a programmer may or may not use (e.g. BERT [46]). Automatic parallelization of Java programs is, for example, considered in Bik and Gannon [51] and Wu and Padua [446].

10.2 SKELETON MODELS

We have seen thus far several patterns or paradigms that are frequently used to express parallelism: divide and conquer, master/slave, data parallelism, scan, etc. Yet more patterns exist that have not been mentioned. The patterns are coded repeatedly in parallel programming, which, altogether, takes a lot of human time. On the other hand, compilers try to recognize patterns in a given program, in order to substitute well-known equivalent implementations.

Taking these two observations together, it seems unreasonable to first let the programmer express a high-level pattern by means of low-level programming constructs, and later let the compiler recognize the pattern in order to devise an efficient implementation. Although this comparison is not fully fair —since compilers recognize local patterns (such as scan), whereas programmers use global patterns (such as data parallelism) as well—it illustrates the principal problem: Expressing well-known high-level patterns with low-level constructs costs programmer time and destroys knowledge that is potentially useful for the compiler.

Skeleton models make frequently used patterns, called *skeletons*, directly available to the programmer, which has several advantages:

- The programming expense is reduced: Since the details of parallel execution are already coded in the skeleton, the programmer only needs to fill in application-specific details.
- Programs become clearer and less error-prone.
- Compilers can exploit the high-level information to devise more efficient implementations.
- Compilers can translate the constructs differently for different architectures, which improves performance portability.

Comparison with other models The aforementioned advantages are not unique to skeleton models; indeed, they are quite the same as those of collective operations and libraries. What distinguishes skeleton models from those approaches is mainly two points:

- In skeleton models, patterns are the sole, or at least chief, constructs for the expression of parallelism.
- Skeletons describe the outer program structure, whereas collective operations and libraries describe individual operations.

It can be argued that data-parallel programming models are a special case of skeleton models, because parallel loops such as *forall* describe patterns into which the programmer fills in details. Skeleton models are more general than parallel loops in that they support both task and data parallelism.

Skeleton models can be considered as coordination models, because skeletons coordinate individual program components. Skeleton models have been put into a separate chapter because their concept of coordination is slightly different. Whereas coordination models separate computation activities from activities of communication, synchronization, and task management, skeleton models separate application-specific details from standard functionality covered by the skeleton. Skeleton functionalities cover the typical coordination tasks, and they may also cover sequential computation. Skeleton models are in general less flexible than coordination models, because they rely on a limited set of patterns. Unlike coordination models, skeleton models emphasize the reuse of coordination code.

In their focus on the outer program structure, skeleton models are related to higher-level models of object-oriented programming, particularly to design patterns. A distinction can be seen in that skeletons describe more elementary and general-purpose patterns, and focus on an efficient implementation.

More detailed description   In the following, we refer to the programming model of the Pisa Parallel Programming Language P3L [334], one of the most advanced skeleton languages. Other skeleton languages are surveyed below.

In P3L, skeletons are the sole language constructs for the expression of parallelism. Skeletons may be *nested*. The approach is therefore reminiscent of structured sequential programming, in which programs are built by nesting constructs such as *if* and *while*. Because of this similarity, nested skeleton models are often called as *structured parallel models*. P3L defines seven skeletons:

- *farm*—a master/slave-like pattern,
- *pipe*—a pipeline as described in Sect. 3.2,
- *reduce*—a reduction,
- *map*—a simple data-parallel pattern (see below),
- *comp*—a composed data-parallel pattern (see below),
- *sequ*—encapsulates sequential code, and
- *loop*—iteratively executes other skeletons.

The *map* construct partitions a set of input data into subsets, applies an operation to each subset independently, and collects the results. The *comp* construct does the same, but additionally splits the computation step into stages with communication in between the stages.

The programmer expresses an algorithm with the help of the skeletons. To be more precise, he or she describes the outer program structure with skeletons, and the details with C. In the example of *map*, the details include the operation to be executed on the subsets, and functions that describe the initial data distribution and the combination of results.

Skeleton programs are translated by a special compiler that replaces the skeleton constructs by appropriate implementations. In the case of P3L, the compiler generates C code with calls to the MPI library. To summarize the skeleton concept:

> Skeleton models provide programming constructs that directly correspond to frequent patterns of parallel execution. The programmer expresses the algorithm in terms of these patterns, and the compiler supplements the details of parallel execution.

Assessment of the model   The skeleton model has similar pros and cons to those of collective operations and libraries. Where applicable, it is an elegant approach, characterized by good programmability, performance, and performance portability. Moreover, performance prediction is comparatively easy.

On the other side, the model is only as good as its language realizations, and, despite much progress, these are not yet mature.

Skeleton languages must overcome significant problems. First of all, they must choose a set of skeletons that are both expressive and easy to implement. Expressive means that it should be easy to formulate algorithms with the skeletons, and that such a formulation should be feasible for many, if not for all, algorithmic problems. Easy to implement means that efficient implementations should exist for a variety of architectures.

The performance advantage of skeletons over other parallel models is partially due to restricting the communication structure of programs. Since skeletons can express certain patterns only, task scheduling and data distribution are simplified. Moreover, skeleton implementations need not be developed anew for each program, but can be reused. Therefore it is worthwhile to put much (human) time into the performance tuning of skeleton implementations. For any skeleton, multiple implementations may exist that are appropriate for different parameters of the machine and program.

Skeleton nesting improves expressiveness. On the other hand, it raises the question as to how the skeleton implementations can be combined. The implementation of an unnested *pipe*, for instance, will typically employ all processors available. If part of the stages is internally data-parallel, however, then it may be profitable to map multiple stages to the same processor, and use the remaining processors in a data-parallel way. It may even be profitable to sequentialize the pipe altogether and rely on data parallelism only. The decision may depend on the particular machine, as well as on parameters of the algorithm such as the amount of computation in the individual stages.

The skeleton model is targeted at applications with a predictable communication structure. It does not support dynamic patterns such as clients that discover their server at run time, or occasional and unpredictable communication between otherwise unrelated tasks. The model relies on optimizing compilers (or other tools) that select and compose skeleton implementations on the basis of performance predictions. Only if the program parameters can be estimated at compile time is an accurate performance prediction possible. The model is typically used in parallel computing, but below we will also see an example from the distributed domain.

Realizations Skeleton models have thus far been developed and implemented in a number of research projects. The various proposals differ, for instance, in the set of skeletons, the sequential programming language, and the user interface. In particular the following projects have been conducted:

- Cole [115] originally introduced the concept of skeletons. He proposed four skeletons and did not allow for skeleton nesting.

- The Structured Coordination Language (SCL) [126] defines a large number of skeletons, many of which deal with data distribution and redistribution.

- The Higher-order Divide-and-Conquer language (HDC) [202] focuses on divide-and-conquer algorithms and uses Haskell as the base language.

- The archetypes project [283, 284] considers patterns as an aid to help programmers develop algorithms. Both general-purpose skeletons and skeletons for specific application classes are being developed.

- The Skeleton-based Integrated Environment (SkIE) [31] is the commercial analog of P3L. It supports the Fortran, C, C++, and Java base languages, and is interoperable with HPF and MPI.

Many projects use imperative base languages such as C, but describe the skeletons in functional languages. Functional languages are a good fit because skeletons correspond to higher-order functions. Bacci et al. [31] describe a graphical user interface for SkIE in which the skeletons are depicted graphically and the programmer builds a program by composing the skeletons on the screen.

To efficiently implement nested skeletons, it is useful to not only select and compose skeleton implementations, but first transform the program. For instance, it may be profitable to transform a *farm* of *pipe*s into a *pipe* of *farm*s, or vice versa. The transformations are usually applied semiautomatically, and are directed by performance predictions. The development of transformation rules is an area of ongoing research [182].

Although P3L and other implementations focus on static environments, in which the parallel execution can be planned in detail by the compiler, the skeleton model is not restricted to this case. Kuang et al. [257] describe a system in which the skeletons are translated into mobile code that runs on a cluster with a varying number of nodes. In this dynamic environment, accurate performance prediction is not possible. Apart from that, the approach has similar pros and cons to the more traditional parallel skeleton models.

10.3 COMPOSITIONAL MODELS

Closely related to the coordination and skeleton models, this group of models represents more a different viewpoint than a distinct approach. Foster [155] describes the concept as follows:

> A programming model is called *compositional* if the "properties of program components are preserved when those components are composed in parallel with other program components".

In particular, correctness-related properties such as determinism are referred to here. Compositionality ensures that the correctness of the whole program can be derived from assertions about the program modules and the composition construct; it is not necessary to take the module implementations into account.

Compositionality facilitates a modular program design, and is therefore advantageous from a software engineering point of view. Moreover, and this aspect is emphasized in many projects, compositionality facilitates the integration of modules that were written with different programming models.

Compositional models resemble coordination models insofar as both impose a strict separation between 1) subfunctionalities that are realized by program modules and 2) the interaction between these modules. Whereas coordination models separate computation activities from coordination activities, compositional models separate elementary functionalities from management functionalities. Since elementary functionalities may correspond to computation activities, and management functionalities may correspond to coordination activities, the borderline between the approaches is blurry. Nevertheless the models differ in that compositional models do not require the modules to be sequential. Instead, they focus on a hierarchical program structure in which lower-level modules encapsulate parallelism too.

Compositional models are related to skeleton models insofar as both build up programs hierarchically, and both eliminate interference between the functionality of a composition construct (skeleton) and the functionality of the inner code. Compositional models differ from skeleton models in that they deploy elementary instead of algorithmic patterns for the composition.

A consequence of the similarity between the compositional and coordination concepts is the use of similar coordination constructs. The IWIM model covered in Sect. 8.2, for instance, uses the same constructs for coordinating sequential computations at the bottom layer as for composing parallel subprograms at higher layers of the program hierarchy. Therefore, it can be classified as both a coordination and a compositional model.

The various compositional models have widely differing characteristics. In the following, we outline three typical proposals: PCN, Opus, and TwoL. References to other proposals are given thereafter.

PCN   The Program Composition Notation (PCN) [100, 159] is an early task-parallel language in which programs are hierarchically composed of modules. At the bottom layer, the modules comprise sequential C or Fortran code, and at higher layers, the modules are composed and coordinated with the help of PCN constructs. For composition, three constructs are provided:

- *Sequential Composition.* The modules are carried out one after another.

- *Parallel Composition.* The modules are carried out in parallel.

- *Alternative Composition.* The modules are prefaced with a guard, and one module with a true guard is executed, as in the CSP model.

PCN is targeted at coarse-grained tasks and provides constructs through which the tasks can interact *during* their execution. To preserve compositionality, the interaction constructs are designed so that they prevent race conditions. The major construct is called the *single-assignment variable*. Such a variable can get assigned a value only once during its lifetime. The variable is initially undefined, and is defined when a process assigns a value. Thereafter the value can be read by any other process, but it can not be overwritten. If a process accesses the variable before it was defined, that process blocks. Other interaction constructs are generalizations of single-assignment variables. In particular, PCN provides a queue construct in which a reader blocks until there is at least one value in the queue. Furthermore it supports arrays of single-assignment variables that are distributed across the processors.

PCN enables the reuse of composition code, but—unlike skeletons—this code is application-specific and not part of the PCN system. In addition to the parallel structure, a PCN programmer specifies the mapping of processes to a virtual processor array. Mapping and parallel structure are specified separately.

Opus Whereas PCN focuses on the convenient expression of task parallelism and the integration of sequential modules into a parallel program, Opus [102] combines task and data parallelism. To be more precise, Opus permits data-parallel modules written in HPF to cooperate in a task-parallel manner.

The concrete mechanism is reminiscent of object-based DSM systems: Modules coordinate their activities by invoking methods of coordination objects called *shared abstractions* (SDAs). Each SDA encapsulates shared data and methods for accessing the data. To guarantee exclusive access, only one method per SDA may be invoked at a time. SDAs are used for both communication and synchronization. The data structures encapsulated within an SDA can be distributed.

Object orientation is a key characteristic of Opus. Objects are not only used for coordination, but they also wrap the data-parallel modules. Computation is driven by mutual method calls, and objects can be created dynamically.

Opus is targeted at heterogeneous environments, and focuses on the integration of coarse-grained data-parallel modules from various application areas. Since method invocation is slower than message passing, the performance is not sufficient for fine-grained task-parallel applications [37].

TwoL   Like Opus, the two-level parallelism model TwoL [151, 355] supports programs in which the outer structure is task-parallel and the inner structure is data-parallel. In many other respects, the models are different. TwoL has been suggested together with a two-step program development method: In the first step, the programmer specifies all parallelism that can be identified in an application. In the second step, an interactive tool decides which parallelism potential is to be exploited, and chooses task scheduling and data distribution. The so-obtained program version is then automatically converted into a C program with calls to the MPI library.

TwoL is classified as compositional because programs are built up hierarchically from independent modules. At the bottom layer, the modules are data-parallel; above, they are composed with task-parallel constructs. The constructs comprise parallel composition, sequential (or pipelined) composition, and various loops. The modules have clear interfaces, which are defined by their input and output parameters. Except for pipelining, communication only takes place at the beginning and end of a module execution, but not in between.

TwoL is targeted at numerical computing. Like skeletons, the model supposes a predictable program structure that can be expressed in the model. For this class of programs, the model combines performance, performance portability, and programmability. Performance portability is supported in that the specification can be reused for different architectures. Programmability is supported in that the programmer describes the algorithm in a high-level specification language and is not concerned with task scheduling and other execution details. A high-level specification language is also provided for the data-parallel modules.

Other models   Compositional models have been suggested for various architectures and classes of applications. To mention a few further examples, Brandes [68] describes a library for message passing between HPF tasks, and Chandy and Rifkin [99] study the composition of objects in Internet applications. Skillicorn [389] extends the concept of compositionality to costs, and suggests a model in which skeleton programs are building blocks for the composition of larger programs.

10.4   FUNCTIONAL PROGRAMMING MODELS

Functional programming is a long-standing research direction of computer science, not specifically tied to parallel computing. Whereas conventional imperative languages describe a program as a sequence of actions, functional languages describe a program as a nest of functions. Functional languages do not know the concept of variables; instead they use identifiers to which a value is assigned once and for all, as to the single-assignment variables of PCN. Each function maps inputs to outputs, and has no other effects. In particular, it cannot modify global identifiers. This property is called side-effect freedom; it ensures compositionality and is thus useful for a modular program design and the verification of correctness.

The input and output parameters of a function may be conventional data —integers, reals, lists, etc.—but they may also be functions themselves. In the latter case, one speaks of higher-order functions; they are permitted in many but not all functional languages.

Functional languages are naturally amenable to a parallel implementation because the programs do not specify the execution order of operations, except that arguments to a function must be evaluated before the function can be applied. Automatic parallelism detection is easy, since the parameters of functions may always be evaluated in parallel. If the parameters are expressions that contain other functions, their parameters may be evaluated in parallel, too, and so on. Thus, automatic parallelization promises to be simpler for functional than for imperative languages, which is a main reason for the research interest in parallel functional programming.

Unfortunately, being able to identify parallel tasks is not sufficient for a gain in performance. Often, too many fine-grained tasks are identified, which introduces a high overhead for process creation. Partially for this reason, parallel functional programming is often researched in the context of shared-memory machines with threads, but even there the overhead is significant. It is thus a challenging problem to identify the *right* parallel tasks, characterized by a reasonable granularity and small communication require-ments. Moreover, task scheduling and data distribution must be accom-plished in a functional setting as well, and the fundamental problems mentioned in Sect. 10.1 have not been overcome either.

For these reasons, the success of functional programming with automatic parallelization was much smaller than originally hoped. The focus of research has thus moved towards languages with explicit support for a parallel execution. The spectrum of such languages is wide and reflects ideas from various models treated in the previous chapters. We will see examples below. First, let us look at basic mechanisms for a parallel implementation.

Implementation Some functional languages are *strict*, while others are not. Strictness means that the output of a function depends on all arguments. If one argument is undefined (or its evaluation does not terminate), then the output of the whole function is undefined, too. An example of a nonstrict language construct is *if–else*, because the undefined argument may be re-ferred to in the branch that is not executed.

The distinction between strict and nonstrict languages is important for a parallel implementation. In strict languages, all arguments of a function are needed and may thus be evaluated prior to invoking the function. In nonstrict languages, not all arguments are needed, and the evaluation of other arguments may slow down the program or even prevent it from terminating.

In both strict and nonstrict languages, a program can be represented by a graph, with inputs in the leaves and intermediate nodes corresponding to function applications. The graph is not a tree, because data may be input to multiple functions. Program execution corresponds to simplifying the graph by stepwise replacement of subgraphs with values. Under certain assumptions, the famous Church–Rosser property ensures that the replacements may be executed in any order, including parallel orders; the overall result is the same.

There are two main strategies for simplifying the graph: top-down, starting from the outermost function; or bottom-up, starting from the arguments. Both approaches have pros and cons. The bottom-up approach tends to expose ample but too fine-grained parallelism, and is moreover unsuited for nonstrict languages. The top-down approach supports nonstrict languages but, as parameters are evaluated by need, is inherently sequential. To exploit parallelism in this approach, one must deploy speculative evaluation, or rely on compiler analysis to identify those parameters that are needed. A frequently used implementation technique is *graph reduction*. Roughly speaking, it combines the top-down approach with a sharing mechanism that avoids the repeated evaluation of common subexpressions.

In both the top-down and bottom-up schemes, the computation is driven by an evaluation strategy. A different approach is taken by *dataflow*. Here the progress of the computation depends on the availability of data, and thus any operation may be executed as soon as all inputs are available. A typical performance problem, again, is excessive fine-grained parallelism. It is tackled by an increased granularity of the operations, called *macro-dataflow*.

Especially in the late 1980s, there was much interest in the development of special-purpose hardware to support the dataflow and graph-reduction models. This research line has been abandoned, because the machines could not compete with the commercial microprocessor designs that are being developed in large-scale and well-funded projects.

Nowadays, parallel functional languages are implemented on standard shared- and distributed-memory parallel machines, with a variety of implementation techniques. To give an example, Chakravarty [94] describes an implementation that exploits both coarse- and fine-grained tasks. Coarse-grained tasks are implemented as processes and run on different processors, whereas fine-grained tasks are implemented as threads and run on the same processor. Threads are useful for latency tolerance.

Functional languages with parallelism constructs   Acknowledging the limits of automatic parallelization, many functional languages contain explicit parallelism constructs. The various languages resolve the tradeoff between programmability and performance differently, and thus there is a whole spectrum of models. A survey is given by Loogen [274], who distinguishes between implicit, controlled, and explicit models.

The implicit class contains, besides automatic parallelization, annotation-based languages and data-parallel languages. An example of a data-parallel language is Sisal, which stands for "streams and iterations in a single assignment language". Sisal is targeted at numerical computing and makes much use of loops and arrays. The language is simple and restrictive from a programmability point of view, but, interestingly, has been shown to be competitive with Fortran in performance [83].

In annotation-based languages, the programmer gives hints for a parallel execution, and the language implementation is free to use or ignore the hints, as with compiler directives. The programmer can, for instance, assert that certain expressions may be evaluated in parallel, or advise that they should be evaluated on a particular processor. Examples of languages in this class include Glasgow parallel Haskell and Concurrent Clean.

In control-based languages, parallelism constructs are not solely hints, but they stipulate how the program is implemented. The constructs are relatively high-level, and there is a clear separation between the core functional program and the parallelism management. An example is para-functional programming, in which the programmer specifies both the parallel tasks and task scheduling.

Finally, the explicit approach exposes to the programmer details of the parallel execution, such as the communication mechanism. The concrete proposals resemble models from previous chapters. For instance, Eden uses a channel-based coordination model, Scampi integrates functional programming with MPI, and D'Caml deploys an RPC-related mechanism [436].

Functional programming has been applied not only to parallel, but also to distributed programming. This stream of work is typically put under the heading of *concurrency*; it is targeted at reactive systems that respond to unpredictable inputs at varying locations. Exemplary languages in this class include Concurrent ML, Erlang, and GOFFIN [95].

In summary, there is not a single model of parallel functional programming, but a variety of proposals that more or less deviate from the original concept. In particular, many models give up or weaken the functional programming ideal that the programmer should not be concerned with implementation details. Several languages even allow for side effects, race conditions, and deadlocks.

Assessment   The pros and cons of parallel functional programming depend on the particular model. Most models place emphasis on programmability and give less consideration to performance. Although the languages are applicable to many areas [418], the functional programming style is unfamiliar to programmers, and algorithms may be hard to formulate if assignment statements are not available. Functional languages place a heavy burden on the run-time system, so decisions concerning the decomposition into parallel tasks and task scheduling are delayed until run time. Functional languages operate on a high level of abstraction, and thus portability is unproblematic.

Because of its conceptual simplicity, functional programming is amenable to formal approaches. Therefore, many research projects in, for instance, program development and verification assume a functional model. In real applications, functional programming is only occasionally used, and it is still open whether the approach will ever enter the mainstream. As Peyton Jones [337] formulates it: "[T]he low-pain/moderate gain tradeoff of parallel functional programming has yet to find an economic niche".

10.5 LOGIC PROGRAMMING MODELS

Like functional programming, logic programming is a stream of computer science that has been developed independently of parallelism. Functional and logic programming are often put under the common heading of declarative programming, since, ideally, the programmer describes *what* is evaluated, but not *how*. While functional languages express a program as a nest of functions, logic languages express a program as a set of logic clauses. In both cases, programs are evaluated by stepwise replacement of syntactic patterns with others until no further replacements are possible.

There are three types of logic clauses: facts, rules, and a goal. Facts and rules together form a database, that is, a collection of mutually conflict-free predicates that are assumed to be true. The goal is a query to the database. Usually the goal contains variables that, during program execution, are bound to concrete values found in the database. Logic programming has a strong theoretical foundation in first-order predicate logic, which provides formal definitions for the concepts. For our purposes, an example should be sufficient:

parent(susan,ben).   (1)

parent(ben,eve).   (2)

ancestor(X,Y):-parent(X,Y).   (3)

ancestor(X,Y):-parent(X,Z), ancestor(Z,Y).   (4)

The program is in Prolog notation, where capitalized words/letters denote variables, and others denote constants. The program expresses the two facts

(1) Susan is a parent of Ben.

(2) Ben is a parent of Eve.

and the two rules

(3) Any X is an ancestor of Y if X is a parent of Y.

(4) Any X is an ancestor of Y if there is a Z such that X is a parent of Z and Z is an ancestor of Y.

The program is started by specifying a goal, say "ancestor(susan, R)". A sequential Prolog implementation evaluates the program from top to bottom and from left to right. At any one time, it has a list of goals and tries to match the goals with entries in the database. If there is no matching entry, then the program terminates with a negative answer. In the example, the list initially consists of the goal "ancestor(susan, R)". Clause (3) matches, binding X to susan and R to Y. Now the right side of clause (3), "parent(susan, Y)", becomes our next goal. Fortunately it matches clause (1), binding Y (and thus R) to ben. Since the goal list has become empty, the program terminates with result R = ben.

The Prolog system can be instructed to look for alternative results. In the example, the initial goal can alternatively be matched with clause (4). This matching binds X to susan and R to Y, and replaces the initial goal by the list of goals "parent(susan, Z), ancestor(Z, Y)". The two goals are evaluated in sequence, binding Z to ben, and Y to eve. Finally the program returns with R = eve.

The example has been simple and thus all proceeded well. In general, the evaluation may run into a dead end in which there is no matching clause for an intermediate goal, even though the original goal may have been solvable. Prolog escapes from dead ends by backtracking, in which it undoes the most recent variable bindings. To give an example, the goal "ancestor(susan, eve)" matches clause (3), binding X to susan and Y to eve. The next goal, "parent(susan, eve)", however, cannot be resolved, so backtracking is deployed. Backtracking releases the bindings of X and Y and goes back to the goal "ancestor(susan, eve)". The goal is now matched with clause (4) and, after a few intermediate steps, succeeds.

Parallelism   There are four sources of parallelism:

- AND parallelism refers to solving multiple goals (from the current list) in parallel. (A goal succeeds if one subgoal *and* the other subgoals succeed.)

- OR parallelism refers to investigating multiple clauses in parallel. (A goal succeeds if one clause *or* another clause succeeds.)

- Search parallelism searches the clause database in parallel.

- Unification parallelism deploys a parallel algorithm to check whether a particular clause matches a particular goal.

The major sources are AND and OR parallelism; the others are not further discussed here. Although parallelism can be detected automatically, standard Prolog programs are not suited for automatic parallelization, since, in violation of the ideal of declarative programming, Prolog programmers take the evaluation order into account when coding a program. Different evaluation orders may lead to different results.

Therefore, special parallel languages have been developed, in which the programmer is aware of the modified evaluation strategy. In many languages, moreover, the programmer controls the parallel execution through explicit constructs. The next subsections describe such constructs and discuss specific problems of AND and OR parallelism.

AND parallelism   This approach raises the problem of how to bind variables that occur in multiple goals. For correctness, each occurrence of the same variable must be bound to the same value, and so communication is needed. In our example, AND parallelism can be used in evaluating the subgoals "parent(X, Z)" and "ancestor(Z, Y)" of clause (4). The example is for illustration purposes only; exploiting the parallelism potential in this particular case is not worthwhile, since 1) the amount of computation is too small to justify the creation of a process for parent(X, Z), and 2) the existence of the shared variable Z forces the second process to wait until the first process has bound the variable.

In general, however, AND parallelism can lead to significant speedups. It is most profitable if the subgoals do not contain shared variables. If they do, then the parallel processes consider the shared variables as communication channels, similar to those in the CSP model. To avoid multiple processes binding the same variable, many languages rely on help from the programmer, who normally knows whether a variable functions as input or output. In the language Concurrent Prolog, for instance, input variables are marked by "?", so that clause (4) is written as

ancestor(X,Y) :-parent(X,Z) , ancestor(Z?,Y) .

If a process tries to bind an input variable such as Z, it is suspended. Nevertheless,the use of shared variables does not sequentialize the execution. In the example, two processes are created immediately and start working in parallel. The second process figures out that the goal "ancestor(Z?,Y)" matches clause (3) and replaces it by "parent(Z?,Y)". Only when it tries to bind Z to susan with clause (1) is its execution suspended until the first process has produced a binding for Z.

Processes can communicate repeatedly, since logical variables may stand for lists. As soon as one entry of the list has been produced, a partner process can consume that entry, and so on.

There are also parallelism constructs for the explicit labeling of sequential and parallel processes. By writing

ancestor(X,Y) :-parent(X,Z) & ancestor(Z?,Y) .

in Parlog, for instance, the programmer requests that the goals "parent(X, Z)" and "ancestor(Z, Y)" be evaluated in sequence. Similar constructs exist for OR parallelism.

OR parallelism This approach only leads to significant speedups if different clauses for the same goal all have a good chance of succeeding. If some of the clauses deal with unlikely exceptional cases, then it would be wasteful to try them out in parallel to promising candidates. With OR parallelism, each clause defines a process; it can be complex due to multiple levels of recursion and backtracking. In the example, OR parallelism exists between clauses (3) and (4)—although, again, its exploitation is not worthwhile.

A frequently deployed variant of OR parallelism is *committed choice*, an adaptation of guards (from the CSP model) to logic programming. Committed-choice languages deploy rules of the form

$$H :- G_1, G_2, \ldots, G_m \mid B_1, B_2, \ldots, B_n.$$

The $G_1, G_2, \ldots, G_m$ are guards; if they evaluate to true, then the rule may be selected for execution. Only one rule for H is selected and the decision, once taken, is never revised. If the need for backtracking arises, then bindings within $B_1, B_2, \ldots, B_n$ may be undone, but bindings within $G_1, G_2, \ldots, G_m$ may not, and neither may alternative rules for H be investigated. The use of committed choice changes the program semantics, since part of the solution space is no longer explored. Parallelism is used by evaluating the guards of different clauses in parallel.

Assessment Parallel logic models are not really competitors of the other models treated in this book, but rather variants of logic programming. In other words, parallel logic models are chiefly targeted at those applications that are traditionally coded in logic languages, such as knowledge-based systems, but not so much at novel applications. A major drawback of logic programming is inefficiency; parallelism reduces but does not eliminate this problem. As usual, the price for higher performance is increased programming expense; the concrete tradeoff depends on the particular model. In parallel logic programming, deadlocks can occur. The languages have been implemented on both shared- and distributed-memory architectures.

Constraint logic programming An important generalization of logic programming, frequently combined with parallelism, is constraint logic programming. Constraint logic rules have the form

$$H :- c_1, \ldots, c_m \Diamond B_1, \ldots, B_n.$$

where H and $B_1, \ldots, B_n$ are defined as usual, and $c_1, \ldots, c_m$ are constraints. A constraint is a relation between data that partially determines their values, for instance $1 < X < Y$. As usual, program execution starts with a goal. In addition to the list of goals, it maintains a set of constraints. A rule is only applied if the new constraints are compatible with the old ones. The result of a program run is either a concrete value as usual, or a set of constraints that collectively describe a range of solutions.

10.6 MORE ON THIS TOPIC

Much research on programming models has been conducted within the theoretical community. Models such as π calculus [297], linear logic [179], Unity [98], and Seuss [300] abstractly capture the most fundamental concepts of computation and communication. They are helping to gain insight into program development, and to prove correctness-related properties of programs. Although the models inspire and influence the design of practical models, the application programmer rarely comes into touch with them directly. Therefore, the theoretical models are not elaborated upon here.

Especially theoretical, but also several practical models advocate a transformational approach to program design. In this approach, the programmer first writes a specification in a high-level notation. Then, he or she refines the specification in a stepwise process, thereby adding more and more detail. The result of the transformation process is a program, which is then translated into executable code by a compiler. The transformation process can be accomplished manually or be supported by tools. In general, the more effort spent in the transformation process, the faster the program runs. Research in transformational approaches addresses issues such as the design of specification languages, automatic support for the transformation process, and techniques for reasoning about the correctness of intermediate steps.

A theoretical foundation for transformational approaches is provided by the Bird–Meertens formalism (BMF) [54, 287]. The application of this theory to parallel programming is discussed in Skillicorn [388], under the heading of *categorical data types*. This approach considers data structures as the central part of a program; the structure of the computation follows the structure of the data. Other transformational approaches are discussed in Gorlatch [181], Kornerup [255], and O'Donnel and Rünger [313].

Integration The various programming models can be integrated with each other. The language Distributed Oz [199], for instance, integrates concepts from object-oriented, functional, and constraint logic programming, as well as mobility. Distributed Oz is targeted at distributed applications; it supports mobile, stationary, and replicable objects.

Gamma The language Gamma (general abstract model for multiset manipulation) [38] is inspired by an analogy between computation and chemical reactions. Like tuple-based coordination models, Gamma centers around a shared medium that holds data objects. A Gamma program consists of a set of rules that resemble chemical reactions. Each rule states that if a set of data with certain properties exists, then these data are replaced by other data. Multiple rules can fire in parallel. To give a simple example, the program

$$\max : x, y \rightarrow y \Leftarrow x \le y$$

determines the maximal element of a nonempty set. The formula says that if there are elements x, y with $x \le y$ then they are replaced by y.

BIBLIOGRAPHICAL REMARKS

Parallelizing compiler techniques are described in a number of textbooks, such as Banerjee [39–41], Kennedy [248], Muchnick [305], and Wolfe [444]. A concise survey is given in Eigenmann and Hoeflinger [140].

The major reference on skeleton models is Pelagatti [334], for another survey see Cole [114]. The compositional approach is described in Foster [155] and Chandy and Taylor [100]. Compositional models that combine task and data parallelism are surveyed in Bal and Haines [37].

For a comprehensive and up-to-date treatment of parallel functional programming see Hammond and Michaelson [197]. In particular, Ch. 3 of that book [274] surveys a large number of languages. The discussion of parallel logic programming in Sect. 10.5 above is based on Vlahavas et al. [433] and Talia [406].

11

Abstract Models

So far, we have considered a variety of programming models for parallel and distributed computing. This chapter is devoted to a different topic. Abstract models, also called computational models, are high-level machine descriptions that are referred to in algorithm design. Whereas the goal in designing programming models is finding constructs that are both useful for the coding of applications and efficient to implement, the goal in designing abstract models is describing classes of architectures in simple but realistic terms. To state it in more detail, abstract model design has the following goals:

- *Reflectivity.* An abstract model should reflect the essential features of the architectures that it describes. A feature is *essential* if its consideration has a significant influence on the performance or other properties of algorithms.

- *Cost Model.* An abstract model should quantify the costs of computation, communication, and synchronization. Since abstract models are primarily used in algorithm design, the cost model plays a more import role for them than it does for programming models.

- *Portability.* The same abstract model should be reflective of a large class of architectures, including future architectures.

- *Simplicity.* The model itself should have a simple definition, so it can be handled easily by the algorithm designer. In particular, the number of parameters should be small.

Regarding the design of a cost model, Skillicorn [389] formulates the following requirements:

- *Accuracy*. The cost estimates should be close to the real costs.

- *Simplicity*. The cost model should depend on only a few parameters of program and architecture.

- *Monotonicity in the Architectural Parameters*. When the architecture is improved, the predicted costs should decrease.

- *Convexity in the Program Parameters*. When the costs of a part of the program decrease, the costs of the whole program should decrease as well.

A cost model's degree of accuracy depends on application characteristics. For programs with a predictable communication structure, accurate cost prediction is feasible. For programs with a dynamic structure, however, only statistical estimates can be used, and the accuracy of the predictions is consequently lower.

As discussed in Ch. 1, the design of abstract models has not yet been an issue in sequential programming, because the von Neumann model was established early and provided a stable architectural basis. Its abstract-model analog, the random access machine (RAM), has been widely accepted among algorithm designers.

In parallel programming, in contrast, there has been much controversy as to which architectural features should be represented in a model, even more as parallel architectures have differed widely. Another problem is the smaller running time of parallel algorithms, due to which constant factors (for instance the memory access costs) have a larger influence. Although the debate is going on, a small number of models have become established now, and are used widely in algorithm design. This chapter focuses on these models, but also mentions many less well-known proposals.

Algorithm design cannot really be separated from programming, and thus abstract models cannot really be separated from programming models. Abstract models are situated at a slightly lower level in the model hierarchy than programming models. Ideally, each programming model corresponds to an abstract model such that algorithms are designed and analyzed in the abstract model and coded in the programming model. The programming model provides more convenient programming constructs which, ideally, can be efficiently compiled into or interpreted in the abstract model. Such a correspondence between programming models and abstract models is useful, since it makes (theoretical) algorithm design results directly applicable to practical programming. Unfortunately, it is realized in only a few cases, whereas the majority of programming models have been developed independently of abstract models. In the few cases, abstract models have been taken as a basis for the development of programming models. We will treat the major approaches in this chapter.

As discussed in Ch. 1, an abstract model is not only useful for algorithm design, but it can also serve as a bridging model that programming-language designers assume and architecture designers strive to support. This aspect has played an important role in the design of many abstract models. Thus the models do not simply describe existing architectures, but moreover prescribe how architectures should be built. In other words, the abstract models identify properties that are desirable from a programming point of view, and at the same time realizable in architectures.

The following models are discussed in this chapter: network models, the parallel random-access machine (PRAM), the bulk-synchronous parallel computer (BSP), LogP, QSM, locality-centric models, graph-based models, and many less well-known proposals. The majority of these models are targeted at parallel as opposed to distributed computing, because algorithm design focuses on single-application performance. An exception is given in Sect. 11.1.

The chapter makes use of the so-called big-O notation, which is defined as follows:

- $f(n) = O(g(n))$ if $f(n) \leq cg(n)$ for some $c, n_0 \geq 0$ and all $n \geq n_0$.
- $f(n) = \Omega(g(n))$ if $f(n) \geq cg(n)$ for some $c, n_0 \geq 0$ and all $n \geq n_0$.
- $f(n) = \Theta(g(n))$ if $f(n) = O(g(n))$ and $f(n) = \Omega(g(n))$.

Thus, the big-O notation describes asymptotic behavior that becomes effective for large values of n. Small constant factors, typically in the order of $c = 2$ or $c = 5$, are ignored for simplicity. In the notation, "O" denotes an upper bound, "Ω" denotes a lower bound, and"Θ" denotes a tight bound. Further information and discussion can be found in any algorithm textbook, for instance in Cormen et al. [118].

11.1 NETWORK MODELS

This section discusses models in which low-level features of the architecture, for instance the topology of the interconnection network and the fact of insecure message transmission, are exposed to the algorithm designer. We discuss three groups of models: traditional parallel network models, network models for special-purpose computing, and distributed network models.

Traditional parallel network models This group of models focuses on the interconnection topology, and describes each parallel architecture as a graph. Nodes correspond to processors or memory modules, and arcs correspond to

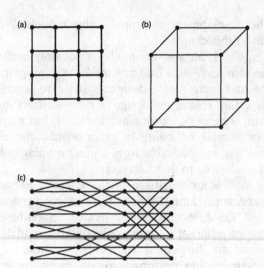

Fig. 11.1   Network topologies: (a) mesh, (b) hypercube, (c) butterfly.

physical connections. Most models assume synchronous operation, that is, the machine carries out a sequence of discrete steps. What exactly can be done in a step depends on the particular model; several variants are in use. For instance, each node may be allowed to receive one input along each of the incoming arcs, carry out an arbitrarily complex computation, and send one output along each of the outgoing arcs. A data transfer between neighbors in the graph takes one step, whereas a data transfer between nonneighbors takes as many steps as there are intermediate nodes.

A key characteristic of any particular network model is the structure of the graph. Frequently used topologies include the mesh, the hypercube, and the butterfly. These models are depicted in Fig. 11.1. The figure shows network instances of a small size. For general definitions and a survey of other topologies, see Leighton [267].

Network models can be direct or indirect. In the former case, each node accommodates computing, storage, and routing functionalities. In the latter case, some of the nodes are sole switches. They do not hold inputs or outputs, and have limited computing and storage facilities. Meshes and hypercubes are typically direct, and butterflies are indirect. Butterflies are used in shared-memory UMA architectures, where the left-column nodes correspond to processors, the right-column nodes correspond to memory modules, and the intermediate nodes correspond to switches.

Network models are parameterized by the number of nodes. Therefore, algorithms are designed and analyzed with respect to two parameters: the number P of processors (nodes), and the input size N. An algorithmic problem is specified by giving the function to be evaluated and the distribution of inputs/outputs to nodes. The execution costs are measured as the number of steps.

Traditional network models were frequently used during the early days of parallel computing. Now they have almost disappeared, for the following reasons:

- The models are based on a store-and-forward routing scheme that moves packets as a whole from node to node. In contrast, many modern architectures deploy wormhole routing (Sect. 2.5) or related schemes. In these schemes, the latency of a message transfer depends much less on the distance in the network. Therefore, traditional network models are no longer sufficiently reflective.

- Network models expose architectural details to the algorithm designer, and are thus difficult to use. Since the algorithm designer must think in terms of individual nodes and communication links, he or she is distracted from the algorithmic problem.

- Lacking portability is a serious drawback. Since algorithms are designed for a particular topology such as the hypercube, they are unlikely to run efficiently on another, for instance on a mesh. The problem is somewhat reduced by the existence of embeddings, which are mappings of one network to another that assign nodes to nodes and arcs to paths. Embeddings have been investigated extensively in research [267].

Network models are appropriate, if at all, for the design of elementary algorithms such as routing, sorting, and broadcast. These algorithms are frequently used, and are usually implemented in libraries. Therefore, it is worthwhile to devise machine-specific and highly optimized implementations.

Another application of network models is studying architectural designs. Architectures are good if algorithms can be implemented efficiently in them. By designing several algorithms on the models, it was, for instance, found that the hypercube performs better than the mesh. In particular, sorting P numbers on a P-processor mesh takes time $O(\sqrt{P})$, where assorting P numbers on a P-processor hypercube takes time $O(\log P)$. Unfortunately, large hypercubes are hard to build, since any embedding of the hypercube structure into a planar circuit leads to long wires.

Network models for special-purpose computing In special-purpose computing, the use of network models is continuing. In this area, lacking portability is unproblematic, because there is a tight binding between hardware and software. Nevertheless the drawback that the models are low-level remains.

A major research topic is reconfigurable architectures. Whereas traditional interconnection networks are fixed, nodes of reconfigurable architectures may dynamically change their set of neighbors. A typical architecture is the reconfigurable mesh. As depicted in Fig. 11.2, each node has four ports and can connect these ports pairwise as coded in a program. Through the

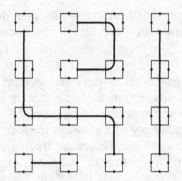

Fig. 11.2 A reconfigurable mesh.

connections, buses of any length and shape can be formed. On reconfigurable architectures, algorithms are executed in steps; each step consists of two phases: 1) All processors connect their ports, thereby forming new buses. 2) The processors communicate along the buses and carry out computations. Any communication along a bus takes a constant (or other small amount of) time, regardless of the network distance.

Another stream of research deals with optical architectures. A major objective is investigating design alternatives for this novel approach.

Distributed network models In distributed computing, algorithm design takes low-level restrictions into account, for instance the absence of a global clock, the possibility of transmission errors, and the local view of processors (processors know their immediate neighbors only, not the overall topology of the network). In particular the following differences between parallel and distributed algorithm design can be observed:

- Distributed algorithm design focuses on unpredictable, and parallel algorithm design on predictable, computations.

- Distributed algorithm design considers networks of arbitrary topology, and parallel algorithm design assumes a homogeneous and regularly structured network.

- Distributed algorithm design considers independent activities that go on at the same time, and parallel algorithm design concentrates on a single application.

- Distributed algorithm design places more emphasis on correctness, and parallel algorithm design on performance.

Like their parallel counterparts, distributed network models describe each architecture as a graph, with processors and memory modules in the nodes, and arcs corresponding to physical connections. The graph may have an arbitrary topology that need not to be known in advance. Several distributed network models assume a synchronous mode of execution, while many others allow for asynchrony. Typical distributed algorithms include: deadlock detection, the provision of logical time, the establishment of a broadcast tree in the network, and leader election (the election of a leader among a set of initially equal processors). These problems are elementary; the application programmer can in most cases rely on libraries to provide the corresponding functionalities.

11.2 PARALLEL RANDOM-ACCESS MACHINE

By far the most popular model in parallel algorithm design is the parallel random access machine (PRAM), introduced in 1978 by Fortune and Wyllie [154].

As illustrated in Fig. 11.3, a PRAM consists of P processors that have access to a global shared memory. Additionally, each processor owns a small amount of local memory for registers and code. The PRAM is a synchronous MIMD model. Each processor is allowed to run a different program, although in practice most PRAM algorithms are SPMD. A PRAM computation is a sequence of steps that are separated by implicit synchronizations of all processors. In a step, each processor may carry out one of the following operations:

- Read one datum from the shared memory into its local memory,

- Write one datum from its local memory into the shared memory, or

- Perform an elementary computation on operands in its local memory.

The PRAM model comes in several variants. They differ in whether multiple processors are allowed to access the same memory cell in a step, and in how the resulting conflicts are resolved. In particular the following variants are distinguished:

- *Exclusive-Read Exclusive-Write (EREW) PRAM*. Simultaneous accesses to the same memory cell are forbidden. The algorithm designer is responsible for meeting this requirement.

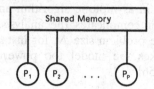

Fig. 11.3 The PRAM model.

- *Concurrent-Read Exclusive-Write (CREW) PRAM.* A cell may be accessed by multiple reads or by at most one write.

- *Concurrent-Read Concurrent-Write (CRCW) PRAM.* Both multiple reads and multiple writes to the same cell are allowed. Multiple writes, of course, are problematic if different processors try to write different values. Several resolution rules have been investigated, for instance:

- *Arbitrary CRCW PRAM.* Any one of the values is written.

- *Priority CRCW PRAM.* The value of the highest-priority writer (for instance the processor with the smallest index) is written.

- *Combining CRCW PRAM.* Each group of writers to the same memory cell takes part in a reduction. The resulting value, for instance the sum, is written.

The PRAM variants differ in power. For instance, a CRCW PRAM can determine the *or* of P boolean values in $O(1)$ steps, whereas the other PRAM variants need time $O(\log P)$ [247].

Assessment The popularity of the PRAM is due to its simplicity. Since the model does not represent architectural details and assumes synchronous execution, algorithm design and analysis are comparatively easy. The PRAM is an appropriate aid to investigate whether a particular application is amenable to parallelization.

With the PRAM, one can quite easily derive a gross estimation of an algorithm's complexity. Nevertheless, the model has been widely criticized for not being sufficiently reflective. In particular, it is unrealistic to assume that an access to the shared memory takes the same amount of time as a local computation. As explained later, the simulation of one PRAM step takes time $O(\sqrt{P})$ on a mesh and $O(\log P)$ on a hypercube if the step involves communication. Thus a PRAM algorithm with complexity $O(P)$ (and much communication) does not necessarily outperform another PRAM algorithm with complexity $O(P \log P)$ (and little communication) on a real architecture. The fundamental problem of the PRAM is its disregard of communication costs, although they are a significant part of real running times. Neither the latency nor the delay caused by network contention is taken into account. Additionally, the model enforces a synchronization after each step, but does not take account of its high costs. Finally, the model disregards the physical division of memory into modules, each of which can only answer a limited number of requests per step.

As an aside, yet another problem arises in asymptotic algorithm analysis. Since the existence of a second parameter complicates the analysis, P is often assumed to grow as a function of the problem size N, for instance as $P = O(N^{\alpha})$ ($\alpha > 0$). This assumption makes the model too powerful, as discussed, for example, by Kruskal et al. [256].

PRAM simulation Although the drawbacks are serious, there are at least three reasons to stay with the PRAM: 1) It is an established model, and a large body of PRAM algorithms has been developed. 2) Future technologies, in particular optical technologies, may enable architectures that come closer to the PRAM ideal. 3) It is hard to devise a substitute, as will be seen in later sections.

Therefore, much research has been conducted on simulating the PRAM on network models. Two major strategies have been worked out: randomized [354] and deterministic [344] PRAM simulation. In both cases, the PRAM program is simulated step by step. The randomized schemes are normally faster, but there is a small risk that the execution of a step may take unusually long.

Randomized schemes simulate a PRAM step in time $\Theta(\sqrt{P})$ on a mesh, and in time $\Theta(\log P)$ on a hypercube or butterfly. Considering an algorithm with sequential time complexity $T(N)$, the parallel time complexity on a PRAM is at best $T(N)/P$, since the same total number of operations must be executed. Due to the simulation delay, the running time on a mesh is thus $\Theta(T(N) \cdot (\sqrt{P}/P))$, and on a hypercube $\Theta(T(N) \cdot (\log P)/P)$. These formulas are disappointing, since they imply that the efficiency (see Sect. 1.3) is limited by, respectively, $O(1/\sqrt{P})$ or $O(1/\log P)$. As noted in Sect. 1.3, one actually hopes for an efficiency of 1. Therefore, a trick has become popular: the use of multithreading. If $\log P$ processes are run on each node of a P-processor hypercube, then the time to simulate one step from each (a total of $P \log P$ steps) is still $O(\log P)$, which translates into the desired efficiency of $O(1)$. Unfortunately, the trick does not work so well on a mesh. Nevertheless, the power of multithreading has given rise to the BSP model, which is treated in Sect. 11.3.

Multithreading can also be implemented in hardware. At the University of Saarbrücken, a computer has been built that, due to the use of multithreading and randomized PRAM simulation techniques, comes close in functionality to a CRCW PRAM [1, 247, 367]. The current version of this SB-PRAM consists of 64 physical processors. 32 virtual processors are mapped onto each physical processor, and the physical processor alternately carries out one instruction from each virtual processor. As discussed in Sect. 11.3, multithreading has limitations and drawbacks. Additionally, the SB-PRAM has been developed in a low-budget university project and therefore uses slow base technologies. For these reasons, the machine cannot compete in speed with commercial computer architectures.

PRAM programming As discussed in the introduction to this chapter, it is useful to have a programming model that corresponds to an abstract model, which·in turn reflects a real architecture. In particular with the SB-PRAM, this vision has become feasible. Therefore, PRAM programming languages have been developed, the best-known being Fork [247].

Fork bears a certain similarity to shared-memory languages, in particular OpenMP. This is not surprising, since the PRAM is a shared-memory model. Fork supports two execution modes, synchronous and asynchronous. In the former, an implicit synchronization is executed after each operation; the latter has no implicit synchronizations. Within a program, synchronous and asynchronous code sections can be mixed.

The programming of asynchronous sections resembles OpenMP programming. So Fork supports private and shared variables, synchronization constructs such as barriers and semaphores, and work sharing. Unlike OpenMP, Fork assumes the number of processes to be constant. All processes are activated at the beginning of a program execution, and process creation constructs are therefore not needed.

The synchronous mode is what makes Fork a PRAM language. This mode simplifies programming, since it eliminates the need for explicit synchronizations. The price for this convenience is a certain performance overhead, and therefore Fork provides asynchronous mode as an alternative. Fork supports a concept of process groups. The groups are either implicitly created in an *if* statement, or explicitly created through a construct called *fork*. In the former case, two process groups are created: the processes that execute the *if* branch, and the processes that execute the *else* branch. Unlike in C* (Sect. 3.1), both groups are active at the same time. In Fork, different process groups are always working asynchronously with each other, whereas the internal operation of the individual groups can be either synchronous or asynchronous, as coded in the program. When a group of processes is split into subgroups, the memory is split accordingly. After the subgroups have finished their work, the parent group is reestablished.

Synchronous and asynchronous groups can be nested. An interesting construct in this context is *join*. It creates a synchronous group by selecting processes according to user-defined criteria. The criteria may include run-time conditions, and thus the size and members of the new group are determined dynamically. The *join* construct is useful for the implementation of parallel critical sections, a technique that is in certain cases more efficient than conventional critical sections.

Fork is a SPMD language, and thus all processes are running the same program. In synchronous mode, moreover, the processes of the same group are running identical instructions at any one time. Fork is based on C and integrates pointer handling. Furthermore, it supports reductions and a scan-like construct called multiprefix. Fork is primarily a teaching tool and a tool for testing parallel algorithms. Nevertheless, several large applications have been coded in the language as well.

The relationship between Fork and the PRAM demonstrates the distinction between a programming model and an abstract model: Whereas a PRAM algorithm designer thinks in terms of individual memory locations and elementary operations, a Fork programmer thinks in terms of data structures and available language constructs.

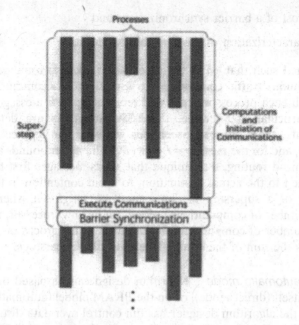

Fig. 11.4 The superstep structure of a BSP computation.

11.3 BULK-SYNCHRONOUS PARALLEL MODEL

Partially motivated by the invention of multithreaded PRAM simulation techniques, the bulk-synchronous parallel model (BSP) was proposed in 1990 by Valiant [422]. BSP has been suggested as a bridging model (Sect. 1.4). It is situated in between the PRAM and network models in the model hierarchy.

BSP describes a computer as a collection of nodes, each consisting of a processor and memory. Unlike network models, BSP does not represent the topology of a particular machine, but models the interconnection network by means of a few parameters (explained later). BSP supposes the existence of a router and a barrier synchronization facility. The router must be able to transfer messages between the nodes, and the barrier synchronization facility must be able to synchronize all or a subset of the nodes. BSP computers are MIMD. Characteristic for the model is a partition of the computation into *supersteps*; see Fig. 11.4. In a superstep, each processor independently performs computations on data in its own memory, and initiates communications with other processors. The communications are guaranteed to complete until the beginning of the next superstep. Thus, BSP differs from the PRAM in a larger step size. Synchronizations only take place at the end of a superstep, not after each individual instruction.

BSP comes with a cost model that involves three parameters:

- P, the number of processors,

- l, the cost of a barrier synchronization, and

- g, a characterization of the available bandwidth.

g is defined such that gh is the time that it takes to route an h-relation under continuous traffic conditions. An h-relation is a communication pattern in which each processor sends and receives up to h messages.

For a particular architecture, the BSP parameters are determined by measurements. More general estimations yield for the hypercube $g = \Theta(1)$, $l = \Theta(\log P)$, and for the mesh $g = l = \Theta(\sqrt{P})$. The upper bounds are achieved with randomized routing, a technique that sends messages first to a random node and then to the actual destination, to avoid contention in the network.

The cost of a superstep is determined as $x + gh + l$, where x is the maximum number of computations carried out by any processor, and h is the maximum number of communications initiated by any processor. The cost of a program is the sum of the costs of the individual supersteps.

Direct and automatic mode   Algorithm design can be based on either the BSP model itself (direct mode), or on the PRAM model (automatic mode). In *direct mode*, the algorithm designer has full control over data distribution and task scheduling. To improve the performance, he or she will try to exploit locality by assigning related data and computations to the same processor. A characteristic feature of BSP is support for latency tolerance. If the algorithm designer is able to identify $x > gh + l$ computations per superstep, then the costs of the program are asymptotically independent of the communication costs.

In *automatic mode*, BSP is not really an algorithm design model in its own right, but more an intermediate step of PRAM simulation. To program a P-processor architecture, the algorithm designer assumes a V-processor PRAM, with V being greater than P by a topology-dependent factor. On a hypercube, for instance, one needs $V \geq P \log P$ to make full use of multi-threading. Consequently, in automatic mode, the algorithm designer must identify more parallelism in an application than is exposed by the target architecture. The simulation translates each PRAM step into one superstep, in which each BSP processor carries out one step from each of V/P PRAM processors. The simulation of a PRAM step has thus costs $O(g \cdot (V/P) + l)$.

Compared with direct mode, automatic mode makes algorithm design more convenient, but has the following performance drawbacks:

- If an application does not possess a sufficient amount of excess parallelism, then performance potential is wasted.

- Locality cannot be exploited, since no distinction is made between local and global accesses. In automatic mode, each memory access is charged a cost of g; whereas in direct mode, some of the accesses have cost 1.

- In addition to the g factor, the simulation itself induces a certain overhead.

How stringent these drawbacks are depends on the particular application and architecture. For applications with low communication requirements or little locality, the second drawback is insignificant [265]. The same holds for architectures with a low value of g. The simulation overhead is a small constant factor; one may be willing to pay this price in return for the greater programming convenience.

In both direct and automatic modes, the BSP model supposes a certain minimum length of a superstep to allow for latency tolerance. Latency tolerance exploits the observation that one h-relation can be routed much faster than h 1-relations. On the hypercube, for instance, either routing a $\log P$-relation or routing a 1-relation takes time $O(\log P)$. If the minimum-step-size requirement cannot be met because either sufficient excess parallelism does not exist (automatic mode) or the application requires tight synchrony (direct mode), then the BSP cost model must be adjusted [390].

Another inaccuracy of BSP is the equal charge for all h relations. This charge does not reflect the observation that incomplete h-relations such as a broadcast can be implemented faster than full h-relations in which each processor sends and receives exactly h packets. There are yet other inaccuracies. Juurlink and Wijshoff [242] give a critical account; they observed deviations of up to 200% between the BSP-estimated and the experimentally measured running times. Clearly, such results depend on the experimental setting; a more optimistic view is given by Goudreau et al. [185].

Assessment   Algorithm design for BSP is harder than for the PRAM, since the additional parameters l and g must be taken into account. Additional parameters are a drawback in general, since they appear in cost formulas, make algorithms less comparable, and require algorithms to adapt themselves to different relative values. Compared with network models, BSP simplifies algorithm design and enables portability.

The superstep structure imposed by BSP is restrictive, since many algorithms, in particular task-parallel algorithms, do not naturally fit into this structure. On the positive side, the superstep structure makes algorithms easier to understand and verify. Deadlocks cannot occur. The superstep structure simplifies algorithm analysis, since supersteps are manageable units and the total costs are determined as a sum.

BSP accounts for the costs of communication and synchronization. The model is reasonably reflective of a wide class of architectures. Locality can be exploited insofar as a distinction is made between data that are stored locally and data that are stored on a remote processor. No distinction is made, however, between data that are stored at neighboring processors and data that are stored farther away in the network. This treatment is reasonable for current architectures, because their communication costs are dominated by the time needed for injecting messages into the network and taking messages out of the network. The omission of network locality may, however, be less appropriate for future architectures that perhaps will have huge processor numbers and a large physical size.

Limitations of latency tolerance and multithreading Except if the ratio between computations and communications is high, the costs of BSP algorithms depend on the parameters g, l. Although BSP advises architecture designers to strive for small values of g, l, there are physical limitations. In [53], Bilardi and Preparata consider architecture design under physical constraints such as the speed of light and a minimum size of deterministic devices. They come to the conclusion that only the mesh and related architectures are scalable in the long run. But the mesh, as noted above, has high values of g, l, namely $\Theta(\sqrt{P})$. Regarding multithreading, Bilardi and Preparata give the following argument, which shows limitations:

A processor that is time-shared by S processes needs physical area $\Omega(S)$ to store their state information. Consequently, a P-processor machine needs area $\Omega(PS)$, and has thus a latency of $\Omega(\sqrt{PS})$. To tolerate this latency, $S = P$ processes per processor are needed. Then, however, the machine has an area of $\Omega(P^2)$ and a latency of $\Omega(P)$. It carries out P^2 operations in $\Omega(P)$ time units. This result is disappointing, since a P^2-processor PRAM can accomplish the same. It as well carries out P^2 operations per step, and, with the previously mentioned PRAM simulation technique, each step needs time $O(P)$. The P^2-processor PRAM can be accommodated within an area of $O(P^2)$, too. Consequently, the use of multithreading leads to no asymptotic improvements under the assumptions of finite speed of light and minimum device sizes. Altogether, multithreading causes three problems:

- A sufficient amount of excess parallelism must be identified in the application.
- Very fast context switching is needed.
- A large bandwidth is required, which may ultimately hit physical limits, as discussed above.

BSP Programming

Since BSP has been proposed as a bridging model, it serves a threefold purpose: 1) it identifies important features that should be supported by computer architects, 2) it is an abstract model for algorithm design, and 3) it is a starting point for the design of programming models. In particular the third aspect has received considerable attention in the BSP research community. In the following, we discuss the major approaches.

BSP libraries Based on the direct mode, BSP libraries have been developed into a quite mature programming model. Several libraries have been implemented, the best-known probably being BSPlib [209]. BSPlib shares a certain similarity with message-passing libraries such as MPI in that the programmer is responsible for partitioning the data among the processes and for organizing all interprocess communication. Only the mapping of processes to processors is handled by the system. BSPlib has been implemented on a variety of shared- and distributed-memory machines. The library provides about 20 functions:

- Elementary functions that return the process identifier, the total number of processes, etc.

- Initialization functions that start and terminate the BSP part of a program.

- A function for barrier synchronization.

- One-sided communication functions that implement the model described in Sect. 4.4 with the modification that the accesses complete until the beginning of the next superstep. In particular, BSPlib provides *put* and *get* routines, and a routine that makes private memory areas accessible to the public.

- Message-passing functions for *send/receive*-like communication. The exact functionality differs from standard *send/receive*: Messages are sent to a *queue* at the receiver, where they arrive before the beginning of the next superstep. In the next superstep, the receiver can take the messages out of the queue; unreceived messages are deleted.

The Oxford BSP Toolset [324] extends BSPlib with profiling, debugging, and performance prediction tools.

In a different research project, the Paderborn University BSP Library (PUB) has been developed [65, 349]. PUB introduces a concept of process groups that is reminiscent of the D-BSP and H-PRAM models treated in Sect. 11.5. Through an explicit construct, the set of processes can be partitioned into subsets, hierarchically. Each process group operates independently and executes separate barrier synchronizations. After all process groups have finished their work, the original group is reestablished. Process groups are useful for the expression of task parallelism. Moreover they exploit the speed of subset synchronization, which is faster than full synchronization on many architectures. Finally, PUB supports collective operations on subgroups.

Other BSP programming models In automatic mode, BSP corresponds to the PRAM, and thus PRAM languages can be used. It has been shown that a PRAM implementation is about equally efficient whether it goes through BSP or not [422]. This good match makes it possible to combine BSP programming and PRAM programming in a single environment. An approach along these lines is suggested by Lecomber [265]

Furthermore, BSP provides a cost model for data-parallel and skeleton languages [452, 453], and can be used in object-based programming [184].

Assessment of BSP programming The availability of matching programming models is an important advantage of the BSP abstract model.

BSP libraries differ from message passing in that the computation is partitioned into supersteps. Therefore, BSP libraries are less flexible than message passing, but facilitate the design of correct programs with predictable performance. This advantage can also be exploited in an MPI system if one follows a BSP-style discipline of programming. A BSP-only library has the additional advantage that the library implementor can exploit the knowledge of the program structure to devise a more efficient implementation [134].

11.4 THE LOGP AND QSM MODELS

The LogP model Motivated by inaccuracies of BSP and the restrictive requirement to follow the superstep structure, LogP has been suggested as an alternative [123]. Like BSP, LogP abstracts from the network topology and describes a machine in terms of a few parameters. The model does not deploy implicit synchronizations. Instead, the processors work asynchronously and communicate via pairwise message exchange. LogP allows for MIMD programming, but many LogP algorithms are SPMD. A machine is described by the following four parameters that give the model its name:

- L, an upper bound on the latency, defined as the period of time during which a message is on the way between source and destination.

- o, the overhead, defined as the time during which a processor is engaged in the transmission or reception of a message. A message transfer thus takes time $L + 2o$. During the overhead time, a processor cannot perform other operations, either computations or communications.

- g, the gap. It measures the bandwidth and is defined as the minimum time interval required between successive sends or receives to avoid overloading the network. LogP imposes a capacity constraint, saying that at most $\lceil L/g \rceil$ messages from or to the same destination may be in the network at any one time. For many architectures $g \geq o$ holds; the time difference $g - o$ may be used for computations but not for communications.

- P, the number of processors.

LogP assumes reliable message delivery, but does not make any further assumptions. So messages may overtake each other, and algorithms must be shown correct for any arrival order that is compatible with the upper bound L.

The original LogP model assumes that all messages are of small size. Alexandrov et al. [14] propose an extension, called LogGP, that provides specific support for long messages.

In algorithm analysis, each message transfer is charged a cost of exactly L. To further simplify the analysis, o and g can be equated at the price of a factor-of-two inaccuracy.

Comparison with BSP   LogP describes real architectures in more detail and more accurately than BSP. The model allows for the use of performance potential that is not represented by BSP, in particular the overlap between computation and communication. LogP does not enforce a specific program structure, and thus algorithms can be formulated more flexibly. On the other side, asynchrony and additional parameters complicate algorithm analysis. Ensuring correctness becomes harder as well, since deadlocks may occur.

QSM   Whereas LogP improves on BSP with respect to reflectivity, QSM [177] improves on it with respect to simplicity. In contrast to BSP, QSM is a shared-memory model. As in BSP, the computation is structured into supersteps, and each processor has its own local memory. In a superstep, a processor performs computations on values in the local memory, and initiates read/write operations to the shared memory. All shared-memory accesses complete until the beginning of the next superstep. QSM allows for concurrent reads and writes. Let the maximum number of accesses to any one cell in a superstep be κ. Then QSM charges costs $\max\{x, gh, \kappa\}$, with x, g, and h being defined as in BSP.

Assessment   The BSP, LogP, and QSM models have been compared from a theoretical point of view in Ramachandran et al. [353]. There it was shown that the models are asymptotically nearly equivalent. More specifically, the reference presents work-preserving simulations of one model by another, for all pairs of the models (with a restriction being applied to LogP). A simulation is called *work-preserving* if the product of the processor number and the running time is the same on the simulated and simulating machines. Most work-preserving simulations require the number V of simulated-machine processors to be larger than the number P of simulating-machine processors. The maximum ratio V/P required in [353] is about $O(\log^4 P)$. The result of [353] implies that algorithms may be designed for any of the models. The resulting running time will be asymptotically the same, provided that a sufficiently high degree of parallelism $V \gg P$ can be identified.

Note that the results are asymptotic, and thus no immediate conclusions can be drawn about the relative power of the models in practice. Which of the models to prefer is still a matter of debate. Probably there will not be a best choice, but different algorithms will be tackled with different models. QSM has a certain simplicity advantage over BSP and LogP, since QSM describes an architecture by only two parameters P, g, and because QSM provides a shared-memory abstraction that eliminates the need for data distribution.

QSM ignores several performance factors: latency, cost for barrier synchronization, and overhead for sending/receiving a message. The model relies on compiler support to reduce the effect of these factors. Grayson et al. [190] provide experimental evidence in support of these design decisions.

11.5 LOCALITY-CENTRIC MODELS

Although BSP and LogP distinguish between local and global memory accesses, they do not represent network proximity. There is a cost difference between neighbor and nonneighbor communication, although it is minor on current architectures. The difference can be exploited to avoid latency, and to thus improve the performance. BSP disregards the potential of network locality, and instead concentrates on latency tolerance. As has been shown before, latency tolerance has limitations. Therefore, alternative models have been suggested that offer the use of network locality.

One of the models is the *hierarchical PRAM* (H-PRAM [205]). It extends the PRAM model by a partition instruction that splits the set of processors into subsets. The so-formed sub-PRAMs work independently of each other, carrying out the same or different algorithms. The sizes of the sub-PRAMs are chosen freely by the programmer, under the condition that the total number of processors must be the same as in the original PRAM. At the end of a partition step, the sub-PRAMs synchronize and the original PRAM is restored. Except for the smaller processor count, a sub-PRAM is defined the same way as the original PRAM. In particular, it may perform partitions. Therefore, a hierarchical program structure arises, giving the model its name.

The H-PRAM model comes in several variants. First, the base PRAM may be EREW, CREW, etc. Second, a distinction is made between private and shared H-PRAMs. In the private variant, the memory is partitioned proportionately along with the processors so that, on a distributed-memory architecture, each memory module is assigned to the same sub-PRAM as the processor it belongs to. The processors of a private sub-PRAM must not access other memory locations than those of their own sub-PRAM. In the shared variant, the memory is not split, and any processor may access any memory location.

The incentive for using the partition construct is a refined cost model that charges less cost to a communication if it occurs within a small sub-PRAM. The cost model represents latency and synchronization costs; both are increasing functions in the number of processors. The synchronization costs are often dominated by the communication costs, and thus the latency is the more important of the two parameters. A read or write to the shared memory takes time $l(P)$ on a P-processor private sub-PRAM, where $l(P)$ depends on the particular architecture. On a mesh, for instance, $l(P) = \sqrt{P}$, and on a hypercube $l(P) = \log P$. The H-PRAM disregards the potential of latency tolerance, and does not explicitly represent the bandwidth.

A related model is the *Y-PRAM* [128]. It extends the PRAM with a partition instruction, too, but the machine may only be split into halves (hierarchically). The cost model represents latency and bandwidth; both are functions in the submachine size.

Similarly, the *decomposable BSP* (D-BSP) model [128] extends the BSP base model with a partition instruction. Submachines may have varying sizes; they behave like smaller BSP computers. In each submachine, the computation is organized as a sequence of supersteps, but the different machines execute independently. On submachine s, the cost of a superstep is $x + hg(s) + l(s)$. Note that the functions g and l depend on the submachine. Often, the dependence can be reduced to the submachine size, simplifying the model.

A refinement of D-BSP, called *Y-BSP*, has been suggested in the same paper [128]. This model includes further details in the cost formula. So the cost of an h-relation depends on not only the maximum number h of messages sent by a processor, but also on the average number. The refinement complicates algorithm analysis and may not be needed, as argued by Bilardi et al. [52].

Different in concept, but also targeted at the representation of network locality, is the *extended BSP* (E-BSP) model [241]. Here, the algorithm designer thinks in terms of processor numbers. A computation is organized into supersteps exactly the same way as in BSP; there is no partition instruction. Network locality is taken into account by a different cost formula. It depends on the particular architecture and reflects both network locality and the cost difference between routing a full and an incomplete h relation. The formula makes the routing costs of a superstep dependent on four parameters: the total number of messages sent, the maximum number of messages sent from the same source, the maximum number of messages sent to the same destination, and a locality parameter. The locality parameter depends on a function that maps the maximum network distance between a pair of source and destination processors to an architecture-dependent value. On a mesh, for instance, the processors can be numbered in such a way that any processors p_1, p_2 with $|p_1 - p_2| = d$ are connected by a path of length $O(\sqrt{d})$. Thus the locality parameter is $\Theta(\sqrt{d})$, where d is the maximum difference of processor numbers for the particular superstep.

Assessment The inclusion of network locality improves the reflectivity of a model. The improvement is most obvious for architectures that have a large processor count. It can also be observed on machines that have less processors than the architecture on which the algorithm has been developed, since neighboring virtual processors can then be mapped onto the same physical processor.

The price for the gain in reflectivity is a loss in simplicity. All suggested models take functions as parameters. With functions, algorithm design and analysis become significantly harder, because the algorithms must adapt themselves to functions of varying shapes, in order to be portable.

Fortunately, this drawback occurs only when an algorithm designer decides to really exploit network locality in a certain part of the algorithm. Otherwise, the models degenerate to the standard PRAM or BSP case, and are thus easier to handle. In other words, the use of network locality is an option in locality-based models, not an obligation.

Except for E-BSP, the models encourage modularity. Thus, as discussed in previous chapters, they support software engineering and correctness. Unfortunately, the models do not only encourage but actually enforce modularity if one wants to exploit locality. This can be overly restrictive: Submachines are in a sense comparable to process groups in MPI. In the author's opinion what is missing in network-locality models is an analog of intercommunicators through which submachines could occasionally communicate. In the current models, the submachines must first synchronize, thereby destroying the program structure for, perhaps, a single communication. E-BSP is less restrictive in this respect, but includes so many parameters that the model is hard to work with.

Memory hierarchy models   Not specific to parallel computing is the existence of memory hierarchies. Let us look into the sequential domain for a moment. There, the standard model, the random-access machine (RAM), does not represent memory hierarchies. It assumes unit-time access to all memory cells, regardless of large cost differences between accesses to cache, main memory, and disks. The differences are unlikely to disappear in the future; in fact they have been growing steadily from one computer generation to the next. Especially for IO-intensive algorithms, the RAM assumption is felt to be too inaccurate, and alternative models have been proposed: the two-level memory model [7], the hierarchical memory model (HMM) [4], the uniform memory hierarchy model [18], and others. Sequential memory hierarchy models share with parallel abstract models the problem that any gain in reflectivity must be paid for by a loss in simplicity. Nevertheless, the higher accuracy seems to be necessary for certain classes of applications.

The concept of locality in memory hierarchies is related to the concept of network locality. In both cases, the access costs grow as a function of physical distance. Latency tolerance is useful in memory hierarchies as well, and thus several parallel algorithms translate into efficient algorithms for memory hierarchies [129, 429].

Memory-hierarchy models have been extended by parallelism, and parallel models have been extended by a representation of memory hierarchy. The best-known combined model is the *parallel disk model* (PDM) [431], which assumes a two-level memory hierarchy with both multiple disks and multiple processors. PDM has gained considerable popularity; see Vitter [431] for a survey of PDM algorithms. A related model is EM-BSP* [129]; it combines PDM with a variant of BSP. Multilevel memory hierarchies are described in, for example, the parallel hierarchical memory model (P-HMM) [432], the parallel memory hierarchy model (PMH) [17], and the LogP-HMM model [271]. The multilevel models tend to be overly complicated, and have only occasionally been used in algorithm design.

11.6 GRAPH-BASED MODELS

For the analysis of task-parallel algorithms, it has been found useful to represent the algorithm as a graph, with nodes corresponding to tasks, and edges corresponding to dependences between the tasks. The graph is directed; an arc indicates that a task must not be started before its predecessor has finished. The graph may be labeled or unlabeled. In the former case, the nodes are marked with the computation costs of the respective task, and the edges are marked with the communication costs that arise if the tasks are mapped onto different processors. The communication costs can be specified in a machine-independent way, for instance by giving the amount of data to be communicated. To be executable, the graph must not have cycles, and is therefore described as a directed acyclic graph (*dag*).

An important step towards the use of dags in algorithm analysis has been made by Papadimitriou and Yannakakis [329]. They describe parallel architectures by a single parameter τ, the cost ratio between a communication and a computation step (*delay model*). Furthermore, they define the costs of an (unlabeled) dag as the length of an optimal schedule (optimal means minimum execution time) that fulfills the following constraints:

1. Each task is executed by at least one processor,

2. At any one time, at most one task is executed per processor, and

3. If there is an edge from u to v in the dag, then either u and v are mapped onto the same processor and v starts at least 1 time unit after u has finished, or u and v are mapped onto different processors and v starts at least τ time units after u has finished.

Determining an optimal schedule for a given dag is NP-complete, but the cited reference presents a simple algorithm that determines an approximation. The approximation is within a factor of two of the optimum, and hence has the same asymptotic running time. With analogous definitions, the same result is achieved for labeled dags. In summary, dags provide a way to estimate the running time of algorithms.

Beyond that observation, dag scheduling is a large research area, surveyed in, for example, El-Rewini et al. [143]. Scheduling research considers, among other topics, more specific classes of graphs, and more accurate machine models, including LogP [64, 275].

An interesting proposal in the context of dag scheduling is the language Cilk [404]. Cilk is C-based and extends C chiefly with three keywords: `cilk`, `spawn`, and `sync`. The concept of the language is simple and can be illustrated with the following example for the computation of the Fibonacci numbers (adapted from [404]):

```
cilk int fib (int n)
{
    if (n<2) return n;
    else
    {
        int x,y;
        x=spawn fib(n-1);
        y=spawn fib(n-2);
        sync;
        return(x+y);
    }
}
```

Because of the keyword `cilk`, `fib` is a so-called Cilk procedure and not a C function. Therefore, `spawn` and `sync` may be used inside. `spawn` corresponds to a function call, but the called function runs in parallel with the calling one. `sync` suspends the parent thread until all children have returned. In the example, `sync` is needed because x and y must not be used before they have been assigned a value.

Cilk is a shared-memory language. The spawned procedures can read and write variables of their parent procedure, and so race conditions and deadlocks may occur. Cilk provides locking mechanisms through which the processes can synchronize their activities. The system also comes with a debugging tool that helps to detect race conditions and deadlocks. In Cilk, the programmer is responsible for the identification of parallel tasks and their synchronization; the scheduling of tasks is accomplished by the run-time system.

A key characteristic of Cilk is the provision of a cost model for performance prediction. It makes use of the concept of threads. In Cilk terminology, a thread is a maximal sequence of instructions that ends with a `spawn`, `sync`, or `return`. Consequently, a Cilk program can be represented by a dag that is embedded in a tree of procedures as depicted in Fig. 11.5 (for a different example than before).

The present version of Cilk is targeted at SMPs, and therefore the communication costs are not represented explicitly. Let T_1 denote the total time needed to execute all threads in the dag, T_∞ the time needed on a longest path through the dag, and T_P the time for a parallel execution on P processors. Then, obviously, the lower bounds $T_P \geq T_1/P$ and $T_P \geq T_\infty$ must hold. Blumofe and Leiserson [60] have found a matching upper bound. They

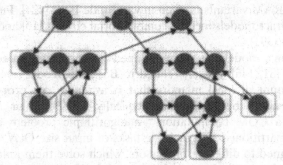

Fig. 11.5 A Cilk program graph. The rounded rectangles stand for Cilk procedures, and the circles stand for threads. Reprinted, by permission from Cilk 5.2 Reference Manual [404]. © 1998 Massachusetts Institute of Technology.

present a scheduling algorithm that implements any Cilk-like dag in such a way that the running time is at most $T_1/P + O(T_\infty)$. The Cilk system makes use of a comparable algorithm, and thus the costs of Cilk programs can be estimated in advance with high accuracy. Only two parameters are needed for the performance prediction, T_1 and T_∞; these parameters are easy to determine.

Cilk has been used in several applications, notably in chess. The language has also been implemented on clusters [61]. A free implementation of Cilk can be obtained from the Cilk home page [112].

11.7 MORE ON THIS TOPIC

The number of abstract models that have been proposed over the years is huge. Many of the models have been targeted at general algorithm design, whereas others have been specifically invented for the investigation of certain phenomena.

Many abstract models are modifications of the PRAM. They improve reflectivity by incorporating features such as

- Asynchrony [116, 175],
- Contention for memory modules [288],
- Contention for individual memory locations [176],
- Cost difference between local and global memory accesses [6],
- Latency tolerance [230],
- Cost advantage of long over short messages [5, 42],
- Global bandwidth restrictions [3], and
- Additional base operations such as scan [57] and selective broadcast [13].

A survey of PRAM variants is given in van Emde Boas [424]. Further notable classes of abstract models include combinatorial circuits [13] and communication skeletons [391].

A well-known model not yet mentioned is the coarse-grained multicomputer (CGM) [81, 145]. Closely related to BSP, this model owes its name to the large amount of local memory that is available per processor. If that amount is denoted by M/P, then, typically, $M/P \geq P$ or $M/P \geq P^\alpha$ is assumed. In a CGM computation, an algorithmic problem of input size $N = \Theta(M)$ is partitioned into multiple tasks of input size $O(N/P)$ each. The tasks are assigned to different processors, which solve them independently in a kind of superstep called a *round*. At the end of each round, the processors communicate, thereby exchanging up to $O(N/P)$ data. CGM differs from BSP in a simplified cost model. Regardless of h, it charges the same communication costs for each round, by combining the parameters g, l into a single value $H_{N, P}$. This cost model is reasonable if the supersteps have a minimum size of $\Theta(N/P)$. The focus of CGM is thus on algorithms with a high computation-to-communication ratio.

Besides the models treated in this book, several classes of fundamentally different models have been suggested: cellular automata [387], spatial machines [149], neural networks [289], genetic algorithms [301], DNA computers [195, 357], quantum computers [440], and others. These unconventional models do not reflect the structure of present mainstream architectures, but suggest and formalize alternative designs. Typically, the designs have been inspired by biological and physical phenomena. Occasionally, the unconventional models have given rise to novel programming models [398].

BIBLIOGRAPHICAL REMARKS

A comprehensive reference on network models and related topics such as routing, embedding, and PRAM simulation is Leighton [267]. Further information on reconfigurable and optical network models can be found in, for example, Akl [13], Middendorf [296], and Trahan et al. [417]. Distributed-algorithm design is covered in depth by Lynch [276] and Wu [445].

For further information on the PRAM model, including programming languages and hardware realizations, see the forthcoming book by Keller et al. [247]. Parallel-algorithm design for the PRAM is also treated in several textbooks, for example in JáJá [229] and Akl [13].

The BSP model is described in Skillicorn et al. [390]; the parameters are discussed in Hill et al. [210]. Further information on BSP, BSPlib, and related work can be found on the Web [74]. Abstract models are surveyed by Maggs et al. [277] and Li et al. [271].

12

Final Comparison

This book has presented a survey of parallel and distributed computing, by covering the diverse set of models that exist in the field. The material has been principally organized by treating each major stream of the field in a separate chapter. This final chapter takes an orthogonal view and reconsiders the models with respect to a few selected criteria.

Degree of abstraction The first criterion is the compromise between reflectivity and abstraction that the models deploy. Reflectivity stands for explicitness about architectural details, and abstraction stands for the omission of these details. Reflectivity expresses a focus on performance, and abstraction expresses a focus on programmability and portability. In this subsection, we classify the models according to their compromise between reflectivity and abstraction. Our classification scheme is thus similar in spirit to the scheme of Skillicorn and Talia that has been outlined in Sect. 1.4. Nevertheless, the schemes differ in that their scheme arranges the models in a linear hierarchy of classes, in which each class has a strictly lower degree of abstraction than its predecessor, whereas our scheme does not attempt to enforce linearity. Giving less emphasis to the introduction of novel classes, the major purpose of our scheme is to highlight some typical compromises.

Table 12.1 presents our scheme. The middle column describes the respective classes by listing typical programmer responsibilities, and the right

TABLE 12.1 Classification of models according to their degree of abstraction.

Class	Programmer responsibilities	Examples
1	Implicit parallelism	Automatic parallelization, functional programming (partially)
2	Identification of parallelism potential	Data-parallel models without placement, logic programming, compositional models, functional programming (partially), skeletons
3	Decomposition (identification of potential), placement	Data-parallel models with placement mobile agents (without communication)
4	Decomposition, high-level coordination	Tuple-based coordination, PRAM, Cilk, structured shared-memory programming,
5	Decomposition, high-level coordination, placement	Distributed objects, parallel mobile code
6	Decomposition, low-level coordination	Thread model, DSM, actor model, BSP
7	Decomposition, low-level coordination, placement	Message passing (all subclasses) sockets, RPC, channel-cased Coordination

column mentions important examples. Many models do not uniquely belong to a single class, because their properties depend on the use of particular features, or differ between submodels. They have nevertheless been inserted into the table for completeness. In other words, the table is meant as an orientation and survey, not as a definitive classification.

Let us now look at the individual classes. In *class* 1, the programmer need not be aware of the parallel execution; all parallelization aspects are managed by tools. Clearly, automatic parallelization (of both imperative and functional programs) belongs to this class. In *class* 2, the programmer identifies parallelism potential, but the tools decide whether the potential is exploited, and manage the details. Together with the parallelism potential, the programmer may give hints on the coordination of the parallel activities. In *class* 3, the programmer is additionally concerned with distribution issues. Class 3 could be further split up in that the programmer may either identify parallelism potential, or actually choose the tasks. Data-parallel models correspond to the former case, and mobile agents to the latter. In *class* 4, the programmer must identify parallel activities and describe their coordination with high-level constructs. The abstraction degree is thus similar to that of class 3, but the focus has moved from distribution to coordination. In *class* 5, the programmer is responsible for both distribution and coordination. *Class* 6 corresponds to class 4, but the coordination must be coded with low-level constructs. Similarly, *class* 7 corresponds to class 5, except that low-level constructs are used. Of course, the borderline between high-level and low-level constructs is fuzzy, and so is the borderline between classes 4 (5) and

6 (7). Classes 6 and 7 could be further divided up into subclasses, according to the particular degree of abstraction. For instance, RPC uses higher-level constructs than sockets do, and thus a refined scheme could put the models into different classes.

Related to the degree of abstraction criterion, programming models differ in their support for structured program design and general software engineering issues. Models with strong emphasis on a structured program design include BSP, object-oriented models, compositional models, skeletons, coordination models, and RPC. The concept of structure has different meanings in these models. Whereas, BSP imposes a structure along the time axis, by dividing the computation into supersteps, the other models focus on clear interfaces between the program components. Yet another aspect of structure is the organization of processes into groups of related activities. This aspect is supported by thread groups in the Java threads model, process groups in MPI, and subspaces in tuple-based models.

Coordination mechanisms In Table 12.1, many models have fallen into the explicit coordination classes 4–7. Besides their degree of abstraction, these models can be classified according to the particular coordination *mechanism* that they deploy. Coordination mechanisms can be divided into communication mechanisms and synchronization mechanisms. We treat the communication mechanisms first, and afterwards discuss the synchronization mechanisms.

Communication mechanisms can be classified into those mechanisms that go through a shared medium, and those that are based on message exchange. The shared medium can be a plain shared memory, or have an internal structure. Shared-medium-based communication may require specific communication routines, or be coded implicitly through statements such as $A[i] = A[i + 5]$. Table 12.2 summarizes the concepts and lists a few examples.

TABLE 12.2 Communication mechanisms.

Basis	Mechanism	Examples
Shared medium	Implicit, plain	Threads, OpenMP, HPF, PRAM
	Explicit, plain	One-sided communication, HPJava
	Implicit, structured	—
	Explicit, structured	Linda, messaging, object-based DSM, parallel mobile code
Message exchange	Message passing	MPI, PVM, Ada
	Channel-based	Occam, Manifold
	Queue-based	Actor model, BSP (partially)
	Connection-oriented	Sockets
	Remote procedure call	RPC, RMI

Message exchange can take the form of message passing, channel-based communication, queue-based communication, connection-oriented communication, and remote procedure calls, as noted in the table. The defining characteristic of *message passing* is the use of matching *send* and *receive* pairs, in which the sender must always name the receiver. In *channel-based communication*, the sender need not know what the receiver is, but sender and receiver must exist at the same time. *Queue-based communication* uncouples sender and receiver so that they need not exist at the same time. Queue-based communication is different from messaging in that each queue is bound to a particular process. *connection-oriented communication* resembles channel-based communication insofar as a connection is established before the actual message exchange takes place, but sender and receiver must actively establish the connection and hence know each other. Finally, a remote procedure call follows a particular pattern: first the caller sends input data, and later the callee sends results back. Examples, again, are given in Table 12.2.

One can consider alternative classification schemes, for example a classification into pairwise, uncoupled, and collective communications. *Pairwise* communications involve exactly two processes. In *uncoupled* communications, the same message may be read by multiple processes, and the partners need not know each other. *Collective communications* follow a certain pattern, and are jointly executed by multiple processes. Collective communications are supported, in one form or the other, by almost all of the programming models discussed (with a notable exception being the very-low level models from Sect. 5.4).

Shared-medium-based communication should not be confused with the existence of a single address space. As an example, distributed-memory implementations of Linda use a shared medium, but there is not single address space. Conversely, object-oriented languages may have a single address space, but the objects communicate by sending messages.

As another difference, some communication mechanisms allow for an overlap between communication and computation, and others do not. Moreover, communication mechanisms may be applicable to the transfer of data, or to the transfer of code.

Since most forms of message exchange imply an implicit synchronization, separate *synchronization mechanisms* are most important for shared-medium-based communication. Two classes can be distinguished: *user-directed synchronizations* and *implicit synchronizations*. The former include mutexes, semaphores, and barrier synchronizations; the latter include lockstep execution (in data-parallel models and the PRAM), and implicit synchronizations at certain points of program execution (for instance in OpenMP).

Parallelism and distribution Another general distinction can be made between models that are targeted at parallel or distributed computing, respectively. We have discussed the difference in Sect. 1.1. To emphasize one aspect, parallel models focus on applications with a predictable structure, and distributed models focus on applications with a dynamic structure. Predictable applications are in particular supported by data-parallel models, skeletons, compositional models, PRAM, and BSP, and to a lesser extent by structured shared-memory programming and message passing. Dynamic applications are in particular supported by thread models, sockets, RPC, tuple-based coordination models, mobile agents, and parallel mobile code. Especially far-reaching support is provided by distributed-object models with dynamic invocation.

Many parallel models emphasize regular computations, and therefore provide special constructs for the expression of frequent patterns. The most obvious example is skeletons; others include the data distribution directives of HPF and the work-sharing constructs of OpenMP. In general, parallel models are more amenable to performance optimization than distributed models, and also to performance estimation.

Another distinction can be made between models that emphasize a local and those that emphasize a global view of the computation. With a *global view*, the programmer thinks in terms of the overall computation. Either there is a single thread of control, or the model is SPMD and emphasizes the overall structure. Programming models with a global view include skeletons, data-parallel models, and collective operations (in any model). With a *local view*, the programmer thinks in terms of the individual processes and their interactions with the environment. While the majority of programming models focuses on the local view, this view is especially dominant in coordination models, client/server models, and mobile agents. In general, distributed models have a stronger focus on the local view than parallel models do. Similarly, distributed programs are typically MPMD, whereas parallel programs are often SPMD.

Parallel models tend to assume a smaller grain size than distributed models; opposite examples are SIMD models on the one hand, and distributed-object models on the other. The differing granularity reflects the differing architectural focus of the models. Whereas distributed models are chiefly targeted at loosely coupled distributed systems, parallel models are targeted at SMPs, NUMA machines, clusters, etc., on which the communication is significantly faster.

Distributed models pay more attention to heterogeneity, openness, and dependability. They assume the existence of multiple applications in the system, whereas parallel models consider one application at a time. In particular the client/server and mobile-agent models support the sharing of resources between different applications.

Despite the differences, it can be observed that parallel and distributed computing are converging more and more into one coherent field. The convergence manifests itself in the fuzziness of the borderlines between the various classes, and in the increasing integration of parallel and distributed models. Here are a few examples:

- Client/server programming uses parallelism within the servers.

- Message passing is integrated with client/server computing in MPI-2.

- The client/server paradigm provides access to supercomputers in systems such as WebFlow (Sect. 6.1).

- Active objects and tuple-based models are used in both parallel and distributed computing.

Programming models and abstract models   In this book, a distinction has been made between programming models and abstract models. While these groups of models serve different purposes, interesting parallels can be drawn. Most importantly, the difference between shared-memory programming and message passing can be observed in both cases. So the PRAM and QSM models provide a shared-memory abstraction, and the LogP and BSP models are based on message exchange. Furthermore, network models and LogP emphasize a local view, and the PRAM emphasizes a global view.

Paradigms   The organization of this book has been model-centric, and so the treatment of paradigms was scattered throughout the book. To give a summary, we have dealt with two major paradigms: *data parallelism* and *task parallelism*. In general, distributed models focus on task parallelism (if they consider parallelism at all), and parallel models support both forms of parallelism, but to a varying degree. Data parallelism plays a large role in data-parallel models, but is also important in structured shared-memory programming and message passing. General forms of task parallelism are supported by thread models, tuple-based coordination models, client/server models, object-oriented models, etc.

On a smaller scale, we have discussed the *pipeline, divide-and-conquer,* and *master/slave* patterns. Other patterns can be identified, but these three patterns are of particular importance for parallel and distributed computing.

Furthermore, we have distinguished the *client/server* and *peer-to-peer* paradigms. Client/server describes an asymmetric relationship between processes, and peer-to-peer a symmetric one. Both paradigms refer to distributed computing, and characterize the overall structure of a computation.

References

1. F. Abolhassan, J. Keller, and W. Paul. On the cost-effectiveness of PRAMs. In *Proceeding of the 3rd IEEE Symposium on Parallel and Distributed Processing*, pages 2–9, 1991.

2. Actor Foundry. Version 0.2.0. Available at http://osl.cs.uiuc.edu/foundry/index.html, Feb. 1999.

3. M. Adler, P. B. Gibbons, Y. Matias, and V. Ramachandran. Modeling parallel bandwidth: Local vs. global restrictions. *Algorithmica*, 24(3–4):381–404, 1999.

4. A. Aggarwal, B. Alpern, A. Chandra, and M. Snir. A model for hierarchical memory. In *Proceedings of the 19th Annual ACM Symposium on Theory of Computing*, pages 305–314, 1987.

5. A. Aggarwal, A. K. Chandra, and M. Snir. On communication latency in PRAM computations. In *Proceedings ACM Symp. on Parallel Algorithms and Architectures*, pages 11–21, 1989.

6. A. Aggarwal, A. K. Chandra, and M. Snir. Communication complexity of PRAMs. *Theoretical Computer Science*, 71:3–28, 1990.

7. A. Aggarwal and J. S. Vitter. The input/output complexity of sorting and related problems. *Communications of the ACM*, 31(9):1116–1127, Sept. 1988.

8. G. Agha, W. Kim, and R. Panwar. Actor languages for specification of parallel computations. In G. E. Blelloch, K. M. Chandy, and S. Jagannathan, editors, *Specification of Parallel Algorithms*, DIMACS Series in Discrete Mathematics and Theoretical Computer Science, pages 239–258. American Mathematical Society, 1994.

9. G. A. Agha. *Actors: A Model of Concurrent Computation in Distributed Systems*. MIT Press, 1986.

229

10. G. A. Agha and N. Jamali. Concurrent programming for distributed artificial intelligence. In G. Weiss, editor, *Multiagent Systems: A Modern Approach to Distributed Artificial Intelligence*, Ch. 12, pages 505–534. MIT Press, 1999.

11. G. A. Agha and W. Kim. Actors: A unifying model for parallel and distributed computing. *Journal of Systems Architecture*, 45(15):1263–1277, Sept. 1999.

12. P. Agrawal and C. J. Sreenan. Get wireless: A mobile technology spectrum. *IEEE IT Professional*, 1(4):18–23, July/Aug. 1999.

13. S. G. Akl. *Parallel Computation: Models and Methods*. Prentice-Hall, 1997.

14. A. Alexandrov, M. F. Ionescu, K. E. Schauser, and C. Scheiman. LogGP: Incorporating long messages into the LogP model for parallel computation. *Journal of Parallel and Distributed Computing*, 44(1):71–79, July 1997.

15. G. S. Almasi and A. Gottlieb. *Highly Parallel Computing*. The Benjamin/Cummings Publishing Company, 1994.

16. B. Alpern and L. Carter. Performance programming: A science waiting to happen. In U. Vishkin, editor, *Developing a Computer Science Agenda for High-Performance Computing*. ACM Press, 1994.

17. B. Alpern and L. Carter. Towards a model for portable parallel performance: Exposing the memory hierarchy. In *Portability and Performance for Parallel Processing*, pages 21–41. John Wiley & Sons, 1994.

18. B. Alpern, L. Carter, E. Feig, and T. Selker. The uniform memory hierarchy model of computation. *Algorithmica*, 12(2/3):72–109, Aug./Sept. 1994.

19. AltaCluster. Available at http://www.altatech.com/systems.html.

20. G. M. Amdahl. Validity of the single processor approach to achieving large scale computer capabilities. In *Proceedings AFIPS Spring Joint Computer Conference*, page 30. Atlantic City, N.J., 1967.

21. W. Amme and E. Zehendner. Data dependence analysis in programs with pointers. *Parallel Computing*, 24(3–4):505–525, May 1998.

22. G. Antoniu, L. Bougé, and R. Namyst. An efficient and transparent thread migration scheme in the PM2 runtime system. In *Workshop Proceedings IPPS/SPDP*, pages 496–510. Springer LNCS 1586, 1999.

23. Applied Parallel Research. *Shared Memory Parallelization User's Guide. Version 2.1*, Apr. 1998. Available at http://www.apri.com/apr_prod_docs.html.

24. F. Arbab. The IWIM model for coordination of concurrent activities. In *1st Int. Conference on Coordination Models, Languages and Applications*, pages 34–56. Springer LNCS 1061, Apr. 1996.

25. F. Arbab, P. Ciancarini, and C. Hankin. Coordination languages for parallel programming. *Parallel Computing*, 24:989–1004, 1998.

26. R. Armstrong, D. Gannon, A. Geist, K. Keahey, S. Kohn, L. McInnes, S. Parker, and B. Smolinski. Toward a common component architecture for high-performance scientific computing. In *8th IEEE Int. Symposium on High Performance Distributed Computing*, 1999. Available at http://www.computer.org/proceedings.

27. K. Arnold, B. O'Sullivan, R. W. Scheifler, J. Waldo, and A. Wollrath. *The Jini Specification*. Addison-Wesley, June 1999.

28. Y. Artsy and R. Finkel. Designing a process migration facility: The Charlotte experience. *IEEE Computer*, 22(9):47–56, Sept. 1989.

29. *The ASCI Blue Mountain 3-TOps System*. Available at http://www.lanl.gov/asci/bluemtn/t_sysnews.shtml.

30. D. Avresky and D. Kaeli. *Fault-Tolerant Parallel and Distributed Systems*. Kluwer Academic Publishers, 1997.

31. B. Bacci, M. Danelutto, S. Pelagatti, and M. Vanneschi. *SkIE*: A heterogeneous environment for HPC applications. *Parallel Computing*, 25:1827–1852, 1999.

32. J. Bacon. *Concurrent Systems: Operating Systems, Database and Distributed Systems: An Integrated Approach*. Addison-Wesley, 2nd edition, 1998.

33. L. Baker and B. J. Smith. *Parallel Programming*. McGraw-Hill, 1996.

34. M. Baker, B. Carpenter, G. Fox, S. H. Ko, and S. Lim. mpiJava: An object-oriented Java interface to MPI. In *Workshop Proceedings IPPS/SPDP*, pages 748–762. Springer LNCS 1586, 1999.

35. M. Baker and G. Fox. Metacomputing: Harnessing informal supercomputers, In Buyya [77], pages 154–185, 1999.

36. H. E. Bal, R. Bhoedjang, R. Hofman, C. Jacobs, K. Langendoen, T. Rühl, and M. F. Kaashoek. Performance evaluation of the Orca shared-object system. *ACM Transactions on Computer Systems*, 16(1):1–40, Feb. 1998.

37. H. E. Bal and M. Haines. Approaches for integrating task and data parallelism. *IEEE Concurrency*, pages 74–84, July–Sept. 1998.

38. J.-P. Banâtre and D. L. Métayer. Gamma and the chemical reaction model: Ten years after. In *Coordination Programming: Mechanisms, Models and Semantics*, pages 3–41. World Scientific Publishing, IC Press, 1996.

39. U. Banerjee. *Loop Transformations for Restructuring Compilers: The Foundations*. Kluwer Academic Publishers, 1993.

40. U. Banerjee. *Loop Transformations for Restructuring Compilers: Loop Parallelization*. Kluwer Academic Publishers, 1994.

41. U. Banerjee. *Loop Transformations for Restructuring Compilers: Dependence Analysis*. Kluwer Academic Publishers, 1997.

42. A. Bäumker, W. Dittrich, and F. M. auf der Heide. Truly efficient parallel algorithms: 1–optimal multisearch for an extension of the BSP model. *Theoretical Computer Science*, 203(2):175–203, Aug. 1998.

43. S. Benkner. HPF+: High Performance Fortran for advanced industrial applications. In *Proceedings of the Int. Conference on High Performance Computing and Networking*, pages 797–808. Springer LNCS 1401, 1998.

44. Beowulf Project Home Page. http://www.beowulf.org.

45. A. J. Bernstein. Analysis of programs for parallel processing. *IEEE Transactions on Electronic Computers*, 15(5):757–763, Oct. 1966.

46. BERT 77 Reference. Available at http://www.plogic.com/bert-des.html.

47. R. A. Bhoedjang, T. Rühl, and H. E. Bal. User-level network interface protocols. *IEEE Computer*, 31(11):53–60, Nov. 1998.

48. L. F. Bic, M. B. Dillencourt, and M. Fukuda. Mobile agents, DSM, coordination, and self-migrating threads: A common framework. Available at http://www.ics.uci.edu/bic/messengers/messengers.html, June 1997.

49. L. F. Bic, M. B. Dillencourt, and M. Fukuda. Mobile network objects. In J. Webster, editor, *Encyclopedia of Electrical and Electronics Engineering*, volume 13. John Wiley & Sons, 1999.

50. L. F. Bic, M. Fukuda, and M. B. Dillencourt. Distributed computing using autonomous objects. *IEEE Computer*, 29(8):55–61, Aug. 1996.

51. A. J. C. Bik and D. B. Gannon. Automatically exploiting implicit parallelism in Java. *Concurrency: Practice and Experience*, 9(6):579–619, June 1997.

52. G. Bilardi, A. Pietracaprina, and G. Pucci. A quantitative measure of portability with application to bandwidth-latency models for parallel computing. In *Proceedings Euro-Par*, pages 543–551. Springer LNCS 1685, 1999.

53. G. Bilardi and F. P. Preparata. Horizons of parallel computation. *Journal of Parallel and Distributed Computing*, 27(2):172–182, June 1995.

54. R. S. Bird. Lectures on constructive functional programming. In M. Broy, editor, *Constructive Methods in Computing Science*, NATO ASI Series, volume F55, pages 151–216. Springer-Verlag, 1989.

55. L. Blackford, J. Choi, A. Cleary, E. D'Azevedo, J. Demmel, I. Dhillon, J. Dongarra, S. Hammarling, G. Henry, A. Petitet, K. Stanley, D. Walker, and R. Whaley. ScaLAPACK User's Guide. Technical Report, Society for Industrial and Applied Mathematics, 1997.

56. G. S. Blair. A convergence of parallel and distributed computing? In Kara et al. [244], pages 1–11, 1996.

57. G. Blelloch. Scans as primitive operations. *IEEE Transactions on Computers*, 38:1526–1538, Nov. 1989.

58. G. E. Blelloch. Programming parallel algorithms. *Communications of the ACM*, 39(3):85–97, Mar. 1996.

59. B. Blount, S. Chatterjee, and M. Philippsen. Irregular parallel algorithms in Java. In *Workshop Proceedings IPPS/SPDP*, pages 1026–1035. Springer LNCS 1586, 1999.

60. R. D. Blumofe and C. E. Leiserson. Scheduling multithreaded computations by work stealing. *Journal of the ACM*, 46(5):720–748, 1999.

61. R. D. Blumofe and P. A. Lisiecki. Adaptive and reliable parallel computing on networks of workstations. In *Proceedings of the USENIX 1997 Annual Technical Conference on UNIX and Advanced Computing Systems*, pages 133–147, Anaheim, Calif., Jan. 1997.

62. N. J. Boden, D. Cohen, R. E. Felderman, A. E. Kulawik, C. L. Seitz, J. N. Seizovic, and W.-K. Su. Myrinet: A gigabit-per-second local-area network. *IEEE Micro*, 15(1):29–36, Feb. 1995.

63. F. Bodin, P. Beckman, D. Gannon, S. Narayana, and S. X. Yang. Distributed pC++: Basic ideas for an object parallel language. *Scientific Programming*, 2(3), 1993.

64. C. Boeres, A. Nascimento, and V. E. F. Rebello. Scheduling arbitrary task graphs on LogP machines. In *Proceedings Euro-Par*, pages 340–349. Springer LNCS 1685, 1999.

65. O. Bonorden, B. Juurlink, I. von Otte, and I. Rieping. The Paderborn University BSP (PUB) Library: Design, implementation and performance. In *Proceedings IPPS/SPDP*, pages 99–104. IEEE Computer Society Press, 1999.

66. M. M. Bonsangue, J. N. Kok, and G. Zavattaro. Comparing coordination models based on shared distributed replicated data. In *ACM Symposium on Applied Computing*, pages 156–165, 1999.

67. P. Bouvry and F. Arbab. Visifold: A visual environment for a coordination language. In *Coordination Languages and Models*, pages 403–406. Springer LNCS 1061, Apr. 1996.

68. T. Brandes. Exploiting advanced task parallelism in High Performance Fortran via a task library. In *Proceedings Euro-Par*, pages 833–844. Springer LNCS 1685, 1999.

69. T. Brandes, F. Brégier, M. C. Counilh, and J. Roman. Contribution to better handling of irregular problems in HPF2. In *Proceedings Euro-Par*, pages 639–649. Springer LNCS 1470, 1998.

70. P. Braun, C. Erfurth, and W. Rossak. An Introduction to the Tracy Mobile Agent System. Technical Report Math/Inf/00/24, Jenaer Schriften zur Mathematik und Informatik, Friedrich-Schiller-Universität Jena, 2000.

71. J.-P. Briot, R. Guerraoui, and K.-P. Löhr. Concurrency and distribution in object-oriented programming. *ACM Computing Surveys*, 30(3):291–328, 1998.

72. T. Brown, K. Jeong, B. Li, S. Talla, P. Wyckoff, and D. Shasha. PLinda User Manual. Available at http://cs.nyu.edu/~binli/plinda/index.html.

73. C. Bryce, M. Oriol, and J. Vitek. A coordination model for agents based on secure spaces. In *Proceedings 3rd Int. Conference on Coordination Models and Languages*, pages 4–20. Springer LNCS 1594, Apr. 1999.

74. BSP Worldwide Home Page. http://www.bsp-worldwide.org.

75. A. Burns and A. Wellings. *Concurrency in Ada*. Cambridge University Press, 2nd edition, 1998.

76. R. Butenuth and H.-U. Heiss. Shared memory programming on PC-based SCI clusters. In *Proceedings of SCI Europe*, Cheshire Henbury Tamwoth House, P.O. Box 103, Macclesfield SK11 8UW, UK, Sept. 1998.

77. R. Buyya, editor. *High-Performance Cluster Computing: Architectures and Systems*. Prentice Hall PTR, 1999.

78. R. Buyya, editor. *High-Performance Cluster Computing: Programming and Applications*. Prentice Hall PTR, 1999.

79. G. Cabri, L. Leonardi, and F. Zambonelli. Reactive tuple spaces for mobile agent coordination. In *2nd Int. Workshop on Mobile Agents*, pages 237–248. Springer LNCS 1477, 1998.

80. G. Cabri, L. Leonardi, and F. Zambonelli. Mobile-agent coordination models for Internet applications. *IEEE Computer*, 33(2):82–89, Feb. 2000.

81. E. Caceres, F. Dehne, A. Ferreira, P. Flocchini, I. Rieping, A. Roncato, N. Santoro, and S. W. Song. Efficient parallel graph algorithms for coarse grained multicomputers and BSP. In *24th Int. Colloquium on Automata, Languages and Programming*, pages 390–400. Springer LNCS 1256, 1997.

82. C. J. Callsen and G. Agha. Open heterogeneous computing in ActorSpace. *Journal of Parallel and Distributed Computing*, 21(3):289–300, June 1994.

83. D. Cann. Retire Fortran? A debate rekindled. *Communications of the ACM*, 35(8):81–89, Aug. 1992.

84. CAPTools Home Page. http://captools.gre.ac.uk/mainpage.htm.

85. L. Cardelli. Mobile computation. In *2nd Int. Workshop on Mobile Object Systems*, pages 3–6. Springer LNCS 1222, 1997.

86. B. Carpenter, G. Fox, and G. Zhang. An HPspmd Programming Model. Available at http://www.npac.syr.edu/projects/pcrc/HPJava, Apr. 1999.

87. B. Carpenter, V. Getov, G. Judd, T. Skjellum, and G. Fox. MPI for Java: Position Document and Draft API Specification. Technical Report JGF-TR-03, Java Grande Forum, Nov. 1998. Available at http://www.javagrande.org/sc98.

88. B. Carpenter, G. Zhang, G. Fox, X. Li, and Y. Wen. HPJava: Data parallel extensions to Java. *Concurrency: Practice and Experience*, 10(11–13):873–877, Sept.–Nov. 1998.

89. N. Carriero and D. Gelernter. Linda in context. *Communications of the ACM*, 32(4):444–458, Apr. 1989.

90. N. Carriero and D. Gelernter. *How to Write Parallel Programs: A First Course*. MIT Press, 1990.

91. N. Carriero and D. Gelernter. Coordination languages and their significance. *Communications of the ACM*, 35(2):97–107, Feb. 1992.

92. N. Carriero, D. Gelernter, and L. Zuck. Bauhaus Linda. In *Object-Based Models and Languages for Concurrent Systems*, pages 66–76. Springer LNCS 924, 1995.

93. H. Casanova, J. Dongarra, C. Johnson, and M. Miller. Application-specific tools. In Foster and Kesselman [158], pages 159–180, 1999.

94. M. M. T. Chakravarty. Lazy thread and task creation in parallel graph-reduction. In *9th Int. Workshop on Implementation of Functional Languages*, pages 231–249. Springer LNCS 1467, 1998.

95. M. M. T. Chakravarty, Y. Guo, and M. Köhler. Distributed Haskell: Goffin on the Internet. In *Proceedings of the 3rd Fuji Int. Symposium on Functional and Logic Programming*, pages 80–97. World Scientific Publishers, 1998.

96. B. L. Chamberlain, S.-E. Choi, E. C. Lewis, L. Snyder, W. D. Weathersby, and C. Lin. The case for high-level parallel programming in ZPL. *IEEE Computational Science and Engineering*, 5(3):76–86, July–Sept. 1998.

97. R. Chandra, A. Gupta, and J. L. Hennessy. COOL. In Wilson and Lu [442], pages 215–255, 1996.

98. K. M. Chandy and J. Misra. *Parallel Program Design: A Foundation*. Addison-Wesley, 1988.

99. K. M. Chandy and A. Rifkin. Systematic composition of distributed objects: Processes and sessions. *The Computer Journal*, 40(8):465–478, 1997.

100. K. M. Chandy and S. Taylor. *An Introduction to Parallel Programming*. Jones and Bartlett Publishers, Boston, 1992.

101. C. Chang, A. Sussman, and J. Saltz. CHAOS++. In Wilson and Lu [442], pages 131–174, 1996.

102. B. Chapman, M. Haines, P. Mehrotra, H. Zima, and J. V. Rosendale. Opus: A coordination language for multidisciplinary applications. *Scientific Programming*, 6(9):345–362, 1997.

103. S. Chatterjee and S. Pawlowski. All-optical networks. *Communications of the ACM*, 42(6):75–83, June 1999.

104. D. Chess, C. Harrison, and A. Kershenbaum. Mobile agents: Are they a good idea? In *2nd Int. Workshop on Mobile Object Systems*, pages 25–47. Springer LNCS 1222, 1997.

105. A. Chien et al. Design and evaluation of an HPVM-based Windows NT super-computer. *The Int. Journal of High-Performance Computing Applications*, 13(3):201–219, Fall 1999.

106. A. A. Chien. Computing platforms. In Foster and Kesselman [158], pages 423–451, 1999.

107. G. Chiola and G. Ciaccio. Lightweight messaging systems. In Buyya [77], pages 246–269, 1999.

108. B. O. Christiansen, P. Cappello, M. F. Ionescu, M. O. Neary, K. E. Schauser, and D. Wu. Javelin: Internet-based parallel computing using Java. *Concurrency: Practice and Experience*, 9(11):1139–1160, Nov. 1997.

109. P. Ciancarini. Distributed programming with logic tuple spaces. *New Generation Computing*, 12(3):251–284, 1994.

110. P. Ciancarini. Coordination models and languages for agents. EASSS 99 Lectures on coordination models and languages. Available at http://www.cs.unibo.it/~cianca/wwwpages/easss.html, July 1999.

111. P. Ciancarini, A. Omicini, and F. Zambonelli. Coordination technologies for Internet agents. *Nordic Journal of Computing*, 6(3):215–240, Fall 1999.

112. Cilk Home Page. http://supertech.lcs.mit.edu/cilk.

113. D. Clark. Are ATM, Gigabit Ethernet ready for prime time? *IEEE Computer*, 31(5):11–13, May 1998.

114. M. Cole. Algorithmic skeletons. In Hammond and Michaelson [197], pages 289–303, 1999.

115. M. I. Cole. *Algorithmic Skeletons: Structured Management of Parallel Computation*. Research Monographs in Parallel and Distributed Computing. Pitman, London, UK, 1989.

116. R. Cole and O. Zajicek. The expected advantage of asynchrony. *Journal of Computer and System Sciences*, 51(2):286–300, Oct. 1995.

117. D. Cooke and S. Hamilton. New directions at NASA Ames Research Center. *Communications of the ACM*, 33(1):63–71, Jan. 2000.

118. T. H. Cormen, C. E. Leiserson, and R. L. Rivest. *Introduction to Algorithms*. MIT Press and McGraw-Hill Book Company, 6th edition, 1992.

119. G. Coulouris, J. Dollimore, and T. Kindberg. *Distributed Systems: Concepts and Design*. Addison-Wesley, 2nd edition, 1994.

120. J. M. Crichlow. *An Introduction to Distributed and Parallel Computing*. Prentice Hall Europe, 2nd edition, 1997.

121. CSP for Java. Available at http://www.rt.el.utwente.nl/javapp.

122. D. E. Culler, A. Dusseau, S. C. Goldstein, A. Krishnamurthy, S. Lumetta, T. von Eicken, and K. Yelick. Parallel programming in Split-C. In *Proceedings of the Conference on Supercomputing*, pages 262–273. ACM, 1993.

123. D. E. Culler, R. M. Karp, D. Patterson, A. Sahay, E. E. Santos, K. E. Schauser, R. Subramonian, and T. von Eicken. LogP: A practical model of parallel computation. *Communications of the ACM*, 39(11):78–85, Nov. 1996.

124. D. E. Culler, J. P. Singh, and A. Gupta. *Parallel Computer Architecture: A Hardware/Software Approach*. Morgan Kaufmann Publishers, 1999.

125. F. Dahlgren and J. Torrellas. Cache-only memory architectures. *IEEE Computer*, 32(6):72–79, June 1999.

126. J. Darlington, Y. Guo, H. W. To, and J. Yang. Functional skeletons for parallel coordination. In S. Haridi, K. Ali, and P. Magnusson, editors, *Proceedings Euro-Par*, pages 55–66. Springer LNCS 966, Aug. 1995.

127. P. de la Torre and C. P. Kruskal. Towards a single model of efficient computation in real parallel machines. *Future Generations Computer Systems*, 8:395–408, 1992.

128. P. de la Torre and C. P. Kruskal. Submachine locality in the bulk synchronous setting. In *Proceedings Euro-Par*, pages 352–358. Springer LNCS 1124, 1996.

129. F. Dehne, W. Dittrich, and D. Hutchinson. Efficient external memory algorithms by simulating coarse-grained parallel algorithms. In *Proceedings 9th Annual ACM Symposium on Parallel Algorithms and Architectures*, pages 106–115, 1997.

130. M. Delves and H. Zima. High Performance Fortran: A status report or: Are we ready to give up MPI? In *Proceedings of the 5th European PVM/MPI User's Group Meeting*, pages 161–171. Springer LNCS 1497, 1998.

131. J. Desharnais, A. Mili, J. Mullins, and Y. Slimani. Semantics of Concurrent Programming, In Zomaya [455], pages 24–58, 1996.

132. Distributed Shared Memory Home Pages. http://www.cs.umd.edu/~keleher/dsm.html.

133. S. Donaldson, J. M. D. Hill, and D. B. Skillicorn. BSP clusters: High Performance, Reliable and Very Low Cost. Technical Report PRG-TR-5-98, Oxford University Computing Laboratory, 1998.

134. S. R. Donaldson, J. M. D. Hill, and D. B. Skillicorn. Predictable communication on unpredictable networks: Implementing BSP over TCP/IP and UDP/IP. *Concurrency: Practice and Experience*, 11(11):687–700, 1999.

135. J. J. Dongarra and D. W. Walker. Constructing numerical software libraries for high-performance computer environments. In Zomaya [455], pages 917–954, 1996.

136. F. Douglis and J. Ousterhout. Transparent process migration: Design alternatives and the Sprite implementation. *Software: Practice and Experience*, 21(8):757–785, Aug. 1991.

137. B. Dreier, M. Zahn, and T. Ungerer. Rthreads: A software distributed shared memory system for distributed execution of POSIX threads. In *Proceedings 3rd Int. Conference on Massively Parallel Computing Systems*, Apr. 1998.

138. P. F. Dubois. Scientific components are coming. *IEEE Computer*, 32(3):115–117, Mar. 1999.

139. M. Eberl, H. Hellwagner, W. Karl, M. Leberecht, and J. Weidendorfer. Fast communication libraries on an SCI cluster. In *Proceedings of SCI Europe*, pages 165–175. Cheshire Henbury Tamworth House, P.O. Box 103, Macclesfield SK11 8UW, UK, Sept. 1998.

140. R. Eigenmann and J. Hoeflinger. Parallelizing and vectorizing compilers. Technical Report ECE-HPCLab-99201, Purdue Univ. School of ECE, High-Performance Computing Lab, 2000.

141. R. Eigenmann, B. Kuhn, T. Mattson, and R. Menon. OpenMP tutorial. Slides available at http://www.openmp.org.

142. H. El-Rewini and T. Lewis. *Distributed and Parallel Computing*. Manning Publications, 1998.

143. H. El-Rewini, T. G. Lewis, and H. H. Ali. *Task Scheduling in Parallel and Distributed Systems*. Prentice Hall, 1994.

144. D. J. Evans and M. Gusev. Systolic and VLSI processor arrays for matrix algorithms. In Zomaya [455], pages 500–536, 1996.

145. F. Dehne, A. Fabri and A. Rau-Chaplin. Scalable parallel computational geometry for coarse grained multicomputers. In *Proceedings ACM Symposium on Computational Geometry*, pages 298–307, 1993.

146. J. Farley. *Java Distributed Computing*. O'Reilly, 1998.

147. P. Feautrier. A parallelization framework for recursive tree programs. In *Proceedings Euro-Par*, pages 470–479. Springer LNCS 1470, 1998.

148. P. Felber and R. Guerraoui. Programming with object groups in CORBA. *IEEE Concurrency*, 8(1):48–58, Jan.–Mar. 2000.

149. Y. Feldman and E. Shapiro. Spatial machines: A more realistic approach to parallel computation. *Communications of the ACM*, 35(10):60, Oct. 1992.

150. J. B. Fenwick Jr. and L. L. Pollock. An efficient tuple space programming environment. In Buyya [78], pages 175–196, 1999.

151. U. Fissgus, T. Rauber, and G. Rünger. A framework for generating task parallel programs. In *Proceedings of the 7th Symposium on the Frontiers of Massively Parallel Computation*, pages 72–80. IEEE Computer Society Press, Feb. 1999.

152. M. J. Flynn. Some computer organizations and their effectiveness. *IEEE Transactions on Computers*, 21(9):948–960, Sept. 1972.

153. Fortran MP Applications Development. Available at http://www.sgi.com/developers/devtools/languages/fortran.html.

154. S. Fortune and J. Wyllie. Parallelism in random access machines. In *Proceedings of the 10th ACM Symposium on Theory of Computing*, pages 114–118, 1978.

155. I. Foster. Compositional parallel programming languages. *ACM Transactions on Programming Languages and Systems*, 18(4):454–476, July 1996.

156. I. Foster and C. Kesselman. Computational grids. In Foster and Kesselman [158], pages 16–51, 1999.

157. I. Foster and C. Kesselman. The Globus toolkit. In Foster and Kesselman [158], pages 259–278, 1999.

158. I. Foster and C. Kesselman. *The Grid: Blueprint for a New Computing Infrastructure*. Morgan Kaufmann Publishers, 1999.

159. I. Foster, R. Olson, and S. Tuecke. Productive parallel programming: The PCN approach. *Scientific Programming*, 1(1):51–66, 1992. Reprinted in D. Skillicorn and D. Talia, editors, *Programming Languages for Parallel Processing*, pages 358–373, IEEE Computer Society Press, 1995.

160. Foundation for Intelligent Physical Agents. Available at http://drogo.cselt.it/fipa.

161. G. Fox, T. Haupt, E. Akarsu, A. Kalinichenko, K.-S. Kim, P. Sheethalnath, and C.-H. Youn. The Gateway system: Uniform web based access to remote resources. In *Proceedings of the ACM 1999 Conference on Java Grande*. ACM Press, 1999. Available at http://www.cs.ucsb.edu/conferences/java99/program.html.

162. E. Freeman, S. Hupfer, and K. Arnold. *JavaSpaces(TM) Principles, Patterns and Practice*. Addison-Wesley, June 1999.

163. A. Fuggetta, G. P. Picco, and G. Vigna. Understanding code mobility. *IEEE Transactions on Software Engineering*, 24(5):342–361, May 1998.

164. M. Fukuda, L. F. Bic, M. B. Dillencourt, and J. M. Cahill. Messages versus Messengers in distributed programming. *Journal of Parallel and Distributed Computing*, 57(2):188–211, 1999.

165. M. Fukuda, L. F. Bic, M. B. Dillencourt, and F. Merchant. Distributed coordination with Messengers. *Science of Computer Programming*, 31:291–311, 1998.

166. S. Fünfrocken. Transparent migration of Java-based mobile agents: Capturing and reestablishing the state of Java programs. In *Proceedings of the 2nd Int. Workshop on Mobile Agents*, pages 26–37. Springer LNCS 1477, 1998.

167. E. Gabriel, M. Resch, T. Beisel, and R. Keller. Distributed computing in a heterogeneous computing environment. In *Proceedings of the 5th European PVM/MPI User's Group Meeting*, pages 180–187. Springer LNCS 1497, 1998.

168. D. G. Galatopoullos and E. S. Manolakos. Parallel processing in heterogeneous cluster architectures using JavaPorts. *ACM Crossroads*, 5(3), Spring 1999. Available at http://www.acm.org/crossroads.

169. E. Gamma, R. Helm, R. Johnson, and J. M. Vlissides. *Design Patterns: Elements of Reusable Object-Oriented Software*. Addison-Wesley, 1995.

170. D. Gannon, P. Beckman, E. Johnson, T. Green, and M. Levine. HPC++ and the HPC++ Lib Toolkit. White paper. Available at http://www.extreme.indiana.edu/hpc++/docs/papers/index.html.

171. D. Gannon and A. Grimshaw. Computational grids, In Foster and Kesselman [158], pages 205–236, 1999.

172. A. Geist, A. Beguelin, and J. Dongarra. *PVM: Parallel Virtual Machine*. MIT Press, 1994

173. V. Getov, S. Flynn-Hummel, and S. Mintchev. High-performance parallel programming in Java: Exploiting native libraries. *Concurrency: Practice and Experience*, 10(11–13):863–872, Sept. 1998.

174. L. A. Giannini and A. A. Chien. A software architecture for global address space communication on clusters: Put/get on fast messages. In *7th IEEE Int. Symposium on High Performance Distributed Computing*, July 1998. Available at http://www.computer.org/proceedings.

175. P. B. Gibbons. A more practical PRAM model. In *Proceedings 1st ACM Symposium on Parallel Algorithms and Architectures*, pages 158–168, 1989.

176. P. B. Gibbons, Y. Matias, and V. Ramachandran. The Queue-Read Queue-Write PRAM model: Accounting for contention in parallel algorithms. *SIAM Journal on Computing*, 28(2):733–769, 1998.

177. P. B. Gibbons, Y. Matias, and V. Ramachandran. Can a shared-memory model serve as a bridging model for parallel computation? *Theory of Computing Systems*, 32(3):327–359, 1999.

178. Gigabit Ethernet Alliance. Gigabit Ethernet Overview, May 1999. Available at http://www.gigabit-ethernet.org/technology/whitepapers.

179. J.-Y. Girard. Light linear logic. *Information and Computation*, 143(2):175–204, June 1998.

180. Globus Project. http://www.globus.org.

181. S. Gorlatch. Stages and transformations in parallel programming. In Kara et al. [244], pages 147–161, 1996.

182. S. Gorlatch and S. Pelagatti. A transformational framework for skeletal programs: Overview and case study. In *Workshop Proceedings IPPS/SPDP*, pages 123–137. Springer LNCS 1586, 1999.

183. J. Gosling, B. Joy, and G. Steele. *The Java Language Specification*. Addison-Wesley, 1996.

184. M. W. Goudreau, K. Lang, G. Narlikar, and S. B. Rao. BOS is boss: A case for bulk-synchronous object systems. In *Proceedings ACM Symposium on Parallel Algorithms and Architectures*, pages 115–125, 1999.

185. M. W. Goudreau, K. Lang, S. B. Rao, T. Suel, and T. Tsantilas. Portable and efficient parallel computing using the BSP model. *IEEE Transactions on Computers*, 48(7):670–689, July 1999.

186. W. C. Graham and S. Majumdar. Performance of scheduling strategies for client-server systems. *Journal of Parallel and Distributed Computing*, 58(3):389–424, 1999.

187. Grasshopper: The Agent Platform. http://www.grasshopper.de.

188. P. A. Gray and V. S. Sunderam. Metacomputing with the IceT system. *The International Journal of High Performance Computing Applications*, 13(3):241–252, 1999.

189. R. S. Gray, D. Kotz, G. Cybenko, and D. Rus. D'Agents: Security in a multiple-language, mobile-agent system. In G. Vigna, editor, *Mobile Agents and Security*, pages 154–187. Springer LNCS 1419, 1998.

190. B. Grayson, M. Dahlin, and V. Ramachandran. Experimental evaluation of QSM, a simple shared-memory model. In *Proceedings IPPS/SPDP*, pages 130–136. IEEE Computer Society Press, 1999.

191. A. Grimshaw, A. Ferrari, F. Knabe, and M. Humphrey. Wide-area computing: Resource sharing on a large scale. *IEEE Computer*, 32(5):29–37, May 1999.

192. W. Gropp, M. Snir, B. Nitzberg, and E. Lusk. *MPI: The Complete Reference*. MIT Press (Scientific and Engineering Computation Series), 1998.

193. R. Guerraoui and M. E. Fayad. OO distributed programming is not distributed OO programming. *Communications of the ACM*, 42(4):101–104, Apr. 1999.

194. Z. Guessoum and J.-P. Briot. From active objects to autonomous agents. *IEEE Concurrency*, 7(3):68–76, July–Sept. 1999.

195. M. Hagiya. Perspectives on molecular computing. *New Generation Computing*, 17:131–151, 1999.

196. M. W. Hall, J. M. Anderson, S. P. Amarasinghe, B. R. Murphy, S.-W. Liao, E. Bugnion, and M. S. Lam. Maximizing multiprocessor performance with the SUIF compiler. *IEEE Computer*, 29(12):84–89, Dec. 1996.

197. K. Hammond and G. Michaelson, editors. *Research Directions in Parallel Functional Programming*. Springer-Verlag London, 1999.

198. M. Hapner, R. Burridge, and R. Sharma. Java Message Service. Version 1.0.2. Available at http://java.sun.com/products/jms/docs.html, Nov. 1999.

199. S. Haridi, P. V. Roy, and G. Smolka. An overview of the design of Distributed Oz. In *Proceedings of the 2nd Int. Symposium on Parallel Symbolic Computation*, pages 13–24. ACM Press, 1997.

200. P. J. Hatcher and M. J. Quinn. *Data-Parallel Programming on MIMD Computers*. MIT Press, 1991.

201. T. Hauser, G. Xiong, and G. Huang. A hierarchical parallelization concept for a high-performance Navier–Stokes solver. Available at http://www.cs.uky.edu/~jzhang/HPSCA/hauser99.html.

202. C. A. Herrmann and C. Lengauer. The HDC compiler project. In A. Darte, G.-A. Silber, and Y. Robert, editors, *Proceedings 8th Int. Workshop on Compilers for Parallel Computers*, pages 239–254. LIP, ENS Lyon, 2000.

203. C. E. Hewitt. Viewing control structures as patterns of passing messages. *Journal of Artificial Intelligence*, 8(3):323–364, 1977.

204. T. Heywood and C. Leopold. Models of parallelism. In J. R. Davy and P. M. Dew, editors, *Abstract Machine Models for Highly Parallel Computers*, pages 1–16. Oxford University Press, 1995.

205. T. Heywood and S. Ranka. A practical hierarchical model of parallel computation. Part I: The model. *Journal of Parallel and Distributed Computing*, 16:212–232, 1992.

206. High Performance CORBA Working Group Home Page. http://www.omg.org/homepages/realtime/working_groups/high_performance_corba.html.

207. High Performance Fortran Forum. High Performance Fortran Language Specification. Available at http://dacnet.rice.edu/Depts/CRPC/HPFF/versions/hpf2/hpf-v20/hpf-report.html, Jan. 1997.

208. G. Hilderink, J. Broenink, W. Vervoort, and A. Bakkers. Communicating Java threads. In *Proceedings of the 20th World Occam and Transputer User Group Technical Meeting*, pages 48–76. IOS Press, 1997.

209. J. Hill, W. McColl, D. Stefanescu, M. Goudreau, K. Lang, S. Rao, T. Suel, T. Tsantilas, and R. Bisseling. BSPlib: The BSP programming library. *Parallel Computing*, 24(14):1947–1980, 1998.

210. J. M. Hill, S. R. Donaldson, and D. B. Skillicorn. Stability of Communication Performance in Practice: From the Cray T3E to Networks of Workstations. Technical Report PRG-TR-33-97, Oxford University Computing Laboratory, 1997.

211. M. D. Hill. Multiprocessors should support simple memory-consistency models. *IEEE Computer*, 31(8):28–34, Aug. 1998.

212. C. Hoare. Communicating sequential processes. *Communications of the ACM*, 21(8):666–677, 1978.

213. C. A. R. Hoare. *Communicating Sequential Processes*. Prentice-Hall International, 1985.

214. T. Hopfner, F. Fischer, and G. Färber. NoWait-RPC: Extending ONC RPC to a fully compatible message passing system. In *Proceedings IPPS/SPDP*, pages 250–254. IEEE Computer Society Press, 1998.

215. R. M. Hord. *Understanding Parallel Supercomputing*. IEEE Computer Society Press, 1999.

216. HPC++ Technical Overview. Available at http://www.extreme.indiana.edu/hpc++/about/index.html.

217. HPCLINE. Available at http://www.siemens.de/computer/hpc/en/hpcline/index.htm.

218. Y. C. Hu, H. Lu, A. L. Cox, and W. Zwaenepoel. OpenMP for networks of SMPs. In *Proceedings IPPS/SPDP*, pages 302–310. IEEE Computer Society Press, 1999.

219. M. Hughes, M. Shoffner, D. Hamner, and U. Bellur. *Java Network Programming*. Manning Publications, 2nd edition, 1999.

220. K. Hwang and Z. Xu. *Scalable Parallel Computing*. McGraw-Hill, 1998.

221. D. C. Hyde. Java and different flavors of parallel programming models. In Buyya [78], pages 274–290, 1999.

222. The IceT Project's Home Page. http://www.mathcs.emory.edu/icet.

223. IMPI Steering Committee. IMPI: Interoperable Message-Passing Interface. Protocol Version 0.0, Jan 2000. Available at http://impi.nist.gov/IMPI.

224. IMPI–Interoperable MPI. Available at http://impi.nist.gov/IMPI.

225. Information Power Grid. Available at http://www.nas.nasa.gov/IPG.

226. M. Ishikawa and N. McArdle. Optically interconnected parallel computing systems. *IEEE Computer*, 31(2):61–68, Feb. 1998.

227. A. Itzkovitz and A. Schuster. Distributed Shared Memory: Bridging the Granularity Gap. Position Paper. Available at http://www.cs.technion.ac.il/Labs/Millipede.

228. A. Itzkovitz, A. Schuster, and L. Shalev. The Millipede Virtual Parallel Machine for NT/PC Clusters. Position Paper, Available at http://www.cs.technion.ac.il/Labs/Millipede.

229. J. JáJá. *An Introduction to Parallel Algorithms*. Addison-Wesley, 1992.

230. J. F. JáJá and K. W. Ryu. The block distributed memory model. *IEEE Transactions on Parallel and Distributed Systems*, 7(8):830–840, Aug. 1996.

231. Java Communicating Sequential Processes. Available at http://www.cs.ukc.ac.uk/projects/ofa/jcsp.

232. Java Grande Forum. Available at http://www. javagrande.org.

233. JavaSpaces Specification Version 1.0.1. Available at http://java.sun.com/products/javaspaces, Nov. 1999.

234. S. Jenks and J.-L. Gaudiot. Nomadic threads: A migrating multithreaded approach to remote memory accesses in multiprocessors. In *Proceedings of the 1996 Conference on Parallel Architectures and Compilation Techniques*, pages 2–11. IEEE, Oct. 1996.

235. Jini Connection Technology. Available at http://www.sun.com/jini.

236. G. Jones and M. Goldsmith. *Programming in occam 2*. Prentice Hall, 1989.

237. JPVM: The Java Parallel Virtual Machine. Available at http://www.cs.virginia.edu/ajf2j/jpvm.html.

238. G. Judd, M. Clement, Q. Snell, and V. Getov. Design issues for efficient implementation of MPI in Java. In *Proceedings of the ACM 1999 Conference on Java Grande*, pages 58–65, 1999. Available at http://www.cs.ucsb.edu/conferences/java99/program.html.

239. A. Judge, P. Nixon, B. Tangney, S. Weber, and V. Cahill. Distributed shared memory, In Buyya [77], pages 409–438, 1999.

240. M. Jurczyk and T. Schwederski. SIMD-processing: Concepts and systems. In Zomaya [455], pages 649–679, 1996.

241. B. H. H. Juurlink and H. A. G. Wijshoff. The E-BSP model: Incorporating general locality and unbalanced communication into the BSP model. In *Proceedings Euro-Par*, pages 339–347. Springer LNCS 1124, 1996.

242. B. H. H. Juurlink and H. A. G. Wijshoff. A quantitative comparison of parallel computation models. *ACM Transactions on Computer Systems*, 16(3):271–318, Aug. 1998.

243. D. Kafura and J.-P. Briot. Actors & agents. *IEEE Concurrency*, 6(2):24–29, Apr.–June 1998.

244. M. Kara, J. Davy, D. Goodeve, and J. Nash, editors. *Abstract Machine Models for Parallel and Distributed Computing*. IOS Press, 1996.

245. W. Karl, M. Leberecht, and M. Schulz. Supporting shared memory and message passing on clusters of PCs with a SMiLE. In *Proceedings Communication, Architecture, and Applications for Network-Based Parallel Computing*, pages 196–210. Springer LNCS 1602, 1999.

246. P. Keleher. The relative importance of concurrent writers and weak consistency models. In *Proceedings of the 16th Int. Conference on Distributed Computing Systems*, pages 91–99, 1996.

247. J. Keller, C. W. Keßler, and J. L. Träff. *Practical PRAM Programming*. John Wiley & Sons, 2000. To appear.

248. K. Kennedy. *Advanced Compiling for High Performance*. Morgan Kaufmann Publishers, 2000. To appear.

249. M. Kirtland. *Designing Component-Based Applications*. Microsoft Press, 1999.

250. S. Kleiman, D. Shah, and B. Smaalders. *Programming with Threads*. Prentice Hall (SunSoft Press), 1996.

251. M. Knapik and J. Johnson. *Developing Intelligent Agents for Distributed Systems*. McGraw-Hill, 1998.

252. Knowledge Interchange Format: Draft Proposed American National Standard (dpANS), NCITS.T2/98-004. Available at http://logic.stanford.edu/kif/dpans.html.

253. P. T. Koch, J. S. Hansen, E. Cecchet, and X. Rousset de Pina. SciOS: An SCI-based software distributed shared memory. In *Proceedings of the 1st Workshop on Software Distributed Shared Memory*, June 1999. Available at http://www.cs.umd.edu/~keleher/wsdsm99.

254. C. H. Koelbel, D. B. Loveman, R. S. Schreiber, G. L. Steele Jr., and M. E. Zosel. *The High Performance Fortran Handbook*. MIT Press, 1994.

255. J. Kornerup. *Data Structures for Parallel Recursion*. PhD thesis, The University of Texas at Austin, Dec. 1997.

256. C. P. Kruskal, L. Rudolph, and M. Snir. A complexity theory of efficient parallel algorithms. *Theoretical Computer Science*, 71(1):95–132, Mar. 1990.

257. H. Kuang, L. F. Bic, M. B. Dillencourt, and A. C. Chang. PODC: Paradigm-Oriented Distributed Computing. In *7th IEEE Workshop on Future Trends of Distributed Computing Systems*, 1999. Available at http://www.computer.org/proceedings.

258. Y. Labrou and T. Finin. A Proposal for a New KQML Specification. Technical Report TR CS-97-03, Computer Science and Electrical Engineering Department, University of Maryland, Baltimore County, Baltimore, Feb. 1997.

259. LAM/MPI Parallel Computing. http://www.mpi.nd.edu/lam.

260. D. B. Lange and M. Oshima. *Programming and Deploying Java Mobile Agents with Aglets*. Addison-Wesley, Aug. 1998.

261. J. R. Larus, B. Richards, and G. Viswanathan. C**, In Wilson and Lu [442], pages 297–341, 1996.

262. J. Laudon and D. Lenoski. The SGI Origin: A ccNUMA highly scalable server. In *Proceedings of the 24th Int. Symposium on Computer Architecture*, pages 241–251, 1997.

263. M. Lauria, S. Pakin, and A. Chien. Efficient layering for high speed communication: The MPI over Fast Messages (FM) experience. *Cluster Computing*, 2(2):107–116, 1999.

264. G. Lawton. Multicasting: Will it transform the Internet? *IEEE Computer*, 31(7):13–15, July 1998.

265. D. Lecomber. *Methods of BSP Programming*. PhD thesis, Oxford University Computing Laboratory, 1998.

266. Legion Home Page. http://www.legion.virginia.edu.

267. F. T. Leighton. *Introduction to Parallel Algorithms and Architectures: Arrays, Trees, Hypercubes*. Morgan Kaufmann Publishers, 1991.

268. C. Lengauer and M. Griebl. On the parallelization of loop nests containing *while* loops. In *Proceedings 1st Aizu Int. Symposium on Parallel Algorithm/Architecture Synthesis*, pages 10–18. IEEE Computer Society Press, 1995.

269. S. M. Lewandowski. Frameworks for component-based client/server computing. *ACM Computing Surveys*, 30(1):3–27, Mar. 1998.

270. B. Lewis and D. J. Berg. *Multithreaded Programming with Pthreads*. Sun Microsystems Press (Prentice Hall), 1998.

271. Z. Li, P. H. Mills, and J. H. Reif. Models and resource metrics for parallel and distributed computation. In *Proceedings 28th Annual Hawaii Int. Conference on System Sciences*, 1995.

272. Y. Lin and D. Padua. On the automatic parallelization of sparse and irregular Fortran programs. In *Proceedings 4th Int. Workshop on Languages, Compilers, and Run-Time Systems for Scalable Computers*, pages 41–56. Springer LNCS 1511, 1998.

273. B. Liskov and L. Shrira. Promises: Linguistic support for efficient asynchronous procedure calls in distributed systems. *ACM SIGPLAN Notices*, 23(7):260–268, June 1988.

274. R. Loogen. *Programming language constructs*. In Hammond and Michaelson [197], pages 63–92, 1999.

275. W. Löwe and W. Zimmermann. Scheduling iterative programs onto LogP-machine. In *Proceedings Euro-Par*, pages 332–339. Springer LNCS 1685, 1999.

276. N. A. Lynch. *Distributed Algorithms*. Morgan Kaufmann Publishers, 1996.

277. B. Maggs, L. Matheson, and R. Tarjan. Models of parallel computation: A survey and synthesis. In *Proceedings of the 28th Hawaii Int. Conference on System Sciences (HICSS)*, volume 2, pages 61–70, Jan. 1995.

278. A. Mainwaring and D. Culler. Active Message Applications Programming Interface and Communication Subsystem Organization. Technical Report UCB CSD-96-918, University of California at Berkeley, 1996.

279. Manifold. Available at http://www.cwi.nl/~farhad/manifold.html.

280. B. D. Martino and C. W. Keßler. Two program comprehension tools for automatic parallelization. *IEEE Concurrency*, 8(1):37–47, Jan.–Mar. 2000.

281. C. Mascolo. MobiS: A specification language for mobile systems. In *Coordination Languages and Models*, pages 37–52. Springer LNCS 1594, 1999.

282. MasPar Computer Corporation. *MasPar System Overview*, Aug. 1994. Document Part Number: 9300-9072, Revision A0.

283. B. L. Massingill and K. M. Chandy. Parallel program archetypes. In *Proceedings IPPS/SPDP*, pages 290–296. IEEE Computer Society Press, 1999.

284. B. L. Massingill, T. G. Mattson, and B. A. Sanders. A Pattern Language for Parallel Application Programming. Technical Report UF CISE TR 99-009, University of Florida, 1999.

285. S. Matsuoka and A. Yonezawa. Analysis of inheritance anomaly in object-oriented concurrent programming languages. In G. Agha, P. Wegner, and A. Yonezawa, editors, *Research Directions in Concurrent Object-Oriented Programming*, pages 107–150. MIT Press, 1993.

286. T. G. Mattson and G. Henry. An overview of the Intel TFLOPS supercomputer. *Intel Technology Journal*, Q1, 1998. Available at http://developer.intel.com/technology/itj/q11998.htm.

287. L. Meertens. Algorithmics: Towards programming as a mathematical activity. In J. W. de Bakker, M. Hazewinkel, and J. K. Lenstra, editors, *Proceedings CWI Symposium on Mathematics and Computer Science*, pages 289–334. North-Holland, 1986.

288. K. Mehlhorn and U. Vishkin. Randomized and deterministic simulations of PRAMs by parallel machines with restricted granularity of parallel memories. *Acta Informatica*, 21:339–374, 1984.

289. K. Mehrotra, C. K. Mohan, and S. Ranka. *Elements of Artificial Neural Networks*. MIT Press, 1996.

290. P. Melliar-Smith and L. E. Moser. Network protocols. In Foster and Kesselman [158], pages 453–478, 1999.

291. The Message Passing Interface Standard. Available at http://www-unix.mcs.anl.gov/mpi.

292. Message Passing Interface Forum. MPI-1: A Message-Passing Interface Standard. Technical Report, University of Tennessee, Knoxville, June 1995. Available at http://www-unix.mcs.anl.gov/mpi.

293. Message Passing Interface Forum. MPI-2: Extensions to the Message-Passing Interface. Technical Report, University of Tennessee, Knoxville, July 1997. Available at http://www-unix.mcs.anl.gov/mpi.

294. M. Metcalf and J. Reid. *Fortran 90/95 Explained*. Oxford University Press, 1996.

295. Microsoft COM Home Page. http://www.microsoft.com/com.

296. M. Middendorf. Bit summation on the reconfigurable mesh. In *Workshop Proceedings IPPS/SPDP*, pages 625–633. Springer LNCS 1586, 1999.

297. R. Milner, J. Parrow, and D. Walker. A calculus of mobile processes. *Information and Computation*, 100(1), 1992.

298. D. Milojicic et al. MASIF: The OMG mobile agent system interoperability facility. In *Proceedings of the 2nd Int. Workshop on Mobile Agents*, pages 50–67. Springer LNCS 1477, 1998.

299. D. Milojicic et al. Trend wars: Mobile agent applications. *IEEE Concurrency*, 7(3):80–90, July–Sept. 1999.

300. J. Misra. An object model for multiprogramming. In *Workshop Proceedings IPPS/SPDP*, pages 881–889. Springer LNCS 1388, 1998.

301. M. Mitchell. *An Introduction to Genetic Algorithms*. MIT Press, Cambridge, 1996.

302. T. Miyazaki. Reconfigurable systems: A survey. In *Proceedings Asia and South Pacific Design Automation Conference*, pages 447–452, 1998.

303. Mole Home Page. http://mole.informatik.uni-stuttgart.de.

304. mpiJava Home Page. http://www.npac.syr.edu/projects/pcrc/HPJava/mpiJava.html.

305. S. S. Muchnick. *Advanced Compiler Design and Implementation*. Morgan Kaufmann Publishers, 1997.

306. M. O. Neary, S. P. Brydon, P. Kmiec, S. Rollins, and P. Cappello. Javelin++: Scalablity issues in global computing. In *Proceedings of the ACM 1999 Conference on Java Grande*, pages 171–180, 1999. Available at http://www.cs.ucsb.edu/conferences/java99/program.html.

307. P. Niemeyer and J. Peck. *Exploring Java*. O'Reilly, 1997.

308. S. Oaks and H. Wong. *Java Threads*. O'Reilly, 1997.

309. Object Management Group. CORBA Whitepapers. Available at http://www.omg.org/library/whitepapers.html.

310. Object Management Group. Supporting Aggregated Computing RFI. Available at http://www.omg.org/techprocess/meetings/schedule/Supporting_Aggreg._Computing_RFI.html.

311. Object Management Group Home Page. http://www.omg.org.

312. Object Space Inc. Voyager ORB 3.0 Developer Guide. Available at http://www.objectspace.com.

313. J. O'Donnel and G. Rünger. A methodology for deriving parallel programs with a family of parallel abstract machines. In *Proceedings Euro-Par*, pages 662–669. Springer LNCS 1300, 1997.

314. A. Omicini. On the semantics of tuple-based coordination models. In *ACM Symposium on Applied Computing*, pages 175–182, 1999.

315. A. Omicini and F. Zambonelli. Coordination of mobile information agents in TuCSoN. *Internet Research: Electronic Networking Applications and Policy*, 8(5):400–413, 1998.

316. A. Omicini and F. Zambonelli. Tuple centres for the coordination of Internet agents. In *ACM Symposium on Applied Computing*, pages 183–190, 1999.

317. Open Distributed Processing Reference Model. ITU-T X.901, ISO/IEC 10746-1. Available at http://enterprise.shl.com/RM-ODP/default.html.

318. OpenMP Architecture Review Board. OpenMP C and C++ Application Program Interface. Version 1.0. Available at http://www.openmp.org, Oct. 1998.

319. OpenMP FAQ. Available at http://www.sgi.com/software/openmp/openmpfaq.html.

320. OpenMP Home Page. http://www.openmp.org.

321. R. Orfali and D. Harkey. *Client/Server Programming with Java and Corba*. John Wiley & Sons, 2nd edition, 1998.

322. R. Orfali, D. Harkey, and J. Edwards. *Client/Server Survival Guide*. John Wiley & Sons, 3rd edition, 1999.

323. S. Ortiz Jr. Active networks: The programmable pipeline. *IEEE Computer*, 31(8):19–21, Aug. 1998.

324. Oxford BSP Toolset. Available at http://www.BSP-Worldwide.org/implmnts/oxtool.

325. V. S. Pai, M. Aron, G. Banga, M. Svendsen, P. Druschel, W. Zwaenepoel, and E. Nahum. Locality-aware request distribution in cluster-based network servers. *ACM SIGPLAN Notices*, 33(11):205–216, Nov. 1998.

326. S. Pakin et al. High-Performance Virtual Machines, 1999. Available at http://www-csag.ucsd.edu/projects/hpvm/doc/hpvmdoc.html.

327. S. Pakin, V. Karamcheti, and A. A. Chien. Fast Messages (FM): Efficient, portable communication for workstation clusters and massively-parallel processors. *IEEE Concurrency*, 5(2):60–73, Apr.–June 1997.

328. C. H. Papadimitriou and J. D. Ullman. A communication-time tradeoff. *SIAM Journal on Computing*, 16(4):639–646, Aug. 1987.

329. C. H. Papadimitriou and M. Yannakakis. Towards an architecture-independent analysis of parallel algorithms. *SIAM Journal on Computing*, 19(2):322–328, Apr. 1990.

330. G. A. Papadopoulos and F. Arbab. Coordination models and languages. In M. Zelkowitz, editor, *The Engineering of Large Systems*, volume 46 of Advances in Computers, pages 329–400. Academic Press, Aug. 1998.

331. N. Parab and M. Raghvendran. *Active messages*. In Buyya [77], pages 270–300, 1999.

332. PARADIGM Project. Available at http://www.crhc.uiuc.edu/Paradigm.

333. J. B. Pedersen and A. Wagner. PVMbuilder: A tool for parallel programming. In *Proceedings Euro-Par*, pages 108–112. Springer LNCS 1685, 1999.

334. S. Pelagatti. *Structured Development of Parallel Programs*. Taylor & Francis, 1998.

335. C. E. Perkins. Mobile networking in the Internet. *Mobile Networks and Applications*, 3:319–334, 1998.

336. C. E. Perkins. Mobile networking through Mobile IP. *IEEE Internet Computing*, 2(1):58–69, Jan./Feb. 1998.

337. S. Peyton Jones. Foreword. In Hammond and Michaelson [197], 1999.

338. G. F. Pfister. *In Search of Clusters*. Prentice Hall, 2nd edition, 1998.

339. Portland Group Home Page. http://www.pgroup.com/prodservpgf77pgcc.htm.

340. M. Philippsen. A survey of concurrent object-oriented languages. *Concurrency: Practice and Experience*. 12(10):917–980, 2000.

341. M. Philippsen, B. Haumacher, and C. Nester. More efficient serialization and RMI for Java. *Concurrency: Practice Experience*. 12(7):495–518, 2000.

342. M. Philippsen and M. Zenger. JavaParty: Transparent remote objects in Java. *Concurrency: Practice and Experience*, 9(11):1225–1242, 1997.

343. G. P. Picco, A. L. Murphy, and G.-C. Roman. Lime: Linda meets mobility. In D. Garlan, editor, *Proceedings of the 21st Int. Conference on Software Engineering*, pages 368–377. ACM Press, May 1999.

344. A. Pietracaprina, G. Pucci, and J. F. Sibeyn. Constructive, deterministic implementation of shared memory on meshes. *SIAM Journal on Computing*. To appear.

345. Polaris Home Page. http://polaris.cs.uiuc.edu/polaris/polaris.html.

346. D. K. Pradhan. *Fault-Tolerant Computer System Design*. Prentice Hall, 1996.

347. I. Pramanick. *MPI and PVM Programming*. In Buyya [78], pages 48–86, 1999.

348. J. F. Prins, S. Chatterjee, and M. Simons. Expressing irregular computations in modern Fortran dialects. In *Proceedings 4th Int. Workshop on Languages, Compilers, and Run-Time Systems for Scalable Computers*, pages 1–16. Springer LNCS 1511, 1998.

349. PUB-Library Home Page. http://www.uni-paderborn.de/~pub.

350. W. Pugh. Fixing the Java memory model. In *Proceedings of the ACM 1999 Conference on Java Grande*, 1999. Available at http://www.cs.ucsb.edu/conferences/java99/program.html.

351. PVM: Parallel Virtual Machine. http://www.epm.ornl.gov/pvm/pvm_home.html.

352. B. Quinn and D. Shute. *Windows Sockets Network Programming*. Addison-Wesley, 1995.

353. V. Ramachandran, B. Grayson, and M. Dahlin. Emulations between QSM, BSP and LogP: A Framework for General-Purpose Parallel Algorithm Design. Technical Report TR98-22, CS Department, University of Texas at Austin, Nov. 1998.

354. A. G. Ranade. How to emulate shared memory. *Journal of Computer and System Sciences*, 42(3):307–326, June 1991.

355. T. Rauber and G. Rünger. A coordination language for mixed task and data parallel programs. In *13th Annual ACM Symposium on Applied Computing*, pages 146–155, Feb. 1999.

356. J.-P. Redlich. *CORBA 2.0: Praktische Einführung für C++ and Java*. Addison-Wesley, 1996.

357. J. H. Reif. Paradigms for biomolecular computation. In *1st Int. Conference on Unconventional Models of Computation*, pages 72–93. Springer, 1998.

358. M. Resnick. *Turtles, Termites and Traffic Jams*. MIT Press, 1994.

359. H. Richardson. Data Parallel Programming in C*. Course Notes, Edinburgh Parallel Computing Centre, 1993.

360. A. Rodman and M. Brorsson. Programming effort vs. performance with a hybrid programming model for distributed memory architectures. In *Proceedings Euro-Par*, pages 888–898. Springer LNCS 1685, 1999.

361. S. Rodriguez, T. Anderson, and D. Culler. High-performance local-area communication using Fast Sockets. In *USENIX Annual Technical Conference*, 1997. Available at http://www.usenix.org.

362. A. Rowstron. WCL: A co-ordination language for geographically distributed agents. *World Wide Web Journal*, 1(3):167–179, 1998.

363. R. Rugina and M. Rinard. Automatic parallelization of divide and conquer algorithms. *ACM SIGPLAN Notices*, 34(8):72–83, May 1999.

364. M. Sagiv, T. Reps, and R. Wilhelm. Solving shape-analysis problems in languages with destructive updating. *ACM Transactions on Programming Languages and Systems*, 20(1):1–50, Jan. 1998.

365. P. Sapaty. *Mobile Processing in Distributed and Open Environments*. John Wiley & Sons, 1999.

366. L. F. G. Sarmenta. An adaptive, fault-tolerant implementation of BSP for Java-based volunteer computing systems. In *Workshop Proceedings IPPS/SPDP*, pages 763–780. Springer LNCS 1586, 1999.

367. SB-PRAM Home Page. http://www-wjp.cs.uni-sb.de/sbpram/sbpram.html.

368. D. J. Scales, K. Gharachorloo, and C. A. Thekkath. Shasta: A low overhead, software-only approach for supporting fine-grain shared memory. *ACM SIGPLAN Notices*, 31(9):174–185, Sept. 1996.

369. A. Scherer, H. Lu, T. Gross, and W. Zwaenepoel. Transparent adaptive parallelism on NOWs using OpenMP. In *Proceedings of the 7th ACM SIGPLAN Symposium on Principles and Practice of Parallel Programming*, pages 96–106, 1999.

370. M. S. Schlansker and B. R. Rau. EPIC: Explicitly parallel instruction computing. *IEEE Computer*, 33(2):37–45, Feb. 2000.

371. I. Schoinas, B. Falsafi, M. D. Hill, J. R. Larus, and D. A. Wood. Sirocco: Cost-effective fine-grain distributed shared memory. In *Proceedings Int. Confer-*

ence on Parallel Architectures and Compilation Techniques, 1998. Available at http://www.computer.org/proceedings.

372. V. J. Schuster. Parallel Fortran for HP systems. Slides of talk at Hewlett-Packard High-Performance Computing User's Group Meeting, Chicago, March 1999, Available at http://www.pgroup.com/presentations/hpcug99/index.htm.

373. Scientific Computing Associates, Inc. Virtual Shared Memory and the Paradise System for Distributed Computing, Apr. 1999. Available at http://www.sca.com.

374. SCIzzL Home Page. http://www.SCIzzL.com.

375. C. L. Seitz. The cosmic cube. *Communications of the ACM,* 28(1):22–33, Jan. 1985.

376. Sequent Computer Systems, Inc. NUMA-Q 2000 Model 320 Specification Summary, 1999. Available at http://www.sequent.com.

377. S. Shah, G. Haab, P. Petersen, and J. Throop. Flexible control structures for parallelism in OpenMP. In *1st European Workshop on OpenMP,* 1999. Available at http://www.it.lth.se/ewomp99/programme.html.

378. H. Shan and J. P. Singh. A comparison of MPI, SHMEM and cache-coherent shared address space programming models on the SGI Origin2000. In *Proceedings of the 1999 Int. Conference on Supercomputing,* pages 329–338. ACM, 1999.

379. R. L. Shuey, D. L. Spooner, and O. Frieder. *The Architecture of Distributed Computing Systems.* Addison-Wesley, 1997.

380. A. A. Shvartsman and P. C. Kanellakis. *Fault-Tolerant Parallel Computation.* Kluwer Academic Publishers, 1997.

381. H. J. Siegel et al. Report of the Purdue Workshop on Grand Challenges in Computer Architecture for the Support of High Performance Computing. *Journal of Parallel and Distributed Computing,* 16:199–211, 1992.

382. J. Siegel. A preview of CORBA 3. *IEEE Computer,* 32(5):114–116, May 1999.

383. Silicon Graphics, Inc. Performance of the Cray T3E Multiprocessor. White Paper. Available at http://www.sgi.com/t3e/performance.html.

384. L. M. Silva, P. Martins, and J. Silva. Merging web-based with cluster-based computing. In *Proceedings of Computing in Object-Oriented Parallel Environments,* pages 119–126. Springer LNCS 1505, 1998.

385. J. A. Simpson and E. S. C. Weiner, editors. *The Oxford English Dictionary.* Oxford University Press (Clarendon Press), 2nd edition, 1989.

386. H. Singh. *Progressing to Distributed Multiprocessing.* Prentice Hall, 1999.

387. M. Sipper. The emergence of cellular computing. *Computer,* 32(7):18–26, July 1999.

388. D. Skillicorn. *Foundations of Parallel Programming.* Cambridge University Press, 1994.

389. D. Skillicorn. The Network of Tasks Model. Technical Report ISSN-0836-0227-1999-427, Department of Computing and Information Science, Queen's University, Ontario, Canada, May 1999.

390. D. Skillicorn, J. M. D. Hill, and W. F. McColl. Questions and answers about BSP. *Scientific Programming*, 6(3):249–274, 1997.

391. D. B. Skillicorn. Communication skeletons. In Kara et al. [244], pages 163–177, 1996.

392. D. B. Skillicorn and D. Talia. Models and languages for parallel computation. *ACM Computing Surveys*, 30(2):123–169, 1998.

393. A. Snavely, L. Carter, J. Boisseau, A. Majumdar, K. S. Gatlin, N. Mitchell, J. Feo, and B. Koblenz. Multi-processor performance on the Tera MTA. In *Proceedings High-Performance Networking and Computing Conference* (*SC98*), 1998. Available at http://www.supercomp.org/sc98/papers.

394. M. Snir, S. W. Otto, S. Huss-Lederman, D. W. Walker, and J. Dongarra. *MPI: The Complete Reference*. MIT Press, 1996.

395. L. Snyder. Type architectures, shared memory, and the corollary of modest potential. *Annual Review of Computer Science*, 1:289–317, 1986.

396. E. Speight, H. Abdel-Shafi, and J. K. Bennett. An integrated shared memory/message passing API for cluster-based multicomputing. In *Proceedings of the 2nd Int. Conference on Parallel and Distributed Computing and Networks*, Dec. 1998. Available at http://www-brazos.rice.edu/brazos/brazos_pub_page.htm.

397. E. Speight and J. K. Bennett. Brazos: A third generation DSM system. In *Proceedings of the 1997 USENIX Windows/NT Workshop*, pages 95–106, 1997. Available at http://www-brazos.rice.edu/brazos/brazos_pub_page.htm.

398. G. Spezzano and D. Talia. A high-level cellular programming model for massively parallel processing. In *Proceedings of the 2nd Int. Workshop on High-Level Programming Models and Supportive Environments*, pages 55–63. IEEE, 1997.

399. R. Steinmetz. *OCCAM 2 : Die Programmiersprache für parallele Verarbeitung*. Huethig Verlag Heidelberg, 2nd edition, 1988.

400. T. Sterling and D. Savarese. A coming of age for beowulf-class computing. In *Proceedings Euro-Par*, pages 78–88. Springer LNCS 1685, 1999.

401. W. R. Stevens. *UNIX Network Programming*. Prentice Hall, 1990.

402. Sun Microsystems, Inc. ONC+ Developer's Guide. Available at http://answer book.cs.nmsu.edu.

403. Sun Microsystems, Inc. Sun Enterprise 10000 Server. Technical White Paper, Sept. 1998. Available at http://www.sun.com/servers/wp.html.

404. Supercomputing Technologies Group, MIT Laboratory for Computer Science. Cilk 5.2 Reference Manual, July 1998. Available at http://supertech.lcs.mit.edu/cilk.

405. N. Suzuki, M. Fukuda, and L. F. Bic. Self-migrating threads for multi-agent applications. In *Proceedings 1st IEEE Int. Workshop on Cluster Computing* (*IWCC*), 1999. Available at http://www.computer.org/proceedings.

406. D. Talia. A survey of PARLOG and Concurrent Prolog: The integration of logic and parallelism. *Computer Languages*, 18(3):185–196, 1993.

407. C. P. Tan, W. F. Wong, and C. K. Yuen. tmPVM: Task migratable PVM. In *Proceedings IPPS/SPDP*, pages 196–202. IEEE Computer Society Press, 1999.

408. A. S. Tanenbaum. *Distributed Operating Systems*. Prentice-Hall, 1995.

409. A. S. Tanenbaum. *Computer Networks*. Prentice Hall, 3rd edition, 1996.

410. S. Thakkar and T. Huff. Internet streaming SIMD extensions. *IEEE Computer*, 32(12):26–34, Dec. 1999.

411. The PIPS Workbench Project. Available at http://www.cri.ensmp.fr/pips.

412. The SUIF 2 Compiler System. Available at http://suif.stanford.edu/suif/suif2.

413. K. Thitikamol and P. Keleher. Thread migration and communication minimization in DSM systems. *The Proceedings of the IEEE*, 87(3):487–497, Mar. 1999.

414. Titanium. Available at http://www.cs.berkeley.edu/projects/titanium.

415. R. Tolksdorf. Laura: A service-based coordination language. *Science of Computer Programming*, 31:359–381, 1998.

416. Top 500 Supercomputer Sites, Nov. 1999. Available at http://www.top500.org/index.html.

417. J. L. Trahan, A. G. Bourgeois, Y. Pan, and R. Vaidyanathan. Optimally scaling permutation routing on reconfigurable linear arrays with optical buses. In *Proceedings IPPS/SPDP*, pages 233–237. IEEE Computer Society Press, 1999.

418. P. W. Trinder, H.-W. Loidl, and K. Hammond. Large scale functional applications. In Hammond and Michaelson [197], pages 399–426, 1999.

419. S. Tucker Taft and R. A. Duff, editors. *Ada 95 Reference Manual*. Springer LNCS 1246, 1997.

420. J.-C. Ueng, C.-K. Shieh, and C.-C. Lin. Design and implementation of Proteus. In *1st Workshop on Software Distributed Shared Memory*, 1999. Available at http://www.cs.umd.edu/~keleher/wsdsm99.

421. Universal Plug and Play Forum. http://www.upnp.org.

422. L. G. Valiant. A bridging model for parallel computation. *Communications of the ACM*, 33(8):103–111, Aug. 1990.

423. R. A. van de Geijn. *Using PLAPACK: Parallel Linear Algebra Package*. Scientific and Engineering Computation Series, MIT Press, 1997.

424. P. van Emde Boas. Machine models and simulations. In J. van Leeuwen, editor, *Handbook of Theoretical Computer Science, Vol. A*. Elsevier Science Publishers and MIT Press, 1990.

425. R. van Nieuwpoort, J. Maassen, H. E. Bal, T. Kielmann, and R. Veldema. Wide-area parallel computing in Java. In *Proceedings of the ACM 1999 Conference on Java Grande*, pages 8–14, 1999. Available at http://www.cs.ucsb.edu/conferences/java99/program.html.

426. M. van Steen, P. Homburg, and A. S. Tanenbaum. Globe: A wide-area distributed system. *IEEE Concurrency*, 7(1):70–78, Jan.–Mar. 1999.

427. C. Varela and G. Agha. A hierarchical model for coordination of concurrent activities. In *Coordination Languages and Models*, pages 166–182. Springer LNCS 1594, 1999.

428. G. Vigna. *Mobile Agents and Security*. Springer LNCS 1419, 1998.

429. U. Vishkin. Can parallel algorithms enhance serial implementation? *Communications of the ACM*, 39(9):88–91, Sept. 1996.

430. Visual KAP for OpenMP. Available at http://www.kai.com.

431. J. S. Vitter. External memory algorithms and data structures: Dealing with massive data. *ACM Computing Surveys*. To appear.

432. J. S. Vitter and E. A. M. Shriver. Optimal algorithms for parallel memory II: Hierarchical multilevel memories. *Algorithmica*, 12(2–3):148–169, 1994.

433. I. Vlahavas, P. Tsarchopoulos, and I. Sakellariou. *Parallel and Constraint Logic Programming*. Kluwer Academic Publishers, 1998.

434. T. von Eicken, D. E. Culler, S. C. Goldstein, and K. E. Schauser. Active messages: A mechanism for integrated communication and computation. In *Proceedings of the 19th Annual Int. Symposium on Computer Architecture*, pages 256–267, 1992.

435. T. von Eicken, D. E. Culler, K. E. Schauser, and S. C. Goldstein. Retrospective on active messages: A mechanism for integrated communication and computation. In S. Barcelona, editor, *Int. Conference on Computer Architecture (25th anniverary)*, pages 83–84, 1998.

436. K. Wakita, T. Asano, and M. Sassa. D'Caml: Native support for distributed ML programming in heterogeneous environments. In *Proceedings Euro-Par*, pages 914–924. Springer LNCS 1685, 1999.

437. J. Waldo. The Jini architecture for network-centric computing. *Communications of the ACM*, 42(7):76–82, July 1999.

438. J. Waldo, G. Wyant, A. Wollrath, and S. Kendall. A note on distributed computing. In *Mobile Object Systems*, pages 49–66. Springer LNCS 1222, 1997.

439. A. C. Weaver. Xpress transport protocol. In Buyya [77], pages 301–316, 1999.

440. C. P. Williams and S. H. Clearwater. *Explorations in Quantum Computing*. Springer, 1997.

441. G. V. Wilson. A glossary of parallel computing terminology. *IEEE Parallel & Distributed Technology*, pages 52–67, Feb. 1993.

442. G. V. Wilson and P. Lu. *Parallel Programming Using C++*. MIT Press, 1996.

443. M. E. Wolf and M. S. Lam. A loop transformation theory and an algorithm to maximize parallelism. In *IEEE Transactions on Parallel and Distributed Systems*, 2(4):452–471, 1991.

444. M. J. Wolfe. *High Performance Compilers for Parallel Computing*. Addison-Wesley, 1996.

445. J. Wu. *Distributed System Design*. CRC Press, 1999.

446. P. Wu and D. Padua. Containers on the parallelization of general-purpose Java programs. In *Proceedings Int. Conference on Parallel Architectures and Compilation Techniques*, 1999. Available at http://www.computer.org/proceedings.

447. P. Wyckoff, S. McLaughry, T. J. Lehman, and D. A. Ford. TSpaces. *IBM Systems Journal*, 37(3):454–474, 1998.

448. D. K. Y. Yau and S. S. Lam. Migrating sockets: End system support for networking with quality of service guarantees. *IEEE/ACM Transactions on Networking*, 6(6):700–716, Dec. 1998.

449. A. Yee. Making sense of the COM vs. CORBA debate. *UNIX Review*, June 1999. Available at http://www.performancecomputing.com/features/9906dev.shtml.

450. K. Yelick, L. Semenzato, G. Pike, C. Miyamoto, B. Liblit, A. Krishnamurthy, P. Hilfinger, S. Graham, D. Gay, P. Colella, and A. Aiken. Titanium: A high-performance Java dialect. *Concurrency: Practice and Experience*, 10(11–13):825–836, Sept.–Nov. 1998.

451. W. Yu and A. Cox. Java/DSM: A platform for heterogeneous computing. *Concurrency: Practice and Experience*, 9(11):1213–1224, Nov. 1997.

452. A. Zavanella. Optimizing skeletal-stream parallelism on a BSP computer. In *Proceedings Euro-Par*, pages 853–857. Springer LNCS 1685, 1999.

453. A. Zavanella and S. Pelagatti. Using BSP to optimize data distribution in skeleton programs. In *Proceedings High-Performance Computing and Networking*, pages 613–622. Springer LNCS 1593, 1999.

454. G. Zhang, B. Carpenter, G. Fox, X. Li, and Y. Wen. The HPspmd model and its Java binding. In Buyya [78], pages 291–309, 1999.

455. A. Y. Zomaya, editor. *Parallel and Distributed Computing Handbook*. McGraw-Hill, 1996.

456. A. Y. Zomaya. Parallel and distributed computing: The scene, the props, the players. In Zomaya [455], pages 5–23, 1996.

457. ZPL Home Page. http://www.cs.washington.edu/research/zpl.

Index

Abstract model, 21, 199ff, 228
Active messages, 44, 107f, 109, 168
Active networks, 143
Active objects, 167ff
ActiveX, 166
Actor Foundry, 171
Actor model, 168ff, 175, 224, 225
ActorSpace, 171
Ada, 93, 125, 154, 225
Affinity scheduling, 80
Alignment, 58
AM, see Active messages
Amdahl's law, 10, 17
AND parallelism, 194ff
API, 21
Applets, 134, 143
Archetypes, 186
ATM, 41, 42
Attribute, 82, 158
Automatic parallelization, 177ff, 224
Availability, 18

Bandwidth, 10, 42
Barrier synchronization, see Synchronization
Beans, 165
Beowulf cluster, 47
Berkeley sockets, 118ff, 126
Big-O notation, 201
BMF, see Bird–Meertens formalism
Bird–Meertens formalism, 197
Block distribution, 59, 61
Blocking communication, 102

Bridging model, 22, 201, 209, 212
Broadcast, 66
BSP libraries, 212f
BSP, 209ff, 222, 224–228
Bulk-synchronous parallel model, see BSP
Butterfly, 202
Bytecode, 129
Byzantine failure, 18

C*, 53, 70
Cache (coherence), 12, 35f, 44
Categorical data types, 197
CC-NUMA, 35f, 49
CDR, 165
Cellular automaton, 222
CGI, 117, 165
CGM, see Coarse-grained multicomputer
Channel, 152
Channel-based coordination, 151ff, 192, 224–226
Checkpointing, 18
Church–Rosser property, 191
Cilk, 219ff, 224
Classification scheme, 25
   El-Rewini and Lewis, 25
   Flynn, 25
   Skillicorn and Talia, 25f, 223
   others, 29
Client/Server, 111ff
   in MPI-2, 126
   in the web, 117
   model, 111ff, 160, 227–228

Client/Server *Continued*
  paradigm, 111ff, 132ff, 167, 228
  system, 10
  two-tier and three-tier, 115f
  with parallelism, 112, 114
Cluster, 2, 4, 45ff, 49
Coarse-grained multicomputer, 222
Code mobility, <u>127</u>ff, 160, 186
Code on demand, 133f
Collaborative computing, 6, 28
Collective operations. 55, 60, <u>65</u>ff, 103, 160,
  183, 226, 227
COM+, 166
COMA architecture, 49
Committed choice, 196
Common object request broker architecture,
  see CORBA
Communicating sequential processes, *see* CSP
Compiler directive, 27, 56, 62, 84, 192
Component, 159
  in scientific computing, 174
Compositional model, <u>186</u>ff, 198, 224–227
Concurrent computing, 5, 28
Concurrent object-oriented languages, 70, 167,
  171, <u>172</u>
Condition variable, 80
Connection-oriented communication, 39, 225f
Connectionless communication, 39
Consistency, 90–92
  release, 90–92
  sequential, 90–92
Constraint logic programming, 196f
Context switch, 77
Conversion of data formats, 106, 165
Coordination, 14, 145
  languages, 146
  model, <u>145</u>ff, 183, 224–228
CORBA, <u>160</u>ff, 175
Cost model, 23, 65, 199, 213
Critical section, 80
Crossbar, 34–35, 44
CSP, <u>151</u>ff, 156, 188, 195f
Cyclic distribution, 59

D-BSP, 213, 217
Dag scheduling, 220
Data dependence, 179
Data distribution, 13, 57
Data parallelism, 51ff
  in object-oriented languages, 70f
  model, 51, 183, 188, 192, 224, 227
  nested, <u>64</u>f, 70
  paradigm, 51, 70, 84, 88, 96, 178, 182, 228

Dataflow, 191
  architecture, 50
Datagram, 40
DCE RPC, 124
DCOM, 160, 166
Deadlock, 14
Decentralized computing, 6, 28
Declarative programming, 193
Delay model, 220
Dependability, 18, 28, 227
Derived datatypes in MPI, 106
DII, 163, 167
Distributed algorithms, 204f, 222
Distributed computing, 2
  comparison with parallel, 3f, 28
  convergence with parallel, 4f, 28, 227
  history, 2f
Distributed objects, <u>159</u>ff, 224–228
  parallelism in, 166
Distributed Oz, 197
Distributed shared memory, 38, 76, <u>89</u>ff, 93f,
  224
Distributed-memory parallel computer, 37f
Divide and conquer, <u>65</u>, <u>104</u>f, 182, 228
DNA computing, 222
Domain decomposition, 70
DSM, *see* Distributed shared memory
Dynamic invocation, 163, 227

E-BSP, 217
Efficiency, 9
Enhanced client/server computing, 132ff, 165
EPIC, 50
Ethernet, 41, 46, 50
Event channel, 165

False sharing, 90f
Fast messages, 44, 47, <u>107</u>f, 109, 168
Fast sockets, 125
Fat client, 115ff, 132
FM, *see* Fast messages
Fork, 207f
Fortran 90/95, 56, 60, <u>69</u>, 71
Functional programming, <u>189</u>ff, 198, 224

Gamma, 198
Gather, 67
Genetic algorithm, 222
Globus, 156, 173
Granularity, 13
Graph reduction, 191
Grid computing, 118, 156
Grid, 48f

Guard, <u>152</u>, 154, 188, 196
Gustafson–Barsis Law, 10f

h-relation, 210
H-PRAM, 213, <u>216</u>
Heterogeneity, 3, <u>17</u>, 28, 227
High-Performance C++, *see* HPC++
HPC++, 173
HPF, <u>56</u>ff, 71, 84, 226
HPF-2, <u>60</u>ff, 71
HPJava, <u>70</u>, 226
HPVM, 47, 92
Hypercube, 202f, 210

IceT, 143
IDL, 123f, 161, 167, 174
IIOP, 165
IMPI, 106, 109
Implementation repository, 164
Incremental parallelization, 89, 98
Inheritance, 82
    anomaly, 158
Inspector/executor, 69
Intercommunicator, 104
Interface Definition Language *see* IDL
Interface repository, 163
Interoperability, 17
Intranet, 48
Irregularity, <u>61</u>, 63, 65, 69, 181
IWIM, <u>154</u>, 187

Java Grande Forum, 108
Java sockets, 122
Java Virtual Machine, *see* JVM
Java, 129f, 143, 165, 171, 182
    applets, 134
    binding for MPI, 108
    Message Service API, 155
    RMI, 166f
    security concept, 130
    sockets, 118, 122
    support for code mobility, 129
    threads, 81ff, 94
JavaParty, 173
JavaSpace, 135, 150–<u>151</u>
Javelin, 118, 135
Jini, 135
Job, 8, 77
JVM, <u>129</u>, 165, 167

LAM MPI, 109
LAN, 39
Latency, 10, 42

avoidance and reduction, 12
    tolerance, 12, 211, 212, 218
Legion, 174
Libraries, 27, <u>65</u>ff, 71, 78
Lightweight protocols, 43, 50, 106
Linda, <u>146</u>ff, 156, 226
Load balancing, 11
Locality, 11, 75, 172–174, 211, 216, 218
LogGP, 214
Logic programming, <u>193</u>ff, 198, 224
LogP, <u>214</u>f, 228
Loop distribution, 180
Loop parallelization, 178ff
Loosely synchronous computing, 56
Loosely coupled distributed systems, 47

Manifold, <u>154</u>, 226
Map construct, 65
Marshaling, 123, 163
Master/slave, <u>104</u>f, 115, 134, 182, 228
Memory consistency, *see* Consistency
Memory hierarchy, 12
    models thereof, 218
    parallel models thereof, 218
Mentat, 173
Mesh, <u>202</u>, 203, 210, 212
Message exchange, 225
Message passing, <u>95</u>ff, 224–228
    comparison with shared memory, 98f,
        109
Message Passing Interface, *see* MPI
Message queuing, 155
Message-driven computation, 170
Message-oriented middleware, 155
Messaging, <u>155</u>f, 156, 226
Messengers, 139
Metacomputing, 48
Method, 82, 158
Middleware, 114
MIMD, 25
Mobile agents, <u>135</u>ff, 170, 224–227
    communication between, 138
Mobile computing, 128
Mobility, *see* code mobility
Model, 19
MOM, *see* Message-oriented middleware
Monitor, 83
MPI Forum, 109
MPI, <u>99</u>ff, 109, 192, 225
    comparison with PVM, 109
MPI-2, 93, <u>100</u>ff, 109
    client/server model, 126
MPMD, 25, 227

Multicast, 50, 66, 122, 156
Multiprefix, 208
Multithreading, 12, 207, 210, 212
   architecture, 50
Mutex, 80
Myrinet, 44, 46, 50

Name server, 124, 162, 167
NCC-NUMA, 37
NESL, 65
Nested data parallelism, 64f, 70
NetSolve, 117
Network models, 201ff, 222, 228
Networked computing, 6, 28
Neural network, 222
NFS, 117, 126
Node, 8
Nonblocking communication, 92, 102, 163, 170
NORMA, 37

Object orientation, 81f
   and parallelism, 157f
   basic concepts, 81f
Object, 82
   adapter, 163, 164
   factory, 165
   serialization, 130, 167
   web, 165
Object-based DSM, 94, 188, 226
Object-oriented models, 157ff, 224–228
Occam, 153f, 226
OMG, 161, 174
ONC RPC, 124
One-sided communication, 92f, 213, 226
OpenMP, 84ff, 93, 182, 208, 226
   interoperability with MPI, 89
Openness, 3, 18, 227
Optical architectures, 50, 222
Opus, 188
OR parallelism, 194, 196
ORB, 161
Orca, 94
Owner-computes rule, 53, 61

P3L, 184
Pairwise communication, 226
Paradigm, 20, 228
Para-functional programming, 192
Parallelaxis, 53
Parallel computing, 1, 226
   comparison with distributed, 3f, 28
   convergence with distributed, 4f, 28, 227f
   history, 1, 28

Parallel disk model, 218
Parallel loop, 54, 56, 183
Parallel mobile code, 139ff, 143, 155,
   224-227
Parallel random access machine, *see* PRAM
Parallel Virtual Machine, *see* PVM
Parallelizing compiler, 177ff, 198
PCN, 187
Peer-to-peer, 126, 136, 160, 167, 228
Performance, 223
π-calculus, 197
Pipeline, 62, 228
Port, 119
Portability, 16, 17, 28, 223
PRAM, 205ff, 222, 224-228
   CRCW etc, 206
   programming, 207
   simulation, 207
Prefetching, 12
Private variable, 88
Process, 8, 77
   groups, 104, 225
   shared memory for, 93
Processing element, 8
Profiling, 13
Programmability, 23, 223
Programming model, 21ff, 200, 228
Protocol, 38, 42
Pseudoparallelism, 5
Pthreads, 79ff, 84, 94
Publish-and-subscribe, 155
PVM, 99ff, 109, 225
   comparison with MPI, 109

QoS, 11, 41, 48
QSM, 215, 228
Quality of service, *see* QoS
Quantum computing, 222
Queue-based communication, 225

Race condition, 14
RAM, *see* Random-access machine
Random-access machine, 200, 218
Randomizing routing, 210
Reconfigurable architectures, 50, 203, 222
Reduction, 55, 60, 66, 68
Redundancy, 19
Reflectivity, 23, 199, 223
Reliability, 18
Remote evaluation, 132f
Remote method invocation, *see* RMI
Remote procedure call, *see* RPC
Rendezvous, 125

Replication, 12
Response time, 10
RMI, 160, 162, 226
Routing, 39
RPC, 122ff, 126, 160, 224–227
  asynchronous, 125

Safety, 18
SAN, 39, 44
SB-PRAM, 207
Scalability, 17, 28
Scalable coherent interface, 44
Scan, 182
Scatter, 66
Scavenging, 8, 46, 48
Security, 18
Self-migrating threads, 139
Semaphore, 81
Serial program, parallel system, see SPPS
Server, 78, 111 See also Client/Server
  concurrent, 113
  connection-oriented, 119
  connectionless, 119–120
  iterative, 113
Servlets, 117
Shared medium-based communication, 225
Shared memory, 73ff
  comparison with message passing, 98f, 109
  in architectures, 24, 33ff, 38
  programming model, 73ff
Shared variable, 88
SIMD, 25
  architecture, 31ff, 49
  programming model, 51, 53ff, 227
Single address space, 33ff, 225
  in programming, 74
Single system image, 4, 15, 28, 34, 45, 47–48
Single-assignment variable, 188
Sisal, 192
Skeleton in CORBA, 163
Skeleton model, 69, 182ff, 187, 198,
    224–227
SMP, 33ff, 49, 75, 202
  clusters programming, 109
Sockets, 118ff, 224–227
Spatial machine, 222
Special-purpose computing, 19, 203
Speedup, 8
  superlinear, 9
Split-C, 94
SPMD, 25, 51, 101, 227
SPPS, 8, 33, 45
Static invocation, 125, 162

Store-and-forward routing, 203
Strictness, 190
Structured parallel programming, 184
Structured shared-memory programming, 84ff,
    93, 224–228
Stub, 123, 162
Supercomputing, 5, 28
Superstep, 209
Symmetric multiprocessor, see SMP
Synchronization, 75
  barrier, 66, 88, 209, 213
  by message exchange, 96
  implicit, 56, 205, 208, 227
  in OpenMP, 88
Systolic array, 50

Task farm, 184
Task management, 74, 79, 103
Task parallelism, 53, 157, 188, 219, 228
Task, 8, 74, 77
  scheduling, 13, 87
TCP/IP, 39ff
Thin client, 115ff, 132
Thread, 8, 77
  group, 83, 225
  model, 76, 224–228
  scheduling, 79, 83
Throughput, 11
Throughput-oriented computing, 8
Time slicing, 79
Titanium, 94
Token ring, 41
Top 500 list, 38, 47
Trader, 162
Transaction, 117
Transformational approach, 197
Transparency, 15, 28, 76, 175
Transparent migration, 142
Transputer networks, 154
Treadmarks, 89, 91f
TSpaces, 149
TuCSoN, 150
Tuple space, 147
Tuple-based coordination, 146ff, 224–228
TwoL, 189

UDP, 40
UMA, 34
Unity, 197
Universal Plug and Play, 135

Vector processors, 50
Very low-level models, 106ff

VIA, 44
Virtual shared memory, 90, 94
VLIW architectures, 50
Volunteer computing, 134, 143
von Neumann bottleneck, 7
von Neumann computer, 22, 25, 200

WAN, 39
WAVE, 139
WebFlow, 118, 228
Where construct, 54

Wireless computing, 50
Work sharing, 85ff, 101, 227
Wormhole routing, 44, 203

XDR, 105, 109, 124, 165

Y-BSP, 217
Yield function, 80

ZPL, 71